THIS BOOK IS THE PROPERTY OF_____

(Your Name)

*Date of Birth*_____

*Basic Number*_____

*Control Number*_____

*Tendency Number*_____

☐ — ☐ — ☐

(Basic Number) (Control Number) (Tendency Number)

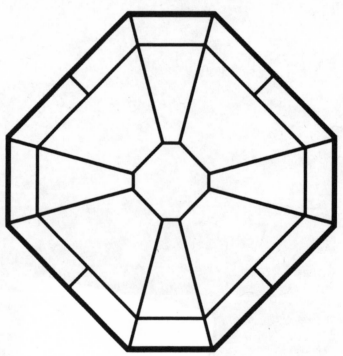

*Your Zodiac Sign*_____

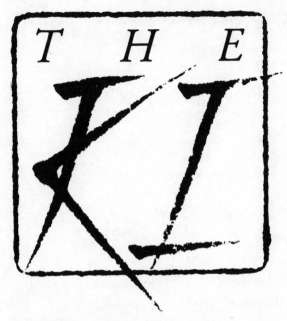

TAKASHI YOSHIKAWA

**An Ancient Oracle
for Modern Times**

THE AQUARIAN PRESS
Wellingborough, Northamptonshire

First published 1986 by St Martin's Press, 175 Fifth Avenue,
New York, NY, 10010, USA
First UK Edition 1988

Designed by Giorgetta Bell McRee/Early Birds

British Library Cataloguing in Publication Data

Yoshikawa, Takashi
  The Ki: an ancient oracle for modern
  times.
  1. Fortune-telling by numbers
  I. Title
  133.3'354   BF1891.N8

ISBN 0-85030-699-X

*The Aquarian Press is part of the Thorsons Publishing Group,
Wellingborough, Northamptonshire,
NN8 2RQ, England*

Printed in Great Britain by Woolnough Bookbinding,
Irthlingborough, Northamptonshire

10 9 8 7 6 5 4 3 2 1

In memory of Patrick C. Meehan

ACKNOWLEDGMENT is due to Viscount Rothermere
for his efforts on my behalf.

THANKS is also due to Terry Blaine and Eugene L. Hanson
for helping me with the language, typing,
and checking of materials prior to publication.

CONTENTS

WHERE TO LOOK
WHEN CONSULTING

PREFACE

Let me tell you a little about the events that first brought me in contact with the Ki, some thirty-five years ago.

As a child growing up in Japan, I had a dream—to go to America. I knew I wanted to do this ever since I was a child, when visitors from that far-off land had come to my family's home bearing a strange, exotic gift that I loved—Hershey's Kisses wrapped in silver paper. They became the symbol of all that America meant to me, the embodiment of a dream. However, making that dream come true proved very difficult. Over the years, I had to abandon my plans several times, as fate stepped in and changed my life: once, at age seventeen, when a ruptured appendix almost took my life, and again when Japan entered World War II.

As a college student I had joined the Army Air Force. During the war, as a young officer, I was a pilot for the army, similar to the navy "kamikaze"—a pilot assigned to suicide missions. The Japanese army sent us all over the Orient—to Formosa, Hong Kong, and finally, Singapore, in search of surplus airplanes. Because of this shortage of planes, the younger officers rarely had the chance to fly. Years later I realized that this "movement"—going to war and traveling in these "directions" throughout the Far East —had actually saved my life.

At the end of the war, my division was sent by the Allies to work for a year on Rempang, an uninhabited island near Singapore. Times were hard and everyone around me was having a different reaction to the new environment. Former leaders seemed less able to lead. Lesser men seemed to take on more responsibility. Individual differences were appearing. Big changes in behavior and communication were occurring. Some men seemed to be more in agreement with the laws of nature and the demands of an environment of scarce food and primitive living conditions than others.

This time was a turning point for me. Life there was extremely difficult. We worked hard, hunted and fished for food, built our own shelters. Survival itself was the goal. It reminded me of the lives of earlier generations—primitive man must have lived this way! But there was one great difference—our ancestors lived on instinct. They had a sensitivity to nature, were able to "read" it. We were "modern men"—civilized, but living in an uncivilized environment—left to fend for ourselves without the well-developed animal instincts that our predecessors had. So, our problems were enormous, not only in learning to survive but also in learning to communicate with each other in those most primitive circumstances. Fear and hunger, faced constantly, brought out the self-protective instincts in all of us. I began to think more for myself, for it was hard to consider others in times like that. I saw that those who were active, who moved around and found enough food and shelter, fared better than those who did not. I noticed that even with similar effort, certain people succeeded in finding what they needed while others failed. People who succeeded, the ones we call "lucky," must have been moving harmoniously with nature, even though they were unaware of how the laws of nature worked. Correct action and movement in relation to their environment seemed to solve their problems. Seeing this connection between man and nature gave me my first insight into a larger view of the world.

When I got back home, feeling free at last and hopeful that life would take a brighter turn, I found that my brother and sister, who had always been stronger and healthier than I, had died from the stresses of war. Later that year, my mother died of a heart attack. Suddenly I found myself alone, wondering again what the future would bring.

A year after my mother's death I was hospitalized with tuberculosis, which in those days was considered as dangerous as cancer. Recovery was doubtful. During the ten months I was hospitalized, my whole life seemed controlled by illness. I thought back to a traffic accident at age five that left me with a neat little scar on my nose. I remembered also the emergency appendectomy at age seventeen that nearly took my life. And now this.

This was a real setback from the beginnings of freedom I had felt when I came home. For the third time in my life, my dream of going to America was out of my grasp. I wondered whether my future would always be clouded by the uncertainty of my physical condition. It seemed that life was always sending me the wrong way.

But why? Why? There I was, twenty-five years old, thinking to myself, "What if I don't recover? How did I get into this condition? *Why is this happening to me now?*" I felt that if this was my life, then I had to accept the situation, but first I had to find out more about it. Why had it happened? What was it that controlled my life? Did I have anything to say about my own future, or was all life controlled by some larger, unknown power? Although I believed this greater power existed, I wasn't sure I could find a way to strengthen my connection to it. But I was determined to try.

Around this time, some friends suggested I see an adviser to find out about the future. I was open to this idea because I had come from a traditional Japanese family. Like many Japanese families, mine had occasionally used divination systems (not unlike *The Farmer's Almanac*) for vital information about matters of importance—moving, building a house, planning a marriage, etc. Consulting an expert was an entirely different matter. I saw several advisers, asking many questions about the past and future, and how the Universe worked. Unfortunately, they only gave me yes or no answers to my questions. I always came away dissatisfied because they would never explain *why* things happen or answer my questions about how their divination systems worked. Since I could not find a teacher or school that satisfied me, I read many books and consulted with other serious students in an attempt to reach a deeper understanding.

I researched a variety of divination systems before coming to one called *Ki* (pronounced "key"), a study of Ki-energies, and a statistical study of the relationships of numbers involved in life. I knew that the Chinese philosophers and scholars had developed their system over thousands of years, and as I began to study intensely, I was amazed to find that their statistics and observations worked when I used the system correctly.

For a period of about ten years, I studied hard and refined the use of this system. Meanwhile, I recovered from my illness. I had learned how to control my life better. I grew strong. My fears diminished. I became able to choose what was right for me. I stopped worrying about the future and began to live more fully in the present.

Once I learned that I could use this system for myself, I felt I needed to see whether the system worked for other people as well. Gradually, I began to find others with similar interests and questions. People told me that my "advice" to them, based on the Ki system, was actually correct a great deal of the time. Suddenly I found all these people referring their friends, family, and business associates to me for answers to their questions about the future. It seemed that everyone wanted to know how to make his dreams come true.

I still thought about coming to America, and finally, after much deliberation, I made the decision to move. When I got to the United States, establishing myself proved much more difficult than I had imagined. It was not until my third trip that I was able to really get myself settled in New York.

As my business here flourished I was able to spend more and more time advising my clients and friends. It took many years to accomplish, but I managed to make my dream come true, even though it seemed so difficult to do. Looking back after all this time, I realize that it is our dreams and desires, however small they may be, that keep us going and give us the strength to carry on. For me, it was the magic of Hershey's Kisses and my childhood dream of coming to America that kept the spark of hope alive in my heart. Throughout all the terrible times, especially during my illness, my desire to make that dream come true burned stronger than any fears I had about life. That dream, coupled with the knowledge I gained from the study of Ki, helped me to find and use inner resources I never knew I had.

You can do the same, using your own dreams as inspiration. Now, after thirty-five years of using the Ki to help others, I would like to share it with you, my readers.

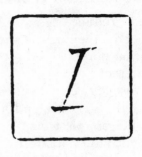

INTRODUCTION

We all have dreams and ambitions and there is a way to make dreams come true—by using the energy that controls the Universe. This energy is called *Ki-energy*. If you know how it works, you can live a more balanced, happier life, whether you are looking for love or success, solutions to personal or business problems, financial rewards or domestic harmony. Understanding Ki-energy gives you a different perspective on how to control your life.

In 1973, John Lennon and Yoko Ono separated. Yoko, remembering that I had predicted they would face this situation a year before it happened, came to see me. My advice to her must have been correct, for in 1975, she reconciled with John. The first day they were together again, they conceived Sean. Also, they got the idea to expand their business investments and were very successful over the next few years building their fortune. For a period of about ten years, from 1973 to September 1982, I advised the Lennons.

I spoke to Tommy Tune in November of 1973, when he was doing the Broadway show *Seesaw*. After I checked his chart, I predicted that he would win the Tony Award the following year. Sure enough, on April 21, 1974, he called to tell me that he was on his way to the theater for the awards ceremony. I watched at home as Tommy, dressed in a white tuxedo, picked up his Tony. It was an especially happy moment for me.

Some years ago, I advised Barry Manilow to consider the field of record producing rather than just singing. Later I found that he had produced Dionne Warwick's successful comeback album. I checked their charts and found that they had excellent communication potential, even though their basic personalities were very different.

My advice to all these people was based on the Ki. So, what exactly is the Ki, and how does it work?

The simplest way I can think of beginning is to describe the science and statistical study of Ki. Well, what is Ki, then? Energies: vital energies, subtle human energies that are the breath of life itself. These Ki-energies show us how desire and morality work for every human being. The ancients in China believed that these Ki-energies were created in the atmosphere by the Five Elements (Wood, Fire, Earth, Metal, and Water). Ki-energies then created our world and were responsible for the birth and death of all creatures on Earth.

These playful energies, as they combine and interact in different patterns, are always changing, yet they repeat according to certain cycles. There is one cycle of Ki-energy that lasts for a year; another cycle lasts one month; still another changes daily. Ki-energies are constantly changing, even down to the minute and second of time.

To keep the discussion practical and simple, this book will focus only on the yearly and monthly Ki-energies and the ways our lives are affected by them. These energies are represented by nine numbers, 1 through 9, which move through their yearly and monthly cycles, combining and forming patterns that are laid out in octagon-shaped charts. There are 108 charts in all (nine numbers times twelve months).

If you study these patterns, as the scholars did thousands of years ago, you will see how these energies guide and shape your life. The Ki is the study of the various Ki-energies and their cycles, which shows how you can use them to your best advantage.

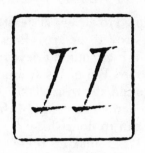

THE BASIS OF THE KI

To begin the study of the Ki, we need to know something about the *Universal Chart,* an octogon-shaped diagram on which the numbers are displayed. It is the fundamental chart of this system and the number positions on it are fixed.

THE UNIVERSAL CHART

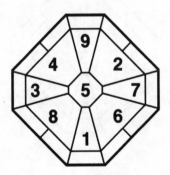

There is an interesting old story surrounding the Universal Chart, called the "Legend of the Turtle Shell." According to tradition in ancient China, civilization had spread out and grown along the coast of the lower and middle streams of the Yellow River (Hwang

Ho). However, at least eight times disastrous floods came and destroyed the area. Because of these periods of destruction, communities couldn't develop smoothly or plan for the future. A man named Wu of Hsia came along, and he made river improvements around the year 2000 B.C. that stopped the flooding. He became emperor as a result of this outstanding achievement, and the land began to flourish.

While making these river improvements, Wu of Hsia encountered a turtle. In the legends of those times God was supposed to have resided in the shell of the turtle and the horns of the water buffalo, so naturally Wu of Hsia was overjoyed, since the turtle was also a symbol of long life and happiness. Noticing an unusual system of black and white circular markings on the turtle's shell, he was inspired by this "sign from above" to carry on and complete his work. Feeling sure that God was on his side, Wu used the inspiration from seeing the turtle's extraordinary markings to begin a basic theory of life that would enable him to rule his country so all would prosper and live long, happy lives. He directed his various scholars to organize and develop ideas that would incorporate their collective knowledge, past observations, and research, using the turtle shell as a focal point.

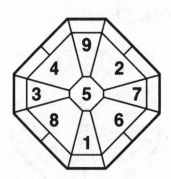

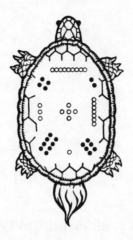

Looking closely at the markings, one can see various black and white dots grouped together as follows:

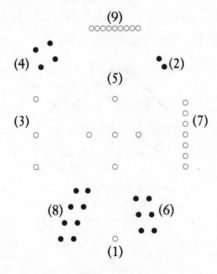

If the shell is represented as a regular square, we find a kind of perfect balance between the numbers, as the sum of the numbers across, up and down, and diagonally in any direction equals fifteen.

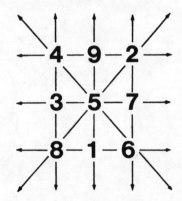

This symmetry was a great surprise to Wu of Hsia. He considered the balanced placement of the nine numbers to be "God-given." Since traditionally, all living things exist facing the sun, the south position was placed at the top. To preserve the turtle shell design, the square configuration was replaced by what is now known as the *Universal Chart.* The Universal Chart represents the Universe and all of life.

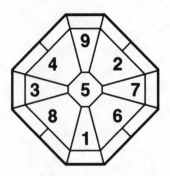

THE FIVE ELEMENTS

What evolved from this early research was a science that taught that the Universe consisted of five basic elements—Wood, Fire, Earth, Metal, Water. The scholars believed that all creatures and natural phenomena were created by these Five Elements. Let's look closely at each element's qualities.

WOOD—This element symbolizes not only Wood itself but all living things. It represents the appearance and the beginnings of growth and is associated with the spring season, activity, and reputation.

FIRE—This element symbolizes heat and burning, the expansion and augmentation of things. It is associated with the summer season, pride, and success.

EARTH—This element symbolizes energy and change, as the Earth gives energy and nourishment for things to appear, work, and disappear again into the Earth. It is associated with the periods between the seasons, dedication, the power to control, and accumulation.

METAL—This element symbolizes maturity and stability. It represents the chill of autumn and harvest, completeness, and entertainment.

WATER—This element symbolizes the phenomenon of fluids, the purification and resolution of things. It is associated with winter, when, after the harvest, Earth goes into hibernation, waiting for the coming spring. It is both independence and insecurity.

All Five Elements affect each other and have interrelationships that are very important. Furthermore, it was found that each element is affected by yin and yang forces—the polar opposites. *Yin* represents the negative pole—the Moon, the female principle, the Earth—and its qualities include darkness, passivity, supportiveness, and receptivity. *Yang* represents the positive pole—the Sun, the masculine principle, Heaven—and its qualities include light, action, leadership, and creativity. Yin and yang forces are always shifting back and forth, one giving way to the other. Before the development of the concept of the Five Elements, Oriental philosophers thought that the Universe was controlled by yin and yang forces alone: an influence would begin, grow to its extreme, then diminish and become its opposite. But it is really these two ideas—the interrelationships of the Five Elements and the interplay of the yin-yang forces—that led to the divination systems we have today.

KI-ENERGY

In ancient Chinese philosophy, the Universe is made up of "Three Circles"—Heaven, Earth, and Human. Ki-energy from Heaven *(Heaven Ki-energy)* is always descending from above, while Ki-energy from Earth *(Earth Ki-energy)* is always rising up from below. Human Ki-energy was created in a combining burst of Heaven Ki-energy and Earth Ki-energy. The Human Ki-energy created our world: minerals, plants, animals, human beings, and all things.

We are affected, then, by two kinds of Ki-energies, from Heaven and from Earth. Heaven Ki-energy controls our *morality*, and Earth Ki-energy controls our *desire*. An understanding of the Ki system helps you to balance these two kinds of energy.

With accumulated observations, scholars associated the elements with the nine Numbers, 1 through 9, which are representations of Human Ki-energy. The following diagram illustrates their associations.

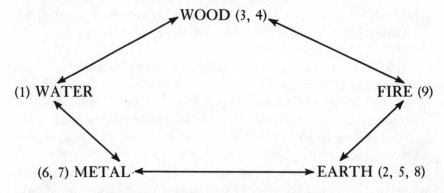

(See the section on Relationships for more information about the reciprocal relationships of the Five Elements.)

Although the progress of science and civilization has caused us to lose our innate sensitivity to many basic connections with nature, we can still see the effects of Ki-energy around us. We notice how the plants and trees respond to the seasons. The Ki-energy of spring brings forth the buds. The Ki-energy of summer blossoms into flowers. In autumn, Ki-energy ripens the fruit and changes the color of the leaves. When the plants and trees meet winter Ki-energy, their leaves fall and die. These natural phenomena are cyclic patterns that repeat according to the laws of nature.

We are subject to the same laws of nature as the plants and trees, but many of us are unaware of how we are affected by them. Changes such as day and night, the four seasons, fair and cloudy weather, wind and rain, heat and cold all influence us both directly and indirectly. We must learn to recognize the changing effects that Ki-energy has upon our lives.

Interestingly enough, as modern science attempts to answer questions about the way the Universe was formed or to find the nature of energy fields, gravity, and so on, the results bear a similarity to the effects of Ki-energy given by the ancient Chinese scholars. Like the quantum field of modern physics, Ki-energy can condense into solid material or disperse again into something tenuous. If there was a "Big Bang," Ki-energy was its basis. If Ki-energy collapses, so will the cosmos.

Literally, the word *Ki* means "ether" and was used in ancient China to denote the energy animating the Universe. The path of this energy in the body is the basis for acupuncture and traditional Chinese medicine. The flow of Ki is also the foundation of the flowing movement of *t'ai chi ch'uan*.

When we add to this the balance or reciprocal relationships of Ki-energy (yin and yang), we realize the great importance of Ki to Chinese thought and culture.

HOW TO FIND YOUR BIRTH CHART

It is of the utmost importance in the study of the Ki system to be able to find the numbers and charts you need. For this book you will see how three of the nine numbers relate to you. Where they appear in your Birth Chart is important.

The first and most important number is the *Basic Number*, which identifies the Ki-energy of your year of birth and tells you, "I am Number . . ." This number reveals your intrinsic nature and is written first, in large print. Influenced by the Yearly Ki-energy, the Basic Number changes once a year, and its position in the chart changes every month.

Second is the *Control Number*, which identifies the Ki-energy of your month of birth. It is the center number in your chart, revealing your spirituality, the driving force behind your personality. It is written second, in small print. The Control Number changes every month.

Last is the *Tendency Number*, which shows the position of your Basic Number during your month of birth. It reveals your habits and likely behavior; it is written third, also in small print. The Tendency Number exerts influence over the Basic Number and also changes every month.

BIRTH CHART	*BIRTH CHART*
*Name:*_____	*Name:*_____
*Date of Birth:*_____	*Date of Birth:*_____
*Basic Number:*_____	*Basic Number:*_____
*Control Number:*_____	*Control Number:*_____
*Tendency Number:*_____	*Tendency Number:*_____

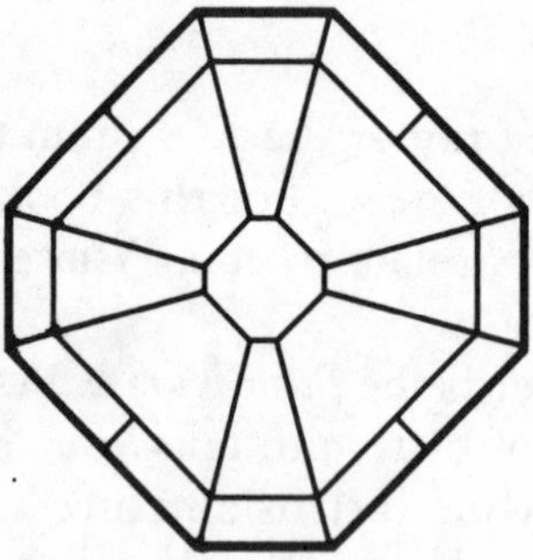

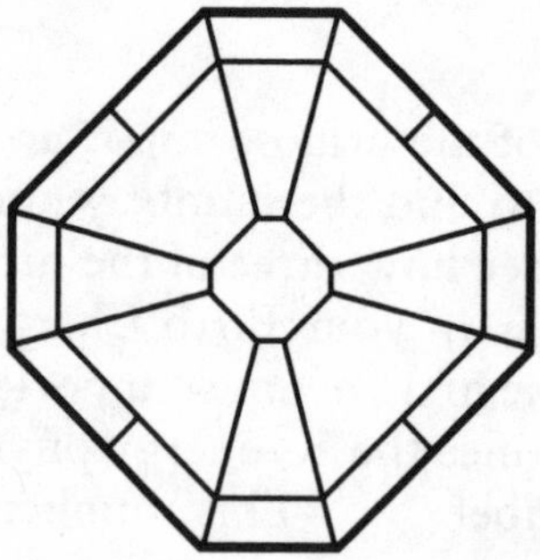

Note Zodiac Sign: *Note Zodiac Sign:*

FINDING YOUR BASIC NUMBER

By now you must be wondering, What is *my* number and how do I find it? This is everyone's first question. All you need to know is your own year of birth, which tells you your basic number. Look on the Basic Number Chart that follows. Find your year of birth. Remember that in the Chinese lunar calendar, the New Year starts around February 4 each year. For example, if your birthday is January 20, 1954, you are Number 2, the Number for 1953. If you are born on or after February 4 of that same year, 1954, you are Number 1.

After you find your Basic Number here, look at the Human Personality Traits Chart (on page 15), which gives an outline of the numbers and their traditional associations. Each number has its own traits, which correspond to our own, and each one of us belongs especially to one of those numbers. For example, if you are Number 1, you are naturally independent; Number 2, dependent;

BASIC NUMBER CHART (YEAR OF BIRTH)*

9	8	7	6	5	4	3	2	1
FEB. 4 1892	FEB. 3 1893	FEB. 4 1894	FEB. 4 1895	FEB. 4 1896	FEB. 3 1897	FEB. 4 1898	FEB. 4 1899	FEB. 4 1900
FEB. 4 1901	FEB. 5 1902	FEB. 5 1903	FEB. 5 1904	FEB. 4 1905	FEB. 5 1906	FEB. 5 1907	FEB. 5 1908	FEB. 4 1909
FEB. 5 1910	FEB. 5 1911	FEB. 5 1912	FEB. 4 1913	FEB. 5 1914	FEB. 5 1915	FEB. 5 1916	FEB. 4 1917	FEB. 5 1918
FEB. 5 1919	FEB. 5 1920	FEB. 4 1921	FEB. 5 1922	FEB. 5 1923	FEB. 5 1924	FEB. 4 1925	FEB. 4 1926	FEB. 5 1927
FEB. 5 1928	FEB. 4 1929	FEB. 4 1930	FEB. 5 1931	FEB. 5 1932	FEB. 4 1933	FEB. 4 1934	FEB. 5 1935	FEB. 5 1936
FEB. 4 1937	FEB. 4 1938	FEB. 5 1939	FEB. 5 1940	FEB. 4 1941	FEB. 4 1942	FEB. 5 1943	FEB. 5 1944	FEB. 4 1945
FEB. 4 1946	FEB. 5 1947	FEB. 5 1948	FEB. 4 1949	FEB. 4 1950	FEB. 5 1951	FEB. 5 1952	FEB. 4 1953	FEB. 4 1954
FEB. 5 1955	FEB. 5 1956	FEB. 4 1957	FEB. 4 1958	FEB. 4 1959	FEB. 5 1960	FEB. 4 1961	FEB. 4 1962	FEB. 4 1963
FEB. 5 1964	FEB. 4 1965	FEB. 4 1966	FEB. 4 1967	FEB. 5 1968	FEB. 4 1969	FEB. 4 1970	FEB. 4 1971	FEB. 5 1972
FEB. 4 1973	FEB. 4 1974	FEB. 4 1975	FEB. 5 1976	FEB. 4 1977	FEB. 4 1978	FEB. 4 1979	FEB. 5 1980	FEB. 4 1981
FEB. 4 1982	FEB. 4 1983	FEB. 4 1984	FEB. 4 1985	FEB. 4 1986	FEB. 4 1987	FEB. 4 1988	FEB. 4 1989	FEB. 4 1990
FEB. 4 1991	FEB. 4 1992	FEB. 4 1993	FEB. 4 1994	FEB. 4 1995	FEB. 4 1996	FEB. 4 1997	FEB. 4 1998	FEB. 4 1999

*The February day in each box shows the day the year changes. This may change your Basic Number if you were born in January or the first few days in February.

Number 3, active; Number 4, tender; Number 5, powerful; Number 6, magnanimous; Number 7, entertaining; Number 8, self-motivated; Number 9, proud. For more details on the Basic Numbers, look at the profiles for the nine general types that follow the chart of Human Personality Traits. Note also the location of your Basic Number on the Universal Chart in the upper left-hand corner of your profile. This is a fixed chart and the permanent position of your basic number on the Universal Chart.

HUMAN PERSONALITY TRAITS

NUMBER	NATURAL PHENOMENON	TRAIT
1	*WATER*	COOL, INDEPENDENT, CONCENTRATING, INTUITIVE, DIPLOMATIC, SERIOUS, CAREFUL, INSIGHTFUL, OBSTINATE, TENACIOUS, WORRISOME, SOCIAL, SELF-PROTECTIVE, INDUSTRIOUS, INSECURE, PATIENT, HARDWORKING, INTIMATE, SELF-ASSERTIVE, MANIPULATIVE
2	*EARTH*	STEADY, SERVING, SACRIFICING, DEPENDENT, DILIGENT, DELICATE, MATERNAL, METICULOUS, FEMININE, FASTIDIOUS, SHREWD, OBSERVING, SUPPORTIVE, CONSERVATIVE, PROVINCIAL, DEDICATED, METHODICAL, DETAIL-MINDED, NOURISHING
3	*THUNDER*	EXPLOSIVE, SUSCEPTIBLE, INSIGHTFUL, ACTIVE, ADVANCING, FRANK, AGGRESSIVE, GROWING, INTENSIVE, IMPATIENT, SENSITIVE, RASH, HASTY, TALKATIVE, PASSIONATE, OUTGOING, STRAIGHTFORWARD, PROGRESSIVE
4	*WIND*	TENDER, IMPULSIVE, CONFIDENT, REPUTABLE, PRUDENT, ADAPTABLE, LIBERAL, STUBBORN, SMOOTH-MANNERED, EMOTIONAL, HARMONIOUS, EVASIVE, CHANGEABLE, CREATIVE, MOODY, OPEN, SCATTERED
5	*EARTH* (Primal Power)	STRONG, SELF-ASSERTIVE, CONTROLLING, HAUGHTY, PERSISTENT, STUBBORN, HUMANE, DETERMINED, EGOISTIC, LATE-MATURING, DESTRUCTIVE, BOLD, TALENTED, FORCEFUL, AGGRESSIVE
6	*HEAVEN*	COMPLETE, STYLISH, MAGNANIMOUS, ORGANIZED, CALM JUDGMENT, UNADAPTABLE, FAITHFUL, CAUTIOUS, PERFECTIONIST, DIGNIFIED, STRONG WILLPOWER, CONFIDENT, LEADERSHIP, RELIABLE, PROUD, RATIONAL, PRUDENT
7	*POND, LAKE*	EASY-GOING, FLEXIBLE, SOCIAL, TALKER (NOT LISTENER), STORMY, HYPER-SENSITIVE, NERVOUS, PASSIONATE, CALCULATING, POLISHED, ENTERTAINING, RESOURCEFUL, EXPRESSIVE, PERSUASIVE
8	*MOUNTAIN*	SEEKING, PERSISTENT, BUILDING UP OF WEALTH, OPINIONATED, SAVING-MINDED, ADVENTUROUS, WILLFUL, FREE, AVARICIOUS, TENACIOUS, REVOLUTIONARY, SELF-MOTIVATING, SELF-INDULGENT, AMBITIOUS, OBSTINATE, ENERGETIC
9	*FIRE*	PROUD, FORESIGHTFUL HONORABLE, IMPULSIVE, SUCCESSFUL, VAIN, INTELLIGENT, FICKLE, STORMY, SELF-CONCERNED, SOPHISTICATED, SELF-CONSCIOUS, ENLIGHTENED, FLAMBOYANT

BASIC NUMBER PROFILES

TYPE ONE

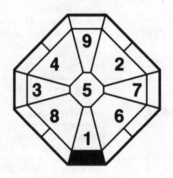

YEAR OF NUMBER ONE*

FEB. 4, 1900–FEB. 3, 1901	FEB. 4, 1954–FEB. 4, 1955
FEB. 4, 1909–FEB. 4, 1910	FEB. 4, 1963–FEB. 4, 1964
FEB. 5, 1918–FEB. 4, 1919	FEB. 5, 1972–FEB. 3, 1973
FEB. 5, 1927–FEB. 4, 1928	FEB. 4, 1981–FEB. 3, 1982
FEB. 5, 1936–FEB. 3, 1937	FEB. 4, 1990–FEB. 3, 1991
FEB. 4, 1945–FEB. 3, 1946	FEB. 4, 1999–FEB. 3, 2000

*Shows basic position of Number One on the Universal Chart.

ELEMENT: Water
NATURAL PHENOMENON: Moving Water
SYMBOLIC NATURE: The natural phenomenon of Water brings forth the idea of a single drop of Water moving down a mountain. It finds another drop and forms a small stream, which in turn joins a larger river and eventually flows into the ocean. Thus the single drop begins its journey from above and flows down to the place beneath—to be stopped only by indentations in the Earth where the Water may be stored. Its journey is often dark and difficult, as it moves around the trees and beneath the rocks and boulders.
ASSOCIATIONS: From this symbolic nature comes an infinite number of associations. Hardship and difficulty are linked to the movement of Water. Social nature and diplomacy are suggested by the ease with which Water joins other Water to grow larger. Sex

is also associated with Water, in its merging or closeness. Water will flow around its obstacles but always keep moving, intent upon reaching its destination. Beginnings of all kinds and their accompanying difficulties, as well as the independence that results from undertakings of one's own are suggested by the single drop of Water about to embark on a journey. Water's unlimited movement can be gloomy, dark and secretive. It can be negative. Insecurity comes from water's constant motion, from not knowing what's going to happen next. It is from this insecurity that independence is born, the courage to face the unknown. Often, independence is accompanied by loneliness.

IN HUMAN LIFE: Generally speaking, Number One has two sides —the gloomy, or negative, and the lively, or positive. There are often distant relationships with one or both of the parents, predominantly with the father. Most Number Ones advance their lives with much effort from childhood. These difficult experiences give them great patience and drive them toward independence. Those powers bring them future success, as a drop of Water eventually creates a great ocean.

Number Ones have a greater chance of succeeding in a venture of their own than through anything they might inherit. They are fiercely independent, talented, and intelligent and dislike being pushed around or confined by anyone or anything. It is easy for them to take the lead in a given situation. They can often relate better to a stranger than to their own blood relations, and thus they are capable of developing a wide circle of acquaintances.

These people must guard against too great an independence, which can lead to overconfident rationalization, and later to loneliness and isolation. They have difficulty finishing things.

GENERAL ADVICE: Lasting success often depends on whether or not good friendships are formed. You shouldn't be afraid of the difficult times in your youth—it is often the lessons learned from these experiences that make for great success later in life. You should listen to what your friends say—and not be overconfident!

TYPE TWO

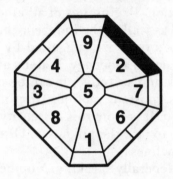

YEAR OF NUMBER TWO*

FEB. 4, 1899–FEB. 3, 1900	FEB. 4, 1953–FEB. 3, 1954
FEB. 5, 1908–FEB. 3, 1909	FEB. 4, 1962–FEB. 3, 1963
FEB. 4, 1917–FEB. 4, 1918	FEB. 4, 1971–FEB. 4, 1972
FEB. 4, 1926–FEB. 4, 1927	FEB. 5, 1980–FEB. 3, 1981
FEB. 5, 1935–FEB. 4, 1936	FEB. 4, 1989–FEB. 3, 1990
FEB. 5, 1944–FEB. 3, 1945	FEB. 4, 1998–FEB. 3, 1999

*Shows the basic position of Number Two on the Universal Chart.

ELEMENT: Earth
NATURAL PHENOMENON: Earth
SYMBOLIC NATURE: Earth is represented symbolically as the Mother of the Universe, as compared with Heaven, the Father. Earth is in the position of receiving energies from above, which are always descending, to nourish and warmly embrace all creatures. To accept energy that is given is one of Earth's most intrinsic qualities, and it is this gentle receptivity that enables the Earth to hold and nurture all life.
ASSOCIATIONS: From these images come an infinite number of associations with patience, quiet, reserve, and diligence in the face of difficulty, as growth and nourishment take time and often involve much hard work. Receptivity gives rise to qualities of dedication, supportiveness, and self-sacrifice, and to service as opposed to leadership. Constancy.
IN HUMAN LIFE: This type of person is often known as the "quiet

person of action." Usually reserved and gentle, such people are capable of great patience, diligence, and devotion. But, like the growth process they represent, they need time to develop their careers. Because of their conservative natures, they build up experience slowly and gradually. Working at first as an assistant to a strong leader (for service is natural to them) gives them a basis from which to grow and learn, and they can reach their goals much more easily in this way.

However, some Number Twos are in a hurry to succeed and want desperately to take the lead or control things their own way. This is a mistake and often leads to failure.

GENERAL ADVICE: Step-by-step development is the best way to your future success.

TYPE THREE

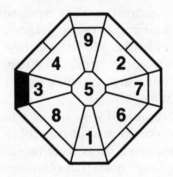

YEAR OF NUMBER THREE*

FEB. 4, 1898–FEB. 3, 1899	FEB. 5, 1952–FEB. 3, 1953
FEB. 5, 1907–FEB. 4, 1908	FEB. 4, 1961–FEB. 3, 1962
FEB. 5, 1916–FEB. 3, 1917	FEB. 4, 1970–FEB. 3, 1971
FEB. 4, 1925–FEB. 3, 1926	FEB. 4, 1979–FEB. 4, 1980
FEB. 4, 1934–FEB. 4, 1935	FEB. 4, 1988–FEB. 3, 1989
FEB. 5, 1943–FEB. 4, 1944	FEB. 4, 1997–FEB. 3, 1998

*Shows basic position of Number Three in the Universal Chart.

ELEMENT: Wood
NATURAL PHENOMENON: Thunder
SYMBOLIC NATURE: The natural phenomenon of Thunder brings forth the idea of a burst of explosive energy, which lights up the entire sky and then is gone. The sound of its rumbling vibrations can be heard even before it is seen. Its presence can be loud enough and powerful enough to frighten and shock even the most fearless. Indeed, Thunder makes a threatening appearance.
ASSOCIATIONS: From this symbolic nature come many associations. Explosive energy, vibrancy, and acute sensitivity are among the most important. From this vibrant nature also come rashness, hastiness, and a certain natural virility. This type of energy often breeds determination and a quest for experience and yet may not include the patience or perseverance necessary to concentrate on one area for very long. Bursts of energy may be spent (not always wisely) on a great variety of things. Thunder can be experimental

and precocious. Explosive activity and sensitivity point toward a tendency to break down, for extreme activity such as this cannot be sustained over long periods of time.

IN HUMAN LIFE: These people are blessed with natural vibrancy and a tremendous amount of energy. Their inclinations lead them into all kinds of different activities and experiences (which they pursue fervently for a time before moving on to something else) and their creation of new opportunities, especially early in life, often finds them successful at a young age.

Their quick determination to take chances can often make them rash or hasty. Always on the move, pushing forward, they may not be cautious enough or aware of surrounding influences that should also be considered. These people have a hard time sitting still in one place for very long. They must develop patience and persistence to accompany their great energy and determination, for they can easily exhaust themselves by trying to do too much, either too soon or all at once.

In human relationships, these people are open and honest, but also highly sensitive because of their nature. They can be lonely at times, since they can alienate others with their frankness and are easily hurt, despite their grandiose appearance. It is hard for them to gain satisfaction through others—for them, it is "What *I* did" that is important. They have to deal with everything by themselves, and their natural prejudice dictates that they will give their energies only to things they really want to do. Even relationships can depend on their convenience, and this self-mindedness can bring them unintentional solitude.

They are often at odds with, or distant from, their fathers; this tendency, coupled with their own abundant energy, leads them to be quite strong and vigorous in their approach to life.

GENERAL ADVICE: Don't bite off more than you can chew. Ladies, don't wear heels that are too high. You may have a long way to run.

TYPE FOUR

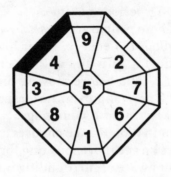

YEAR OF NUMBER FOUR*

FEB. 3, 1897–FEB. 3, 1898	FEB. 5, 1951–FEB. 4, 1952
FEB. 5, 1906–FEB. 4, 1907	FEB. 5, 1960–FEB. 3, 1961
FEB. 5, 1915–FEB. 4, 1916	FEB. 4, 1969–FEB. 3, 1970
FEB. 5, 1924–FEB. 3, 1925	FEB. 4, 1978–FEB. 3, 1979
FEB. 4, 1933–FEB. 3, 1934	FEB. 4, 1987–FEB. 3, 1988
FEB. 4, 1942–FEB. 4, 1943	FEB. 4, 1996–FEB. 3, 1997

*Shows basic position of Number Four on the Universal Chart.

ELEMENT: Wood
NATURAL PHENOMENON: Wind
SYMBOLIC NATURE: The natural phenomenon of Wind brings forth the idea of movement, constant movement that cannot always be seen or heard. Unlike Water, which obviously moves downward, Wind tends to move every which way, without a regular pattern, and quite invisibly. Wind can be fierce as a gale or gentle as a whisper. Its nature is such that it may carry other things from place to place, making relationships easier and helping life to renew itself.
ASSOCIATIONS: From this symbolic nature several associations suggest themselves. Gentle, easy movement that is always ongoing and touches all things indicates real tenderness and affection within a broad social framework. Communication flows quietly and is made simpler by this gentility, which is its natural gift. Strong emotion is indicated by the variation in the Wind's speed

and direction—like the turbulent, changing feelings of people. Intimacy is deepened by emotion; distance is suggested by the lack of deeper communication. Confidence is suggested by the strength of the wind as it pushes a sail or carries pollen. Also, indecision is indicated (trying to "catch the wind") that makes for a lack of clarity, which in turn creates doubt. Gentility often hides a stronger desire or worldly-mindedness that can show itself as greed or pleasure seeking.

IN HUMAN LIFE: These people feel the need to take care of others. They are "tender-touching," affectionate, and loving, usually with a large social circle. Their gentle nature and easy manner make communication easier, and for this, they are greatly appreciated by others.

Generally speaking, these people's lives are much influenced by emotion, and they very often act on their emotional impulses alone. They are very giving, and in their care for other people, they earn a good reputation and the confidence of others. They have a better chance of winning the confidence of others than they have of making a great fortune. Often, success for them comes as the result of efforts they have made on someone else's behalf.

It's hard to describe their nature definitively, for they are indeed like the Wind and can easily change their minds. Their easy willingness to move around or follow a whim can create problems. Indecision, as when they cannot get something clear in their minds, creates doubt and confusion. This can surface in marriage, where indecision, lack of interest, or a changing mind causes grief.

Although such people are often accused of being "too easy" by those with stronger desires than they, their easy appearance may hide or obscure their real wants, which can be very deep-seated and self-serving indeed! It's difficult for other people to read their minds, because they have predetermined direction inside, yet seem indecisive on the outside.

GENERAL ADVICE: Be generous and *give first*. Don't expect to receive from others before you give.

TYPE FIVE

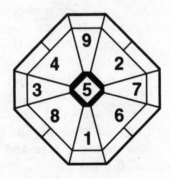

YEAR OF NUMBER FIVE*

FEB. 4, 1896–FEB. 2, 1897	FEB. 4, 1950–FEB. 4, 1951
FEB. 4, 1905–FEB. 4, 1906	FEB. 4, 1959–FEB. 4, 1960
FEB. 5, 1914–FEB. 4, 1915	FEB. 5, 1968–FEB. 3, 1969
FEB. 5, 1923–FEB. 4, 1924	FEB. 4, 1977–FEB. 3, 1978
FEB. 5, 1932–FEB. 3, 1933	FEB. 4, 1986–FEB. 3, 1987
FEB. 4, 1941–FEB. 3, 1942	FEB. 4, 1995–FEB. 3, 1996

*Shows the basic position of Number Five on the Universal Chart.

ELEMENT: Earth
NATURAL PHENOMENON: Primal Power.
SYMBOLIC NATURE: The status of Number Five is different from that of the other eight numbers and is considered to be by far the most powerful number of all. As a larger, primal power, it rises up from Earth and possesses both creative and destructive capabilities. Also, Number Five represents the human being as the center of his own world.
ASSOCIATIONS: Birth and death, as examples of creativity and destruction, are images, as are all natural disasters. Primal power (as for strength and power) that is inherited or "God-given" is indicated. In human beings, Number Five is the great controller —both the concept of power or control over others as well as the control of the self. From this come the ideas of ego, strength, boldness, leadership potential, greatness of talent and ability.

Creativity abounds, but with it comes its opposite, destruction. As Number Five may create or constantly renew itself, so it may also destroy another number or itself if opposed. This two-sided creative/destructive potential must always be in balance for the great power of Number Five to be harnessed and used constructively.

IN HUMAN LIFE: Most of these people spend childhood growing up in difficult family surroundings. It is unusual for them to have help from their families as they move out into the world. The best way for them to build their future is outside their families; often, they are helped by strangers. This gives them a certain boldness and strength in worldly matters. Their nature is to eventually possess great talent. Some of them have a wildness or roughness about them and will labor hard. Their state of mind is indomitable, and their perseverance consistent, especially in career matters. This contributes to their strong talents. They have a fatalistic approach to gambling and in money matters try to make their fortune at a single stroke.

GENERAL ADVICE: Win or lose? The choice is yours.

TYPE SIX

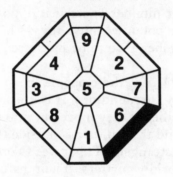

YEAR OF NUMBER SIX*

FEB. 4, 1895–FEB. 3, 1896	FEB. 4, 1949–FEB. 3, 1950
FEB. 5, 1904–FEB. 3, 1905	FEB. 4, 1958–FEB. 3, 1959
FEB. 4, 1913–FEB. 4, 1914	FEB. 4, 1967–FEB. 4, 1968
FEB. 5, 1922–FEB. 4, 1923	FEB. 5, 1976–FEB. 3, 1977
FEB. 5, 1931–FEB. 4, 1932	FEB. 4, 1985–FEB. 3, 1986
FEB. 5, 1940–FEB. 3, 1941	FEB. 4, 1994–FEB. 3, 1995

*Shows basic position of Number Six on the Universal Chart.

ELEMENT: Metal

NATURAL PHENOMENON: Heaven

SYMBOLIC NATURE: Heaven is represented symbolically as the Father of the Universe, as compared with Earth, the Mother. Heaven is the active, creative principle, the giver of life, of energy. Heavenly energy was described by the scholars as always descending from above, animating the Universe and all its creatures.

ASSOCIATIONS: Heaven suggests constancy, clarity and perfection. The center of the spirit order, organization and omnipotence are indicated. (Nothing can be bigger than Heaven!) Also, pride, completeness and independence. Rigidity leads to lack of adaptability. Heaven can be merciless or arrogant. It is positive, active, determined and dignified.

IN HUMAN LIFE: These people are usually born into a most powerful period in the lives of their parents. However, as they grow, the parents' fortunes tend to decline, and they may face difficult times until middle age.

Number Sixes have noble attitudes and highly organized, efficient minds, which give them the power to conquer any difficulty. Sometimes, they are too defensive, and their overly cautious attitude can cause them to lose opportunities. They often feel uncomfortable in social situations because of the calculating part of their natures. Their mode of expression, which is very direct and not at all smooth, can offend others without any real intention to do so. They must be careful to consider other people's wants.

These people are often discontented because it is never easy for them to adjust their minds or personalities in order to compromise quickly. Number Sixes must always do things their own way and should take care that, in so doing, they do not isolate themselves.

Pride plays an important role in their lives. On the one hand, their great sense of pride makes them think that everything they do is right, perhaps alienating others in the process; on the more positive side, their pride enables them to be strong enough to persevere calmly and patiently in difficult times.

GENERAL ADVICE: Give an apple to someone if he wants an apple, even if you think a peach is right for him.

TYPE SEVEN

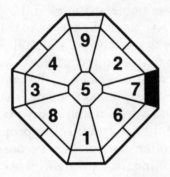

YEAR OF NUMBER SEVEN*

FEB. 4, 1894–FEB. 3, 1895	FEB. 5, 1948–FEB. 3, 1949
FEB. 5, 1903–FEB. 4, 1904	FEB. 4, 1957–FEB. 3, 1958
FEB. 5, 1912–FEB. 3, 1913	FEB. 4, 1966–FEB. 3, 1967
FEB. 4, 1921–FEB. 4, 1922	FEB. 4, 1975–FEB. 4, 1976
FEB. 4, 1930–FEB. 4, 1931	FEB. 4, 1984–FEB. 3, 1985
FEB. 5, 1939–FEB. 4, 1940	FEB. 4, 1993–FEB. 3, 1994

*Shows basic position of Number Seven on the Universal Chart.

ELEMENT: Metal
NATURAL PHENOMENON: Pond or Lake
SYMBOLIC NATURE: The natural phenomenon of the Lake or Pond brings forth the idea of Water coming together or being stored in one place. This gives nourishment to all creatures and helps them to grow strong. This strength brings richness and happiness.
ASSOCIATIONS: These images suggest associations with joy, delight, rejoicing, pleasure, entertainment, affection, and money. Also, ripples on the Lake give rise to the idea of nervousness, which is often associated with this nature.
IN HUMAN LIFE: Most of these people have very social personalities and are good speakers and entertainers. Their sharp minds are aided by their self-interested calculations, which are quite strong. But they tend to be nervous and can be prone to wanton behavior.

Their nature makes them naturally flexible and easygoing. If their families overindulged them when they were young, they will be spoiled, haughty, and extravagant. This can lead to their downfall. Number Sevens are respected because they are quick-witted and able to sense what others are thinking.

Because they are optimistic, they are less likely to finish projects, less likely to examine their own conduct. They are less tenacious. Number Sevens need to be given the chance to learn independence, to develop their careers. Once they learn it, their natural self-interest helps them to improve their lives considerably. Their easy, adaptable natures make them very social but not always sincere, very open and frank but quick to change their minds.

GENERAL ADVICE: Money is important, but there are many other things in life that are as important, especially the development of sincerity, which can improve everything about your life. Beware of arrogance!

TYPE EIGHT

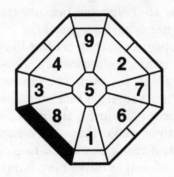

YEAR OF NUMBER EIGHT

FEB. 3, 1893–FEB. 3, 1894	FEB. 5, 1947–FEB. 4, 1948
FEB. 5, 1902–FEB. 4, 1903	FEB. 5, 1956–FEB. 3, 1957
FEB. 5, 1911–FEB. 4, 1912	FEB. 4, 1965–FEB. 3, 1966
FEB. 5, 1920–FEB. 3, 1921	FEB. 4, 1974–FEB. 3, 1975
FEB. 4, 1929–FEB. 3, 1930	FEB. 4, 1983–FEB. 3, 1984
FEB. 4, 1938–FEB. 4, 1939	FEB. 4, 1992–FEB. 3, 1993

*Shows basic position of Number Eight on the Universal Chart.

ELEMENT: Earth
NATURAL PHENOMENON: Mountain
SYMBOLIC NATURE: The natural phenomenon of the Mountain brings forth the idea of the accumulation of the Earth, built up in one place to become the tall, majestic, strong, unmoving, and physically imposing Mountain. From atop the Mountain, one can see much in all directions, but the Mountain itself definitely stays in one place.
ASSOCIATIONS: High-mindedness comes from the vantage point of the far-reaching view, as does its opposite, haughtiness. Stability, stubbornness, strength, and tenacity are associated with the immovability of the Mountain. Proud loneliness and splendid isolation also suggest themselves, although they may be cultivated in self-defense. The image of accumulation is often thought to show possible inheritance or succession. But the building of a mountain

is not always a smooth and continuous process, and stagnation can result.

IN HUMAN LIFE: Number Eights can appear obstinate on the outside but are really gentle on the inside. They are easily liked, and, in many ways, easy to relate to. At times, their self-motivation makes for childish actions. Their persistence and desire to monopolize relationships give rise to intense jealousies, which quickly heat up and cool down.

The greedy side of their nature makes them prone to unprincipled or unscrupulous behavior when their own self-interest is involved. Because they change their minds in this manner, people think them insincere. They have a two-sided character—tender, but greedy. Their motivations shift back and forth between these two powerful forces.

Where affection is concerned, Number Eights look for change and adventure. In money matters they are apt to take chances with grace. They are good at figures, are saving-minded, and tend to be possessive.

Often, these people are more successful later in life if their early years are spent rushing around trying to build up wealth or position for themselves. This kind of effort takes enormous energy, and with time, these people learn to use their energies more effectively. Also, they need the help of a stronger or more influential person to accomplish what they want; they alone don't have all the power it takes.

GENERAL ADVICE: If you know how to be loyal to a stronger person and can be patient, your life will improve greatly. As the Mountain remains steadfast, you must learn to weather all storms and wait for the right time to act. And then, act decisively!

TYPE NINE

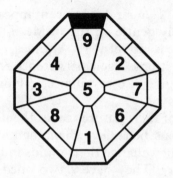

YEAR OF NUMBER NINE*

FEB. 4, 1892–FEB. 2, 1893	FEB. 4, 1946–FEB. 4, 1947
FEB. 4, 1901–FEB. 4, 1902	FEB. 5, 1955–FEB. 4, 1956
FEB. 5, 1910–FEB. 4, 1911	FEB. 5, 1964–FEB. 3, 1965
FEB. 5, 1919–FEB. 4, 1920	FEB. 4, 1973–FEB. 3, 1974
FEB. 5, 1928–FEB. 3, 1929	FEB. 4, 1982–FEB. 3, 1983
FEB. 4, 1937–FEB. 3, 1938	FEB. 4, 1991–FEB. 3, 1992

*Shows basic position of Number Nine on the Universal Chart.

ELEMENT: Fire

NATURAL PHENOMENON: Fire

SYMBOLIC NATURE: The natural phenomenon of Fire brings forth the idea of external brightness and heat, internal darkness and coolness. Bright and beautiful is the colorful flame, and the strong crackling sound of Fire as it burns reminds us of its power. When it has exhausted itself, it returns to emptiness.

ASSOCIATIONS: The image of Fire indicates brightness, far-sighted intelligence, fame, and success. Fire's appearance points to great beauty and a good sense of taste. The sounds associated with Fire demonstrate the kind of self-revelation that is sometimes known as "star quality." The heat of Fire shows its passion, and its burning, frenzy, impatience, and contempt. Its brightness shines with self-confidence, while its constant flickering shows its fickleness. Too much of a display points to vanity.

IN HUMAN LIFE: These people are intelligent and have good

foresight and determination. They are very capable of leadership on high levels. Their fickleness makes them easily angry so they might lose their chance to complete important tasks and fulfill their promise of leadership. Number Nines may proceed impulsively, with not enough consideration for those around them—making loyalty impossible. Often, these individuals find themselves in an emergency without devoted followers to support them; they must learn to listen to the advice and needs of others. To complete projects, they need constancy, prudence, and patience.

Number Nines tend to have an air of superiority about them, as they feel they are the best, brightest, and sharpest. Their self-confidence can become excessive, crossing over into vanity and lack of consideration for others.

GENERAL ADVICE: If you can develop greater generosity and greater benevolence, you can attain anything.

FINDING YOUR CONTROL NUMBER

The center number on the Monthly Charts is called the *Control Number.* It changes every month according to the Rule of Number Movement on page 318 and is found by looking up your month of birth on the following monthly charts. Again, people born early in the month should be careful. Depending on your day of birth, you may have to refer to the Dates the Months Change chart for the exact day that the months change during your year of birth according to the Chinese lunar calendar.

For example, Julie Andrews, who was born on October 1, 1935 (Basic Number 2), would be considered a September birthday, since the month change occurs on October 8 that year. A good rule of thumb is that if your birthdate occurs between the first and ninth of a given month, you should check the Dates the Months Change chart on pages 40–42 to see which month your birthdate is in.

Once you have found your month of birth, look at the following monthly charts. Find your Basic Number at the top of the appropriate monthly chart (Chart A for Basic Numbers 1, 4, and 7; Chart B for Basic Numbers 3, 6, and 9; and Chart C for Basic Numbers 2, 5, and 8). Then locate your month.

This chart is your Birth Chart. Copy it onto your worksheet

MONTHLY CHART SYSTEMS
CONTROL NUMBERS
CHART A

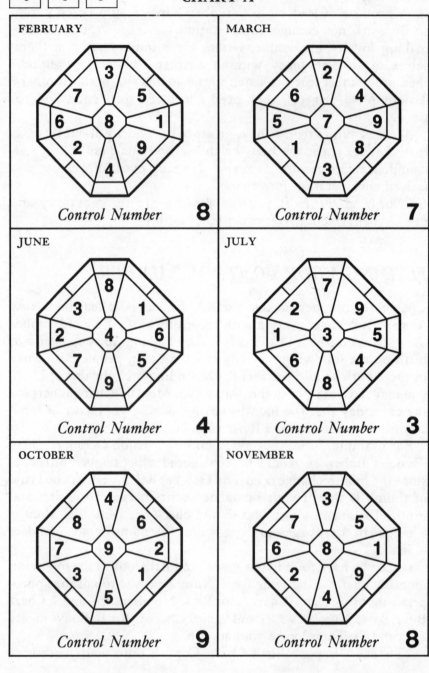

FEBRUARY

Control Number **8**

MARCH

Control Number **7**

JUNE

Control Number **4**

JULY

Control Number **3**

OCTOBER

Control Number **9**

NOVEMBER

Control Number **8**

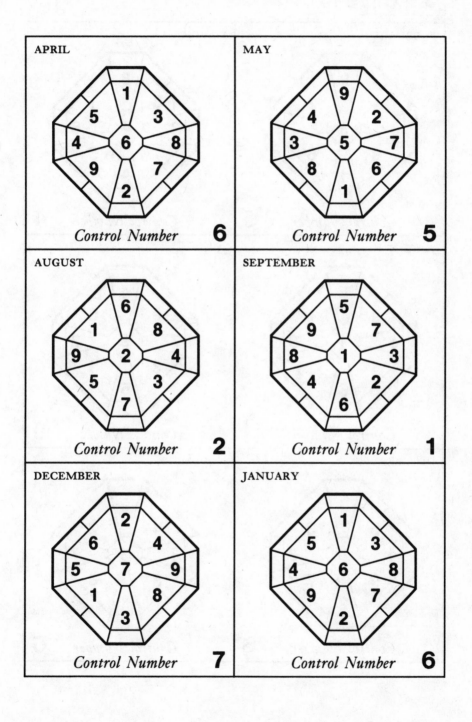

APRIL

Control Number **6**

MAY

Control Number **5**

AUGUST

Control Number **2**

SEPTEMBER

Control Number **1**

DECEMBER

Control Number **7**

JANUARY

Control Number **6**

CHART B

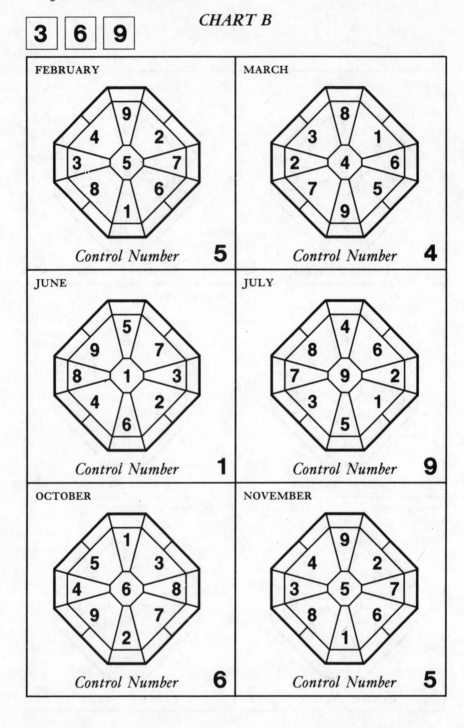

3 **6** **9**

FEBRUARY

9
4 2
3 5 7
8 6
1

Control Number **5**

MARCH

8
3 1
2 4 6
7 5
9

Control Number **4**

JUNE

5
9 7
8 1 3
4 2
6

Control Number **1**

JULY

4
8 6
7 9 2
3 1
5

Control Number **9**

OCTOBER

1
5 3
4 6 8
9 7
2

Control Number **6**

NOVEMBER

9
4 2
3 5 7
8 6
1

Control Number **5**

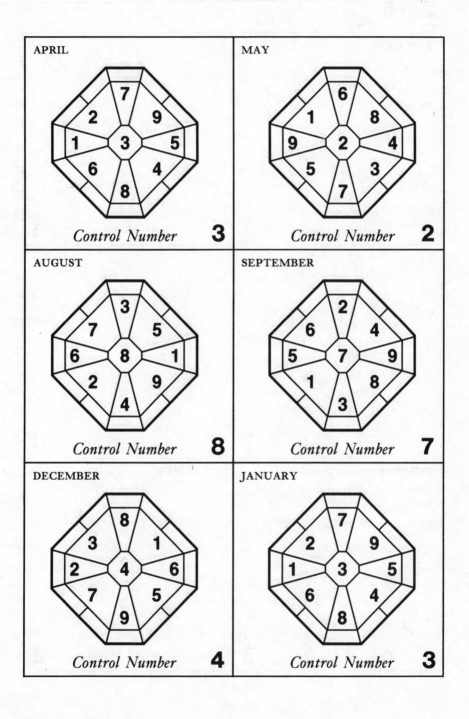

APRIL

7 2 9 1 3 5 6 4 8

Control Number **3**

MAY

6 1 8 9 2 4 5 3 7

Control Number **2**

AUGUST

3 7 5 6 8 1 2 9 4

Control Number **8**

SEPTEMBER

2 6 4 5 7 9 1 8 3

Control Number **7**

DECEMBER

8 3 1 2 4 6 7 5 9

Control Number **4**

JANUARY

7 2 9 1 3 5 6 4 8

Control Number **3**

CHART C

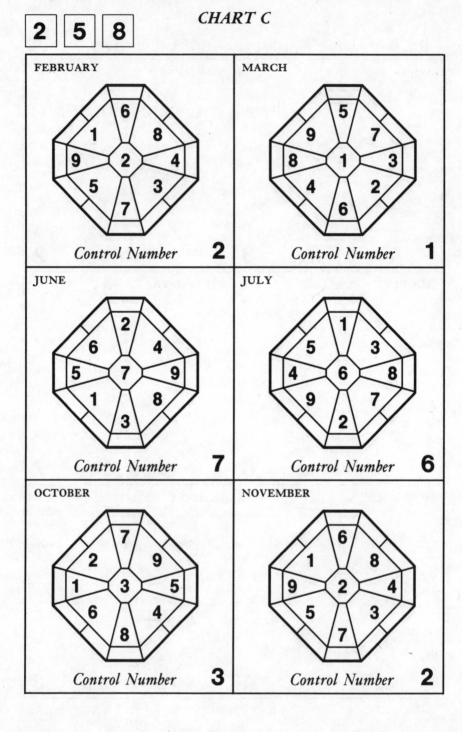

2 **5** **8**

FEBRUARY

6
1   8
9   2   4
5   3
7

Control Number **2**

MARCH

5
9   7
8   1   3
4   2
6

Control Number **1**

JUNE

2
6   4
5   7   9
1   8
3

Control Number **7**

JULY

1
5   3
4   6   8
9   7
2

Control Number **6**

OCTOBER

7
2   9
1   3   5
6   4
8

Control Number **3**

NOVEMBER

6
1   8
9   2   4
5   3
7

Control Number **2**

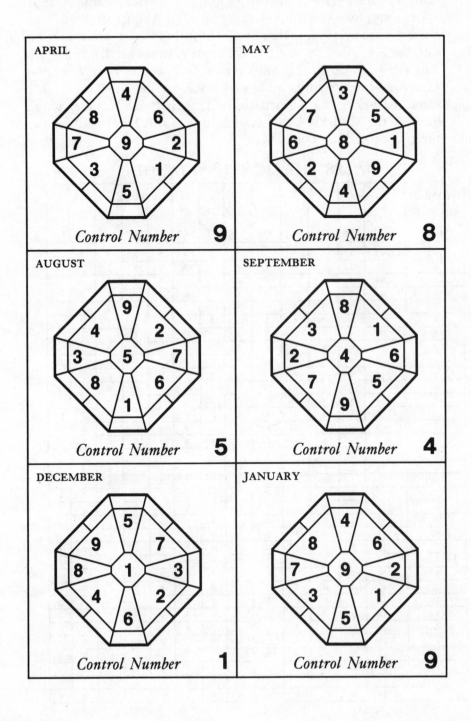

chart and memorize it! Its center number is your *Control Number*.

Let's say, for example, you were born on August 30, 1946. Your Basic Number is 9. Looking on the Monthly Chart, your monthly number is 8. Now by going to the chart systems for 3, 6 and 9, you will see your Control Number is 8. Got it? Let's try one more example—the system is quite easy once you get the hang of it. If someone was born on April 10, 1951, their Basic Number would be 4. By the Monthly Chart system for 1, 4 and 7, you will see that their Control Number is 6.

DATES THE MONTHS CHANGE

NUMBER OF THE YEAR	YEAR	FEB	MAR	APR	MAY	JUN	JUL	AUG	SEP	OCT	NOV	DEC	JAN
9	1892	4	5	4	5	5	7	7	7	8	7	7	5
8	93	3	5	4	5	5	7	7	7	8	7	7	5
7	94	4	5	5	5	6	7	7	8	8	7	7	5
6	95	4	6	5	6	6	7	8	8	8	8	7	6
5	96	4	5	4	5	5	7	7	7	8	7	6	5
4	97	3	5	4	5	5	7	7	7	8	7	7	5
3	98	4	5	5	5	6	7	7	8	8	7	7	5
2	99	4	6	5	6	6	7	8	8	8	8	7	6
1	1900	4	6	5	6	6	8	8	8	9	8	7	6
9	1	4	6	5	6	6	8	8	8	9	8	8	6
8	2	5	6	6	6	7	8	8	9	9	8	8	6
7	3	5	7	6	7	7	8	9	9	9	9	8	7
6	4	5	6	5	6	6	8	8	8	9	8	7	6
5	5	4	6	5	6	6	8	8	8	9	8	8	6
4	6	5	6	6	6	7	8	8	9	9	8	8	6
3	7	5	7	6	7	7	8	9	9	9	8	8	7
2	8	5	6	5	6	6	7	8	8	9	8	7	6
1	9	4	6	5	6	6	8	8	8	9	8	8	6
9	10	5	6	6	6	7	8	8	8	9	8	8	6
8	11	5	7	6	7	7	8	9	9	9	8	8	7
7	12	5	6	5	6	6	7	8	8	9	8	7	6
6	13	4	6	5	6	6	8	8	8	9	8	8	6
5	14	5	6	6	6	7	8	8	8	9	8	8	6
4	15	5	7	6	7	7	8	9	9	9	8	8	7
3	16	5	6	5	6	6	7	8	8	9	8	7	6
2	17	4	6	5	6	6	8	8	8	9	8	8	6
1	18	5	6	6	6	6	8	8	8	9	8	8	6
9	19	5	7	6	7	7	8	9	9	9	8	8	7
8	20	5	6	5	6	6	7	8	8	9	8	7	6
7	21	4	6	5	6	6	8	8	8	9	8	8	6
6	22	5	6	5	6	6	8	8	8	9	8	8	6
5	23	5	7	6	6	7	8	9	9	9	8	8	7
4	24	5	6	5	6	6	7	8	8	8	8	7	6
3	25	4	6	5	6	6	8	8	8	9	8	8	6

NUMBER OF THE YEAR	YEAR	FEB	MAR	APR	MAY	JUN	JUL	AUG	SEP	OCT	NOV	DEC	JAN
2	1926	4	6	5	6	6	8	8	8	9	8	8	6
1	27	5	6	6	6	7	8	8	9	9	8	8	6
9	28	5	6	5	6	6	7	8	8	8	8	7	6
8	29	4	6	5	6	6	8	8	8	9	8	7	6
7	30	4	6	5	6	6	8	8	9	9	8	8	6
6	31	5	6	6	6	7	8	8	9	9	8	8	6
5	32	5	6	5	6	6	7	8	8	8	8	7	6
4	33	4	6	5	6	6	8	8	8	9	8	7	6
3	34	4	6	5	6	6	8	8	8	9	8	8	6
2	35	5	6	6	6	7	8	8	9	9	8	8	6
1	36	5	6	5	6	6	7	8	8	8	8	7	6
9	37	4	6	5	6	6	8	8	8	9	8	7	6
8	38	4	6	5	6	7	8	8	8	9	8	8	6
7	39	5	6	6	6	6	8	8	8	9	8	8	6
6	40	5	6	5	6	6	7	8	8	8	8	7	6
5	41	4	6	5	6	6	7	8	8	9	8	7	6
4	42	4	6	5	6	6	8	8	8	9	8	8	6
3	43	5	6	6	6	7	8	8	8	9	8	8	6
2	44	5	6	5	6	6	7	8	8	8	7	7	6
1	45	4	6	5	6	6	7	8	8	9	8	7	6
9	46	4	6	5	6	6	8	8	8	9	8	8	6
8	47	5	6	6	6	6	8	8	8	9	8	8	6
7	48	5	6	5	6	6	7	8	8	8	7	7	6
6	49	4	6	5	6	6	7	8	8	9	8	7	6
5	50	4	6	5	6	6	8	8	8	9	8	8	6
4	51	5	6	6	6	6	8	8	8	9	8	8	6
3	52	5	6	5	6	6	7	8	8	8	7	7	6
2	53	4	6	5	6	6	7	8	8	9	8	7	6
1	54	4	6	5	6	6	8	8	8	9	8	8	6
9	55	5	6	6	6	6	8	8	8	9	8	8	6
8	56	5	5	5	5	6	7	7	8	8	7	7	5
7	57	4	6	5	6	6	7	8	8	8	8	7	6
6	58	4	6	5	6	6	8	8	8	9	8	7	6
5	59	4	6	5	6	6	8	8	8	9	8	8	6
4	60	5	5	5	5	6	7	7	8	8	7	7	5
3	61	4	6	5	6	6	7	8	8	8	8	7	6
2	62	4	6	5	6	6	7	8	8	9	8	7	6
1	63	4	6	5	6	6	8	8	8	9	8	8	6
9	64	5	5	5	5	6	7	7	7	8	7	7	5
8	65	4	6	5	6	6	7	8	8	8	8	7	6
7	66	4	6	5	6	6	7	8	8	9	8	7	6
6	67	4	6	5	6	6	8	8	8	9	8	8	6
5	68	5	5	5	5	6	7	7	7	8	7	7	5
4	69	4	6	5	6	6	7	8	8	8	7	7	6
3	70	4	6	5	6	6	7	8	8	9	8	7	6
2	71	4	6	5	6	6	8	8	8	9	8	8	6
1	72	5	5	5	5	5	7	7	7	8	7	7	5
9	73	4	6	5	6	6	7	8	8	8	7	7	6

NUMBER OF THE YEAR	YEAR	FEB	MAR	APR	MAY	JUN	JUL	AUG	SEP	OCT	NOV	DEC	JAN
8	1974	4	6	5	6	6	7	8	8	9	8	7	6
7	75	4	6	7	6	6	8	8	8	9	8	8	6
6	76	5	5	5	5	5	7	7	7	8	7	7	5
5	77	4	6	5	5	6	7	8	8	8	7	7	6
4	78	4	6	5	6	6	7	8	8	9	8	7	6
3	79	4	6	5	6	6	8	8	8	9	8	8	6
2	80	5	5	4	5	5	7	7	7	8	7	7	5
1	81	4	6	5	5	6	7	7	8	8	7	7	6
9	82	4	6	5	6	6	7	8	8	8	8	7	6
8	83	4	6	5	6	6	8	8	8	9	8	7	6
7	84	4	5	4	5	5	7	7	7	8	7	7	5
6	85	4	5	5	5	6	7	7	8	8	7	7	5
5	86	4	6	5	6	6	7	8	8	8	8	7	6
4	87	4	6	5	6	6	8	8	8	9	8	7	6
3	88	4	5	4	5	5	7	7	7	8	7	7	5
2	89	4	5	5	5	6	7	7	8	8	7	7	5
1	90	4	6	5	6	6	7	8	8	9	8	7	6
9	91	4	6	5	6	6	7	8	8	9	8	7	6
8	92	4	5	4	5	5	7	7	7	8	7	7	5
7	93	4	5	5	5	6	7	7	8	8	7	7	5
6	94	4	6	5	6	6	7	8	8	8	7	7	6
5	95	4	6	5	6	6	7	8	8	9	8	7	6
4	96	4	5	4	5	5	7	7	7	8	7	7	5
3	97	4	5	5	5	6	7	7	7	8	7	7	5
2	98	4	6	5	6	6	7	8	8	8	7	7	5
1	99	4	6	5	6	6	7	8	8	9	8	7	6
9	2000	4	5	4	5	5	7	7	7	8	7	7	6

THE UNIVERSAL CHART*

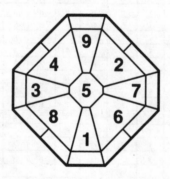

*This is a fixed chart.

FINDING YOUR TENDENCY NUMBER

Now that you have found your Basic Number and Control Number, you can find your Tendency Number, which shows the position of the Basic Number in your Birth Chart. It comes from a comparison of the Birth Chart with the Universal Chart. Before we can really study our Birth Charts closely, we must look at the Universal Chart again, which gives us all nine numbers as they appear in their original permanent positions. (See section on the Universal Chart)

To help in finding your own Tendency Number, let's use Jack Nicholson's Birth Chart as an example.

Born: April 27, 1937   *Written:* **9**-3-2
Basic Number: 9
Control Number: 3
Tendency Number: 2

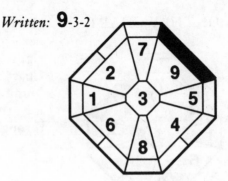

The Basic Number is written first in large print. The Control Number is written second in smaller print, and the Tendency Number is written last, also in small print.

Born in 1937, he has as his Basic Number 9.

YEARLY CHART

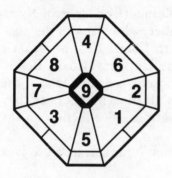

Chart of 1937—Always, the number for that year is placed at the center of the chart. This chart represents the yearly Ki-energy in effect from Feb. 4, 1937, through Feb. 3, 1938. (Basic Number 9 controls the year 1937.)

MONTHLY CHART

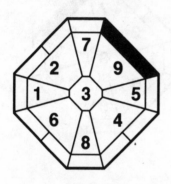

Chart for April 1937—Basic Number 9, on April 27, is in the upper-right position on the Monthly Chart. The Monthly Control Number, 3, is in the center, during the period from April 5, through May 5, 1937.

UNIVERSAL CHART

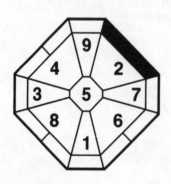

Compared with the Monthly Chart, the Universal Chart shows that Basic Number 9 "sits" in the 2 position on the Universal Chart during the month of April. Therefore, the Tendency Number is 2.

So, to find your Tendency Number, refer to your Birth Chart and compare it with the Universal Chart. Locate the position of your Basic Number in your Birth Chart. The number that appears in that same position in the Universal Chart is your Tendency Number.

If your Basic Number is 4, and your Control Number is 6, your Tendency Number is 3, **4**–6–3.

YOUR CHART   UNIVERSAL CHART

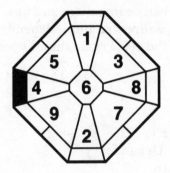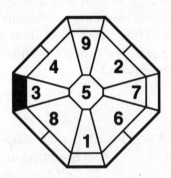

These three numbers, the Basic Number, Control Number, and Tendency Number, and their position in the Monthly Charts, are the bases for the study of the 108 Personality Types that follows. The better we know ourselves, our vehicles, and our intended destination, the easier it is to gain control over our lives.

In reading through the book, you will find many celebrity examples given for each Number. At least one of these celebrity types will have the same set of Numbers as you, which means that you may share many similar characteristics with that person. The success or failure of all these celebrities depended on their ability to understand and use their own strength and weakness in either a positive or negative way. You can do the same. Using your energy in the correct way makes it possible for you to realize your dreams and ambitions. Let's look at nine celebrity examples from the 108 Personality Types—one for each Basic Number—to see how each type relates to its three Numbers.

DOLLY PARTON Born: January 19, 1946 **1**–6–9
Basic: 1 Independence
Control: 6 Willpower, Faith
Tendency: 9 Pride, Success

As a drop of water carries on through hardships to flow into the ocean, so her willpower drove her independence with pride, like a stormy fire, through difficult beginnings to great success. The wonderful thing is that she managed to keep her charm and femininity; even the hard times couldn't change that. But despite a basically harmonious attitude, many of this type suffer in their personal relationships because they can be impatient and unadaptable. This comes from their strong willpower and independence. (See January type of Number 1 in the 108 Personality Types for more details.)

MARILYN MONROE Born: June 1, 1926 **2**–8–8
Basic: 2 Maternal Instinct, Dependency
Control: 8 Self-motivated Spirit
Tendency: 8 High Pursuits

As for many of this type, it was very difficult for her to balance her maternal instincts with her self-motivated ambition and high pursuits. She had a great drive toward success, but was not independent; she really needed someone who could help her realize her dreams. She might have reached her goal more easily if she had been aware of how to use her dedicated, yet dependent, nature. (See May type of Number 2 in the 108 Personality Types.)

PRINCESS DIANA Born: July 1, 1961 **3**–1–7
Basic: 3 Sensitive
Control: 1 Independent Spirit
Tendency: 7 Easygoing

Troubling circumstances upset her sensitive nature, but her generally easygoing attitude helps her conquer problems. Hardworking and optimistic, she knows what she wants and puts in great effort to achieve it. But her determination can occasionally make her view of reality inflexible. To protect her sensitive nature, she associates only with those who make her feel comfortable. Yet her social life is also important and she often expends great energy on it. Tradition and family assume tremendous importance in her life, but as she gains experience her somewhat narrow focus will enlarge and make her a leader of independent spirit.

(See July type of Number 3 in the 108 Personality Types.)

LEE IACOCCA   Born: October 15, 1924   **4**–9–9
Basic: 4   Creative
Control: 9   Proud
Tendency: 9   Foresightful

As far-reaching as the wind, his creative mind is eager to explore new ideas, and he considers his originality very important. Unfortunately, he has a tendency to become overextended and to lose focus, which can lead to a loss of control and cause him much irritation.

This man has a great deal of foresight coupled with the power to persuade. But if people are not persuaded to agree with his opinions, he is apt to get upset.

His pride does not always leave room for others to exercise control, yet he needs the input and affection of others to restore his energy.

His difficulties with Henry Ford II (September 4, 1917. **2**–5–2, see p. 127) were due to lack of communication between them and his hurt pride when forced to resign, which probably led to the gutsy move to rebuild Chrysler.

(See October type of Number 4 in the 108 Personality Types.)

ELIZABETH TAYLOR   Born: February 27, 1932   **5**–2–8
Basic: 5   Power to control (stubborn, humane)
Control: 2   Maternal
Tendency: 8   Self-motivated

Who can control the power of an empress? Elizabeth Taylor can. The problem is that there is always an ongoing battle between her personal power and her maternal instinct. She never gives up until she's fully satisfied, but she can hurt herself easily in the process. She develops her life through her self-motivated ambitions. She has clear judgment, especially when she has enough attention from others, but she must always keep a balance between her power and affection.

(See February type of Number 5 in the 108 Personality Types.)

NAPOLEON BONAPARTE   *Born:* August 15, 1769   **6**–8–3

Basic:	6	Dignified
Control:	8	Ambitious
Tendency:	3	Aggressive

Like the power of heaven, this man's dignity and aggressive ambition transformed his high ideals to a superiority complex that led to leadership, fame and eventual egomania. With a mind that was always working, he was able to actualize all but final dreams.

Excessive aggressiveness can lead this type to make disorganized decisions. For Napoleon, this tendency could have caused his failures during the Russian ordeal.

This type is usually magnanimous and stylish, qualities which attract opportunity. This self-assurance and honesty were with him to the end.

Self-motivated energy and a respect for dignity combined with his size consciousness to make him strive for the power and recognition he received.

(See August type of Number 6 in the 108 Personality Types.)

CLINT EASTWOOD   *Born:* May 31, 1930   **7**–5–7

Basic:	7	Hyper-Sensitivity
Control:	5	Persistence
Tendency:	7	Sociability

He possesses a complicated combination of personality traits and balancing them is the basis of attaining what he wants. Ex-

tremely sensitive and self-protective, he is also gregarious and sociable. He is serious about all his projects, giving them full attention to ensure their success. Although self-assertive and somewhat calculating, his approach to other people is one of innocence and trust. If not aware of this duality of his character, he can be duped easily. In public, he is easy-going and a good conversationalist, and his social inclinations have led him to expect a life of luxury. But since he spends so much energy on entertaining, he must depend on someone else to re-energize him. Consequently, he places great importance on an unstructured way of life, rather than trying to fit into an existing framework.
(See May type of Number 7 in the 108 Personality Types.)

JACQUELINE KENNEDY ONASSIS   *Born:* July 28, 1929
8–6–7
Basic: 8   Self-motivation, Freedom
Control: 6   Willpower, Dignity
Tendency: 7   Flexibility, Passion

She is very ambitious but cannot be swayed into doing anything that goes against her own will. She does not have patience enough to deal with overly complicated matters. People often misjudge her as a "playgirl" because she is able to give vent to her feelings and is passionate, but she really has great willpower and a strong sense of responsibility toward developing her own life. She behaves like a lady. She also makes no bones about trifling matters and is very flexible in managing her affairs.
(See July type of Number 8 in the 108 Personality Types.)

LIZA MINNELLI *Born:* March 12, 1946   **9**–4–1
Basic: 9   Proud
Control: 4   Emotional
Tendency: 1   Insecure, Self-protective

Her pride burns brightly, but she must always be on guard against the waters of insecurity, which try to wash away her fiery self-confidence. She is smart enough to pursue the necessary knowledge to help build up her career, but it may take some time for her to feel fully satisfied about it. It's not easy for people to unravel her introverted emotions because she is proud and very self-protective. Unless they keep an open mind, these people can drive themselves into a tight corner, which makes them quite frustrated. Sometimes this frustration can be used positively on the stage to make a great success. If these individuals can overcome insecurity and use their considerable patience, they can achieve anything in time.

(See March type of Number 9 in the 108 Personality Types.)

Now let's see what effect the Basic Numbers, Control Numbers, and Tendency Numbers have had upon other famous personalities.

Many powerful female celebrities have the same Tendency Number (6). These women have the tendency of Number Six to be rigid, proud, and independent.

GRETA GARBO
September 18, 1905
5–4–6

GLORIA SWANSON
March 27, 1899
2–1–6

MAE WEST
August 17, 1892
9–8–6

DIANA ROSS
March 26, 1944
2–1–6

CAROL CHANNING
January 20, 1922
7–6–6

FANNY BRICE
October 29, 1891
1–9–6

NATALIA MAKAROVA
November 21, 1940
6–5–6

MARY MARTIN
December 1, 1913
6–5–6

People who become successful very young often have the same Basic Number, Control Number, and Tendency Number. Most of these had early success. All share the hardworking personality of Number Three.

CHARLIE CHAPLIN
April 16, 1889
3–3–5

MICHAEL BENNETT
April 8, 1943
3–3–5

ELVIS PRESLEY
January 8, 1935
3–3–5

Two great successes in the world of hair design were born in different months but still have the same Basic Number, Control Number, and Tendency Number. This type of person is strong, independent, intuitive, and insightful; good qualities for success in the fashion field.

KENNETH
(Kenneth E. Battelle)
April 19, 1927
1–6–9

VIDAL SASSOON
January 17, 1928
1–6–9

Many people with Basic Number Seven have artistic sensitivity and strong organizing natures. These people are successful in the art and entertainment fields.

ARTHUR FIEDLER
December 17, 1894
7–7–5

STEPHEN SONDHEIM
March 22, 1930
7–7–5

ANDREW LLOYD WEBBER
March 22, 1948
7–7–5

ALVIN AILEY
January 5, 1931
7–7–5

LAWRENCE WELK
March 11, 1903
7–7–5

STEVE ALLEN
December 26, 1931
7–7–5

People who were born in the same year (1924):

JIMMY CARTER
October 1, 1924
4–1–8

GEORGE BUSH
June 12, 1924
4–4–5

ED KOCH
December 12, 1924
4–7–2

Notice that Carter, Bush, and Koch all have Basic Number Four, but that their Control Numbers (center of chart) for their months of birth are different. Even though many qualities may be similar, each of these men has his own ideas and attitudes about how to live his life.

As these examples show, each person has a variety of numbers in combination, just as every human being is composed of a variety of elements. Oriental philosophy says that we are created by energies known as "desire" and "morality." Desire produces our activities and ambitions, as well as the entire range of our emotions—joy, anger, love, worry, sadness, etc. Morality is our conscience and conduct. Both desire and morality have their positive and negative aspects—we need to strike a balance between the two. When the movement of desire controls too much, our ambitions spread out and seem limitless; we ruin our chance for success. When morality controls too much, we lose our spirit for activity, our drive.

Each Number is made up of part desire, part morality. For example, Number One is independent, and yet anyone who carries through to a goal independently must face isolation. Isolation brings insecurity. These are two sides to Number One—independence and insecurity.

It is most important to know how to put your number to practical use as you develop your life. Even insecurity can be positive, for many insecure people develop great patience, which can be an asset. Managing smoothly helps you to keep a positive outlook and stay healthy in the process.

However, life is a long run, and you simply cannot run against nature. Forcing yourself along, under pressure, is no way to live. The best way is to use every special ability you have, to develop your own individual quality. That is why scholars have always stressed the importance of knowing yourself, for it is self-knowledge that frees you and unleashes all your potential.

I focus here on two ways of using the Ki to improve your life. First, by learning about yourself and others, you can use communication to develop good relationships. Since life is really an accumulation of encounters with people, you cannot go through it alone. Your relationships with lovers, friends, family, business associates, and others are very important (explained in detail in Chapter IV, Relationships).

The second way to use the Ki involves what I call *Direction of Movement*. This tells you how to find the right time and place to get what you want. It is really helpful at times in your life when you have to make important decisions like deciding when to change jobs or where to move. Often disappointments in life are caused by wrong movement at the wrong time, and I'm sure you have all experienced the frustration of a period when nothing goes right. This book gives an introduction to Direction of Movement so that you may understand it easily and use it in a constructive way (see "Direction of Movement").

We are all creatures of desire. It is our desires that drive us toward our goals in life. Whether or not we achieve these goals depends on many things—how much energy we use, how patient we are, how persistent an effort we make in our own behalf. Success gives us self-confidence and spurs us on. Defeat brings disappointment. But our desires always demand our attention, and reaching personal satisfaction is very important to everyone.

This is why the Ki can be so helpful. Because you are faced with so many choices in life, you need to consider every decision you make very carefully. Whether it is a personal relationship or a question of where to locate a new business, the outcome of your choice will continue to shape your future for a long time. You can use the information given in this book as a guide to what's best for you in any circumstance, based on knowledge of yourself, the time and place, and other people involved. With every success, you gain self-confidence. Feeling self-confident enables you to build a brighter, stronger future.

Historically speaking, this knowledge accumulated over thousands of years in ancient China and was further developed in Japan. Originally, the Ki was handed down secretly from the sovereign leaders of one generation to the next, the knowledge considered the key to becoming a leader. During the early seventeenth century, a period of civil war in Japan when many clans were struggling for supremacy, Tokugawa Ieyasu succeeded in unifying the country by using the study of Ki. He became the first shogun, who founded the dynasty of the Tokugawa family. It was not until 1867, when the Tokugawa dynasty came to an end, that knowledge of the Ki became available to the masses. The history of the Orient was actually controlled for many years by the working of the Ki behind the scenes.

The most important message of the Ki is the same one given by the ancients: "Know yourself. Know your strengths and weaknesses and how to use them. Knowing the right way to proceed can make life entirely different."

Along the way, this book will show you history, examples, charts, instructions, comparisons, celebrity numbers, direction, and stories drawn from my personal experiences over the years. I hope you will find as much joy and richness in the discoveries you will make as I have found (and still find) by using the Ki. May each of you learn, with this book's help, how to control your life.

RECAP

To Find Your Basic Number

1) Look up the year of your birth on the chart on p. 13. The number of the year is your Basic Number.

2) This number is written first and larger than the others.

To Find Your Control Number:

1) Turn to pages 34–39 and locate the page with your Basic Number in boldface in the upper left-hand corner.

2) Find the square for the month of your birth. If your birthday falls in the first nine days of the month, check the Dates the Months Change chart on page 40 to see whether your birthday belongs to the preceding month.

3) This is your Birth Chart, and the number in the center is your Control Number.

To Find Your Tendency Number:

1) Turn to the chart that gave you your Control Number, pages 34–39.

2) Note the position of your Basic Number on that chart.

3) See what number appears in the corresponding position on the Universal Chart at the bottom of the page. That is your Tendency Number.

YOUR   *YOUR*
YEARLY CHART   *MONTHLY CHART*

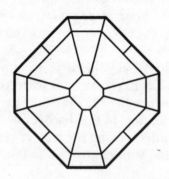 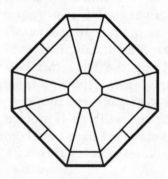

THE UNIVERSAL CHART

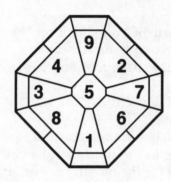

RELATIONSHIPS

WHAT MAKES RELATIONSHIPS WORK?

If you know how to express yourself, you can change your world. Many of us do not realize what effect we have on others because we feel that what we are doing is right. If we were truly seeing ourselves and others correctly, we would not be having difficulty in our relationships.

> How can I handle my child? He's a good boy but I can't reach
>   him.
> Why does my boyfriend cheat on me?
> How can I run a business with people who refuse to accept
>   responsibility?

I am often presented with questions like these. The answers are never simple, but they all boil down to the same point: relationships. When we are hurt, or too sensitive, or feeling lost and unable to express ourselves, we've temporarily lost our ability to relate. It doesn't mean that we (or others!) are bad, mean, crazy, or anything else—just means that we have ceased to understand each other. Having good relationships means really knowing yourself and being able to express yourself to another; it also means seeing others and accepting them for what they are. When we relate poorly, we experience pain, separation, loneliness, and confusion.

Ideal relationships are a special blend of give and take that feels right. They have a very natural movement to them; they are a perfect exchange of feelings that gives one a sense of real happiness. Discovering a true friend, having someone you feel you've known all your life, is like finding a rare and precious jewel. Trust, understanding, and affection between people are gifts that only time can give us, and true friendship showers them upon us abundantly.

SIX INDICATORS TO HELP GUIDE YOU IN RELATIONSHIPS

No person or system can give perfect relationships to someone else —that kind of understanding has to be developed slowly and patiently by the people involved. However, as this book will show, there are at least six conditions that point the way toward understanding the fundamentals of good relationships, using the combinations of the numbers in the charts. These six are:

1. Reciprocal relationships of the Five Elements
2. Family background and blood relationships
3. Control Number
4. Tendency Number
5. Attraction Number (Basic Numbers)
6. Business connections

It is important to know how many of these conditions exist in your relationships with others. You quickly begin to see which combinations are more compatible with your own (tending to make relationships easier) and which are less (tending to make relationships more difficult).

THE RECIPROCAL RELATIONSHIP OF THE FIVE ELEMENTS

Scholars in ancient China gave us a very simple way to express the relationships between the Five Elements. Two of these relationships are mutually nourishing, or *energizing;* one is a brother/sister type, or cooperating; and two are mutually opposed, or *conflicting.* Look at the following chart. Once you find your Basic Number and Element (see p. 15) you can determine how each of these

Reciprocal Relationships involves different numbers for you. If you are Number 8, you are energized by Number 9 and give energy to Numbers 6 and 7; you cooperate with 2; you control Number 1 and are controlled by Numbers 3 and 4.

RECIPROCAL RELATIONSHIPS OF THE NUMBERS

ELEMENT	WATER	EARTH	WOOD	WOOD	EARTH*	METAL	METAL	EARTH	FIRE
NUMBER	1	2	3	4	5	6	7	8	9
RELATIONSHIPS	6	9	1	1	9	2	2	9	3
ENERGIZING (RECEIVE FROM) ☺	7					8	8		4
ENERGIZING (GIVE TO)	3	6	9	9	6	1	1	6	2
	4	7			7			7	8
COOPERATING		8	4	3	2	7	6	2	
					8				
CONFLICTING (CONTROLS)	9	1	2	2	1	3	3	1	6
☹			8	8		4	4		7
CONFLICTING (IS CONTROLLED BY)	2	3	6	6	3	9	9	3	1
	8	4	7	7	4			4	

*Number 5, the Primal Power, chooses relationships, but cannot be chosen by anyone else. Pages 72–82 have more detailed information on the different combinations of the numbers.

Now let's look at each of these relationships individually.

ENERGIZING RELATIONSHIPS

Water gives Wood the energy to grow.
Wood receives energy from Water.
Wood gives Fire the energy to burn.
Fire receives energy to burn from Wood.
Fire leaves the ashes, which become the Earth.
Earth receives energy from Fire.
Earth forms the Mountain, to hold Metal.
Metal receives energy from Earth.
Metal touches the cold air, to make Water.
Water receives energy from Metal.

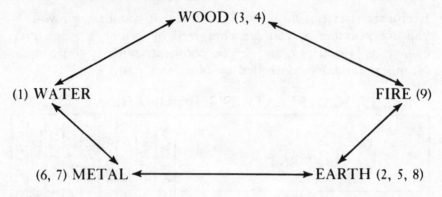

If you are Water (1), your nourishing relationships are with Wood (you supply the energy needs of Numbers 3 and 4) and Metal (you are supplied by Numbers 6 and 7).

CONFLICTING RELATIONSHIPS

Water extinguishes Fire.
Fire makes Metal melt.
Metal cuts into Wood.
Wood drains energy up out of the Earth.
Earth stops Water from moving.

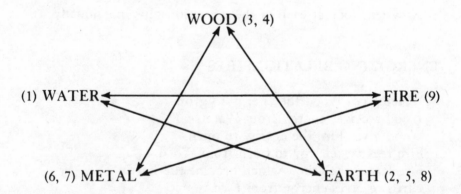

The same Water element (1) here would be in control of the Fire element (9) and controlled by Earth (2, 5, 8). Which of the conflicting relationships applies to you?

COOPERATING RELATIONSHIPS

Numbers with the same element have what is called a *cooperating relationship*, along the lines of brother and sister. These are Wood (3 and 4), Metal (6 and 7), and Earth (2, 5, and 8).

Although a comparison of the elements is necessary, the Basic Number alone is not enough to ensure what will constitute good or poor relationships among people. There are many other important aspects that must be considered before determining whether a person is good for you or not. All six of the conditions must be taken into account.

FAMILY BACKGROUND AND BLOOD RELATIONSHIP

An illustrator, Mr. L (born on May 14, 1937), who had been married and divorced twice, came to me for advice. I found that his former wives had virtually identical charts: their Basic Numbers (9) and their Monthly Control Numbers (3) as well as their Tendency Numbers (2) were the same. When asked for whom in his family he felt the deepest affection, he replied without hesitation, "My grandmother." A comparison of his grandmother's chart with those of his ex-wives revealed the following:

MR. L
May 14, 1937
9–2–3

MR. L'S GRANDMOTHER
May 1, 1892
9–3–2

FIRST WIFE
April 14, 1946
9–3–2

SECOND WIFE
January 20, 1947
9–3–2

My answer to Mr. L was, "You have the same Basic Number (9) as your grandmother and ex-wives. When people have the same Basic Number, that sometimes makes for a very comfortable combination and sometimes not. Since your Control Number is different from your ex-wives', this combination makes for possible communication difficulties.

You cannot expect the same amount of affection (or more) from your ex-wives as you had in your blood relationship with your grandmother, even though your ex-wives have the same type of personality and similar ways of expressing their affection."

Later on, he asked me about five different lovers, but from my interpretation of his numbers, I did not give him the "thumbs-up" sign until two years after his divorce. At last he had met the right kind of woman! They have now moved to California and are making a happy life together.

MR. L
May 14, 1937
9–2–3

NEW LOVE
Mar. 1, 1953
2–2–5

Why is this combination such a good one?

Their Basic Numbers, 2 and 9, show a mutually nourishing relationship of the Five Elements. Their Control Numbers (2) are the same, which makes communication easier.

Harry Truman, Franklin Roosevelt, Lyndon Johnson, and Theodore Roosevelt are all rather well known as being their mothers' favorite children. The most interesting to examine is Truman's case, which is quite an unusual illustration of a blood relative's role in communication.

Harry, his mother and sister, wife Bess and daughter Margaret all have the same Monthly Control Number. I wish everyone could be born into, and marry into, as good a network of relationships as did Harry S. Truman!

HARRY S. TRUMAN
May 8, 1884
8-8–5

MOTHER
November 25, 1852
4-8–1

SISTER
August 12, 1889
3-8–9

WIFE BESS
February 13, 1885
7-8–4

DAUGHTER MARGARET
February 17, 1924
4-8–1

The romance between Harry and Bess is a famous one. Here's how the charts show how easy communication was for people in Harry's family:

1. When you look at the charts of Harry and his mother and sister, they all have the same Monthly Control Number (8), allowing for open communication. Their blood relationship contributed additionally to this openness. If Harry had enough affection from them, it's likely that he'd have been very comfortable with and attracted to a person who possessed the same type of combination. Bess had it.

2. Harry's Basic Number (8) and Bess's Basic Number (7) show an excellent reciprocal relationship of the Five Elements (see the chart on page 59).

3. Their Control Numbers are the same (8).

4. Bess had the same Control Number as Harry's mother and sister. Her chart shows the compatability with Harry's family background and blood relationships.

In Theodore Roosevelt's case, both his marriages were completely influenced by his mother. His first wife (who died) and his second wife both had the same Basic Number, Control Number, and Tendency Number as his mother.

THEODORE ROOSEVELT
October 27, 1858
7–9–3

MOTHER
July 8, 1834
4–3–6

FIRST WIFE, ALICE
July 29, 1861
4–3–6

SECOND WIFE, EDITH
August 6, 1861
4–3–6

Even though his own Basic Number and Control Number have no real connection to the Basic Number and Control Number of his wives, he must have felt extremely comfortable with this combination, which is exactly the same as his mother's. His wives must have given him the right kind of affection, the kind he was used to and expected.

Lyndon Johnson also married a woman whose chart was like his mother's; although the women's Basic Numbers are different, their Control Numbers are the same:

LYNDON JOHNSON
August 27, 1908
2–5–2

WIFE LADY BIRD
December 22, 1912
7–7–5

MOTHER REBECCA
June 26, 1881
2–7–9

So, Lyndon and Lady Bird shared compatible Basic Numbers (2 and 7), and the family connection is there as well.

Moving along to President Reagan; his wife Nancy's birthday is on July 6, 1921, so her chart would be the same as that of Jane Wyman, who was the President's first wife. If this is indeed the case, we might assume that President Reagan was influenced by some chart in his family background. Perhaps his mother's?

RONALD REAGAN
February 6, 1911
8–2–2

NANCY REAGAN
July 6, 1921
7–4–8

JANE WYMAN
January 4, 1914
6–4–7

THE CONTROL NUMBER

Even if their basic personalities are different, people with the same Control Numbers can understand each other more easily. Liking or disliking the person makes no difference. For this modern generation, whose people tend to move quickly, strongly, and individually according to their own desires, good communication saves a great deal of energy and time. The ease of communication that exists when the Control Numbers are the same shows the importance of this particular aspect in chart interpretation. (Note especially the Harry Truman example.)

Jeane Kirkpatrick, who was the U.S. Ambassador to the United Nations and a close staff associate of President Reagan's, shares his chart and Control Number as well:

RONALD REAGAN
February 6, 1911
8-2-2

JEANE KIRKPATRICK
November 19, 1926
2-2-5

Here, the Control Numbers (2) are the same and the Basic Numbers (2 and 8) have a cooperative-element relationship. This combined to make communication between the two much easier.

ELIZABETH TAYLOR
February 27, 1932
5-2-8

These charts of Elizabeth Taylor's ex-husbands show that each of two husbands have the same Control Number.

MIKE TODD
June 2, 1909
1-5-1

RICHARD BURTON
November 10, 1925
3-5-3

EDDIE FISHER
August 10, 1928
9-8-6

JOHN W. WARNER
February 18, 1927
1-8-7

As shown here, Mike Todd and Richard Burton have the same powerful Control Number, even though their Basic Numbers are different. Eddie Fisher and John W. Warner also have the same Control Number and different Basic Numbers. I would think Miss Taylor is looking for the same kind of comfortable relationship she had with a member of her family. It could be her father or someone else who had the same Control Number as one of her four husbands. Although she will look for this kind of comfort, I don't think she can reach full satisfaction this way. I would recommend that she form a relationship with someone who has a Control Number 2, like her own. This could lead to an easier relationship. However, her Number 5 is an extremely strong number, so any relationship should be carefully considered before entering it.

THE TENDENCY NUMBER

People with the same Tendency Number share an approach or attitude toward life and may find they have similar habits. This can contribute to agreeable relationships, especially if some other aspect of the chart (Element, Control Number, attraction, or family background) is also in harmony.

An example of people working together with the same Tendency Number (in this case, Number 8) is the combination of President Carter and Vice President Mondale.

JIMMY CARTER
October 1, 1924
4–1–8

WALTER MONDALE
January 5, 1928
1–7–8

In addition to sharing the same Tendency Number, they have compatible Basic Numbers (4 and 1). (see Reciprocal Relationships of the Five Elements, p. 59).

A second example of a long-term working relationship that was very fruitful is that between John Wayne and director John Ford, whose careers intermingled often over many years.

JOHN WAYNE
May 26, 1907
3–2–6

JOHN FORD
February 1, 1895
7–6–6

Having the same Tendency Number (6) made them a good combination, as illustrated by the many successful movies they made together. The attraction of their Basic Numbers also made for a strong, enduring relationship.

ATTRACTION NUMBER

Attraction is shown by the opposite pairs of numbers as they appear on the Universal Chart (1 and 9, 2 and 8, 3 and 7, 4 and 6). Number 5, in its central location, shows the intrinsic connection of the Control Number with all the pairs of numbers. A larger, primal power, Number 5 chooses relationships that can be under its control.

UNIVERSAL CHART

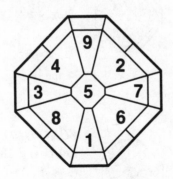

People whose Basic Numbers occur in pairs of opposites on the Universal Chart are said to have Attraction Numbers. Some famous examples follow:

PRINCE CHARLES
November 14, 1948
7-8-4

PRINCESS DIANA
July 1, 1961
3-1-7

7 and **3**

JOHN F. KENNEDY
May 29, 1917
2-8-8

JACQUELINE KENNEDY ONASSIS
July 28, 1929
8-6-7

2 and **8**

WARREN BEATTY
March 30, 1937
9-4-1

DIANE KEATON
January 5, 1946
1-7-8

9 and **1**

JOHN LENNON
October 9, 1940
6-6-5

YOKO ONO
February 18, 1933
4-8-1

6 and **4**

Of the examples, the Kennedys had a compatible-element relationship (Earth, 2 and 8) in addition to the Attraction Numbers. For all the others, it seems that attraction is the only condition these couples share(d). Their Elements, Control Numbers, and Tendency Numbers are really not compatible, and family background cannot be determined by looking at these charts alone. Usually, attraction without one or more other conditions being favorable (especially the Control Number) only lasts as long as the passion does. These days, when attraction plays such an important part in people's getting together, we must be careful—for attraction alone can be dangerous if it dissolves into manipulation instead of blossoming into love.

BUSINESS CONNECTIONS

It's easier to work together if the basic natures of colleagues are compatible and there is good communication. Here are some examples of successful partnerships:

ROBERT DENIRO
August 17, 1943
3-8-9

MARTIN SCORSESE
November 17, 1942
4-8-1

(Basic Number, with cooperative elements 3 and 4, and same Control Number 8, makes for good communication.)

JOHN HUSTON
August 5, 1906
4-3-6

HUMPHREY BOGART
January 23, 1899
3-3-5

(Basic Numbers, with cooperative elements 4 and 3, and same Control Number 3.)

MARGOT FONTEYN
May 18, 1919
9-2-3

RUDOLF NUREYEV
March 17, 1938
8-1-3

(Basic Numbers, with nourishing element 9 and 8, and same Tendency Number 3.)

Wouldn't it be wonderful if you had easy business relationships all the time? But what if you don't have any of the six relationship connections in common and you must do business with someone?

You must find a way to overcome your difficulties and misunderstandings to arrive at mutually agreeable decisions. If you know yourself and study the type of person you are dealing with, you have a better chance of accomplishing your goals. By trusting your intuition, you can succeed even in situations where communication is not naturally good.

The Japanese have recently been credited with the ability to communicate efficiently in their business relationships. This type of communication is known in Japan as *Wa* communication. Wa communication means putting aside all aggressive behavior, personal bias, and selfish interests to work as part of a team. Wa is moderate and well-balanced and has harmony as its goal. The success of the Japanese businessman over the years may be at least partly attributed to the importance given Wa communication in Japanese society.

This book does not deal specifically with Wa, but understanding the 108 Personality Types and learning to use the six conditions for relationships will naturally lead to this type of communication. The key here is to understand others, even if their Control Numbers, Tendency Numbers, and Basic Numbers may not allow for easy communication.

THE COMBINATION OF THE NUMBERS

When comparing the Numbers of people, it is important to consider the many different combinations that are possible. The Reciprocal Relationships of the Numbers chart on page 59 will be of great help, though it shouldn't be your only source of judgment. Combining different Numbers has varying effects on communication. Here are some comparisons that you may use to see what the Numbers can be like with one another.

NUMBER 1 AND NUMBER 1

Both have an independent approach with respect and seriousness. They can develop smoothly together, depending upon how harmonious they can keep things. If something is bothering one or the other, both can easily lose balance. This combination is good for business, friendship, and equal partnership, but if one tries to control the other, there might be difficulty.

NUMBER 1 AND NUMBER 2

Neither one feels close to the other at the beginning of this relationship. Gradually, Number 2, who is dependent, learns how to follow Number 1, and this makes them closer. But, since this is a "one side depends on the other" type of connection, they cannot expect to share enough positive reinforcement for the future. The conservative Number 2 may restrain the positive spirit of Number 1.

NUMBER 1 AND NUMBER 3

Number 1 has intellectual facility and a brilliant talent for business maneuvers. Number 3 does not possess this power but instead brings insight to a situation and is a shrewd judge of talent. As a result, this combination makes for a good friendship and can be very productive in business. In the ideal situation, Number 1 leads Number 3 to a certain point at which Number 3 must learn to (or at least pretend to) accept responsibility for the situation if there is to be a productive result.

NUMBER 1 AND NUMBER 4

Separately, these numbers possess a lack of rapid determination in making decisions. However, when joined together they gain strength of mind, a result of the serious thought of Number 1 and the practical wisdom of Number 4. This combination of qualities also contributes to a very pleasant sociability.

NUMBER 1 AND NUMBER 5

Number 5 has a haughty attitude and tremendous persistence. When Number 5 gets together with Number 1, Number 1 loses the ability to think his own way. This increases the insecurity of Number 1. Not a particularly good combination.

NUMBER 1 AND NUMBER 6

Number 1 has the gift of intimately touching another's heart-strings, so it's easy for this type of person to develop relationships. Number 6 is not a person to play games easily but can choose a comfortable way by using his calm judgment. This combination is good for business and friendship.

NUMBER 1 AND NUMBER 7

Both have a good talent for sociability. Number 1 can be understanding, and Number 7 is a convincing speaker. If they choose to help each other, they can make quite a satisfying pair in business and in friendship.

NUMBER 1 AND NUMBER 8

Number 8 is willful, suspicious, and self-indulgent. Number 1 will be irritated by Number 8's gravity and will find it difficult to remain openminded. Trust will not be easy between these two; it will require a great deal of energy. They may exhaust one another!

NUMBER 1 AND NUMBER 9

Number 9 has an impulsive nature and frank manner. Number 1 is the opposite of Number 9—careful, discreet, judicious in nature. Their minds are very different, so it is difficult for them to understand each other well. The key is in what each one wants, but this combination is not easy.

NUMBER 2 AND NUMBER 2

Both have the same ideas about life. Steady, conservative—they can rely on each other. But neither is easily adaptable and that limitation can cause them difficulty in dealing with problems. They need to compromise sincerely with one another.

NUMBER 2 AND NUMBER 3

Number 2 is steady and conservative. Number 3 is always seeking new projects, wanting to make things happen. Number 2 can hardly follow Number 3's rapid movement and considers it dangerous besides. Number 2's circumspection irritates Number 3. In this case, Number 3 has to have the patience to allow for Number 2's steadiness and cautious behavior.

NUMBER 2 AND NUMBER 4

Number 4 possesses practical wisdom about how to get along in the world, but no perseverance in following his own advice. Number 2 has a more conservative approach to life but doesn't always know the best way to get along. These two will criticize each other easily. Number 2 will consider Number 4 too smart-mouthed, and Number 4 will think of Number 2 as slow or stupid. This is a difficult combination.

NUMBER 2 AND NUMBER 5

Number 5 has considerable persistence and leadership ability, while Number 2 possesses a more dependent nature, making for a good balance between the two. However, after Number 2 is encouraged to build up self-confidence, he will no longer be comfortable being controlled by Number 5. Time may eventually upset the good balance between them.

NUMBER 2 AND NUMBER 6

This combination can be like a traditional masculine (6) and feminine (2) relationship. Number 6 has confidence and can be reliable. Number 2 is nourishing and steady. If Number 6 is in the position of leadership, this can be a very good combination. If Number 2 leads, it could be less so.

NUMBER 2 AND NUMBER 7

Number 7 has flexibility and good judgment by calculation, as compared with Number 2's steadiness and sincerity. They are most compatible when Number 7 is in a leadership position. They can attain more that way in business or partnership together.

NUMBER 2 AND NUMBER 8

This is a brother-sister type of relationship or friendship. Number 8 has great self-motivation, stubbornness, and tenacity. Fortunately, Number 2 has the insight and sincerity needed to understand Number 8's nature. Number 2's great dedication makes it easy for Number 8 to open his mind and heart in friendship.

NUMBER 2 AND NUMBER 9

Number 9 has clear judgment, great foresight, and can be flamboyant. Number 2 possesses sincerity and steadiness, and, though undemonstrative, will willingly sacrifice pleasures in the pursuit of a goal or relationship. These numbers are able to give positive influences to one another.

NUMBER 3 AND NUMBER 3

Both are very sensitive and passionate. They have leadership potential and foresight. If they plan together, with the same objectives and timing, they will make good progress. But sometimes their haste may cause them to lose patience with one another, a potential source of problems. Discretion is a must!

NUMBER 3 AND NUMBER 4

Generally speaking, the very direct, frank expression of Number 3 will make communication between the two numbers difficult. But the tender-hearted, harmonious, and adaptable Number 4 will work toward understanding. On the other hand, Number 4's indecisiveness is helped by Number 3's radical decisions. This combination is good, but only when both are accepting of one another.

NUMBER 3 AND NUMBER 5

Both have an "I did it my way" type of individuality. Number 3 expresses himself very openly and quickly. Number 5 tries to control others. It's not easy for these two to get along with one another.

NUMBER 3 AND NUMBER 6

Both are very active in their ways, with a strong sense of motivation. Number 3 is active but impatient; Number 6 tempers activity with calm judgment. This balance is good. But if they become overactive, it is difficult for Number 6 to stay magnanimous.

NUMBER 3 AND NUMBER 7

Both of these numbers are rapid-speakers and -doers. If they share the same purpose, they may succeed in their goals quickly. But in the area of friendship, discretion is needed. Since they are both very sensitive, they must be careful in their relationship.

NUMBER 3 AND NUMBER 8

Number 3 clearly expresses what he wants to say and cannot pretend he feels or thinks something he doesn't. Number 8 will hold a grudge, even over a trifling matter, and cannot overcome past impressions easily. If Number 3 hits a sensitive nerve in Number 8, Number 8 will hide his dissatisfaction for a long time to the detriment of the relationship. This combination has to be very careful—they may just be too different to share open expression.

NUMBER 3 AND NUMBER 9

Both have insight and intelligence. They can build a relationship that is in tune with itself. Number 9 is the better leader in this team. It's an excellent combination for new intellectual developments.

NUMBER 4 AND NUMBER 4

Both have great practical wisdom, and a highly individual style, bordering on idiosyncratic. Their relationship will be smooth and noncommittal. There is less risk and a tendency for things to be too easy, so they cannot expect a lasting union in the future.

NUMBER 4 AND NUMBER 5

Number 4 has practical judgment. Number 5 makes more self-motivated decisions than the easygoing Number 4. It is difficult for either side to achieve satisfaction in this relationship.

NUMBER 4 AND NUMBER 6

Number 6 has great dignity. To him, it's very important to move according to his own judgment. Number 4 moves by emotion. Understandably, it's often difficult for them to find common ground.

NUMBER 4 AND NUMBER 7

Generally, this combination is good. Both have a social nature and easily find agreement. Number 4 has a tenderhearted sociability, and Number 7 has an adaptable social nature. When these two look at each other, they wonder whether the other is sincere about his expression. Yet they will continue to feel each other out.

NUMBER 4 AND NUMBER 8

Number 4 has a tenderhearted nature and is a good mixer. Number 8 has a more obstinate character. This combination will not achieve closeness or understanding easily.

NUMBER 4 AND NUMBER 9

This is a good combination. Number 4 has a harmonious, adaptable mind. Number 9 has a flamboyant mind, intelligence, and clear judgment. These two combine smoothly.

NUMBER 5 AND NUMBER 5

Both are very egotistic and stubborn. They argue easily; it's difficult for either to give up even an inch to the other. Only when they have a common purpose can they make a good team. But it will always be difficult for them to share.

NUMBER 5 AND NUMBER 6

Number 5 is very discriminating as to what suits him. Number 6 has an understanding of Number 5's strong, positive nature and an ability to look at it calmly. This calm judgment makes Number 5 accept Number 6 more easily, knowing that Number 6 can withstand Number 5's turbulent nature.

NUMBER 5 AND NUMBER 7

Number 7's calculated flexibility can negotiate with Number 5's strong presence and one-track mind. This makes Number 5 respect Number 7. To Number 5, Number 7 appears more "polished."

NUMBER 5 AND NUMBER 8

This combination does not make for easy communication in the beginning, because they both are stubborn and strongly persistent by nature. As time goes on, Number 5 begins to recognize and admire the way that Number 8 conveniently controls his decision-making process. For Number 5, decision-making is always definite, the way he wants it.

NUMBER 5 AND NUMBER 9

The interesting aspect of this combination is that the intelligence, sharp judgment, and refined nature of Number 9 attracts Number 5, whose impulsive, unpolished energies meet a complementary match. Number 9 admires Number 5's great personal control, compared with Number 9's fickleness.

NUMBER 6 AND NUMBER 6

Both have the same character, so they accept each other more easily. Both have great pride, so as long as they respect one another, all is well. If one hurts the other's pride, big problems will ensue. They have to negotiate with calmness.

NUMBER 6 AND NUMBER 7

Both are similar in nature, allowing for easy exchange. Number 6 is very magnanimous but is often hurt by his cautiousness. Number 7's nervousness is hidden by his easy sociability. These two must be careful to consider their inner feelings when relating to one another.

NUMBER 6 AND NUMBER 8

Number 6 and Number 8 have a kind of fated relationship between them, as the mountain has to Heaven. Through their connection to one another, each is better able to see his own existence and purpose. They can rely on each other for good communication. Number 6 is the more natural leader of the two.

NUMBER 6 AND NUMBER 9

Both are intelligent. Number 6 has realistic, calm judgment. Number 9 relies on his sound mind but tends to be fickle. It's not easy for these two to decide on something agreeably.

NUMBER 7 AND NUMBER 7

Both are similar-minded. There is less passion between them than like-mindedness. Somewhere, they are hiding a portion of themselves, which they feel they must keep under control. Because they are both calculating, they usually do not open up to one another.

NUMBER 7 AND NUMBER 8

This is a "good teamwork" combination. Number 7 is flexible while Number 8 possesses self-motivation, strength, and obstinacy, but also a childish jealousy. There is a certain essence that attracts them—the possibility of a real give-and-take relationship. Number 7 is gentle in appearance while sturdy in spirit; Number 8 is obstinate on the outside but soft within.

NUMBER 7 AND NUMBER 9

These numbers are attracted to a flamboyant life. They are often attracted to similar things, making closeness easy in the beginning of the relationship. But as time goes on, it becomes apparent that their natures are very different. Number 9 thinks Number 7 is all talk and no substance; Number 7 thinks Number 9 is too vain and proud. At this point, neither will concede at all to the other.

NUMBER 8 AND NUMBER 8

An understanding relationship between the like-minded makes trust so much easier. But both are willful, jealous, stubborn, and very self-indulgent, resulting in mistrust between the two. They need to control their self-indulgence and willfulness to make this combination work.

NUMBER 8 AND NUMBER 9

Their reciprocal relationship is to help each other. Number 8 is fated to be helped by Number 9 and to respect Number 9's talent for making clear decisions. Number 9 respects Number 8's self-motivated mind and efforts.

NUMBER 9 AND NUMBER 9

This combination has liveliness and clear-mindedness on its side. But they are wise to feel each other out as to what they're thinking. The success of this combination depends upon what type of leadership the two can agree upon.

FAMILY GAME SHEET

Do you have good harmony with your family? Understanding each other is very important.

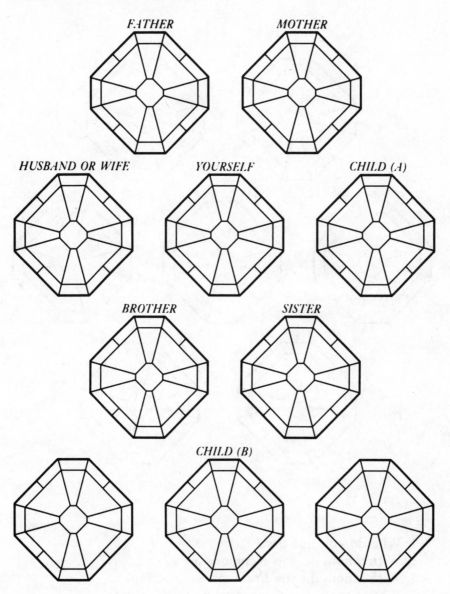

LOVERS GAME SHEET

How you express yourself in your relationship with your lover(s).

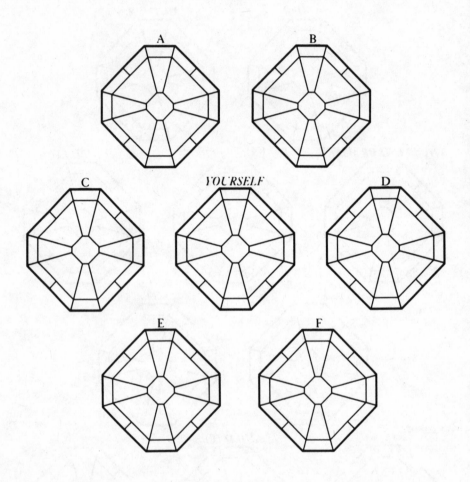

1. Who do you like best?
2. With whom do you communicate most easily?
3. With whom do you find most satisfaction?
4. Who is the best lover according to the charts?

BUSINESS GAME SHEET

How to interact with people in your business field. If you understand other's personality types, you can manage to communicate with them more easily, and you can better develop your business.

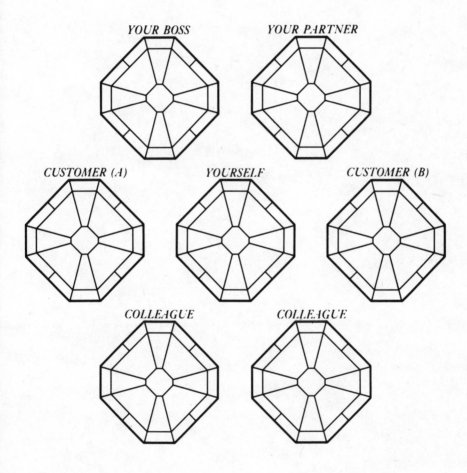

YOUR BOSS   *YOUR PARTNER*

CUSTOMER (A)   *YOURSELF*   *CUSTOMER (B)*

COLLEAGUE   *COLLEAGUE*

Note: You win if you handle them wisely.

THE 108 PERSONALITY TYPES

The 108 Personality Types are the key to improving our under-standing of ourselves and others. If you fall in love with someone, you cannot change that person's basic nature, however, if you know yourself and your own chart and study the chart of the other person, communication can be improved. Problems of understanding, which can exist even when there is great affection between people, as in families, are the source of much pain and loneliness today. By studying the 108 Personality Types, we can become more aware of what causes the problems in such relationships. Perhaps we can learn to act with greater discrimination and insight to avoid unnecessary problems in the future.

Again, the most important thing here is to know yourself. Once you begin to see what you are, you can begin to see others better, too. What does the other person want? How much can you afford to give? How often are you trying to give the other person what you think is best for him, instead of what he really wants? These questions are difficult to answer. For a person dying of thirst in a desert, a drop of water is worth more than diamonds or gold. We must be careful to understand our own desires and use this under-standing in our communication. The charts give a foundation for working with these ideas.

They also show just what kind of nature you have and how that nature can be made to best serve your choice of career or lifestyle. When a real effort is made, learning to use what you have to your own best advantage is often the difference between success and failure. Let's look at a few examples of this, before we begin our discussion of the 108 Personality Types in detail.

In the *Chicago Tribune Magazine*, in 1981, a poll was taken, and the "Ten Best and Ten Worst" presidents of the United States were selected. In 1983, a survey was conducted by a professor at Pennsylvania State University, also concerning the American presidency. In judging the merits of any president, it is often difficult to separate the personality of the man from the many other factors influencing his decisions—the Congress, the Supreme Court, and the historical background of the times during his term in office. However, the personality of the president himself is very important.

Two controversial presidents had the following characteristics in common, as shown by their charts and numbers:

RICHARD M. NIXON
January 9, 1913
7–6–6

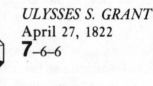

ULYSSES S. GRANT
April 27, 1822
7–6–6

Both Nixon and Grant share strong powers of intuition. Both can also be stubborn and lack adaptability. Each of these presidents had a major scandal occur during his administration. Perhaps if Richard Nixon had known his own weakness, the rigidity of attitude that led to Watergate could have been avoided entirely. On the positive side, his strong intuitive sense led to the breakthrough reopening of diplomatic relations with the People's Republic of China.

Many people with this type of intuitive power are working successfully in the arts, where the intuitive sense has a different kind of creative outlet. This is not to say that they are incapable of holding political office, only that, if they choose that career, they must be more aware of their own strengths and weaknesses. For it is in the greater awareness of ourselves that we become more able to control our lives.

Here are some examples of people with the same numbers as Nixon and Grant:

RICHARD M. NIXON **7**-6–6
(JANUARY)
Cary Grant—January 18, 1904
George Balanchine—
January 22, 1904
Edouard Manet—January 23,
1832
Carol Channing—January 30,
1922

ULYSSES S. GRANT **7**-6–6
(APRIL)
Immanuel Kant—April 22, 1724
David Frost—April 7, 1939

Francis Ford Coppola—April 7,
1939
Giorgio Di Sant'Angelo—May
5, 1939

(See **7**–6–6 in the section following for more information on this type of person. Make sure you check for the proper month, January or April, for there are some differences between the two.)

FEBRUARY 1-8-7

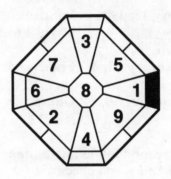

DATES THE MONTHS CHANGE

FEBRUARY 4–MARCH 5, 1900	FEBRUARY 4–MARCH 5, 1954
FEBRUARY 4–MARCH 5, 1909	FEBRUARY 4–MARCH 5, 1963
FEBRUARY 5–MARCH 5, 1918	FEBRUARY 5–MARCH 4, 1972
FEBRUARY 5–MARCH 5, 1927	FEBRUARY 4–MARCH 5, 1981
FEBRUARY 5–MARCH 5, 1936	FEBRUARY 4–MARCH 5, 1990
FEBRUARY 4–MARCH 5, 1945	FEBRUARY 4–MARCH 5, 1999

PASSIONATE	*WILLFUL*
INDEPENDENT	*WEAK DECISION-MAKERS*
EASYGOING	*CALCULATING*
SOCIABLE	*SELF-INDULGENT*

This type of Number 1 person is usually very positive. They are often active people who like to work as hard as they play. Their easygoing manner makes them at home in most social situations, where they can use their considerable skills as conversationalists.

The willfulness of this type is often obscured by the easygoing manner. The desires they have are usually in their own interest, and they are shrewd enough to know who will be of use to them in attaining their goals. Their self-indulgence is tempered by their carefree attitude.

They often have a great capacity to love, to the point of loving more than one person at a time. Their touching is usually soft and gentle, but their passions rise and cool with equal intensity. It is difficult for this type to stay in a first marriage. The men are frequently attracted to strong women but will balk at any attempt at control by them. Women of this type like good-looking, intellectual men and like to control their husbands if possible. Both the men and the women feel very strongly about their personal freedom.

Decision making is not a strong suit for these people. Because they are afraid to lose anything, especially money or their pride, they can easily become upset. But even though they may be unhappy for a while, their easygoing manner protects them. They do not worry or stay depressed for long.

Sound financial planning is integral to their nature, but they are self-indulgent and love to spend money for their own pleasure. They enjoy the attention that their spending sprees can afford them. However, if they become too attached to money and position, it can lead to difficulty.

CHARLES DARWIN—February 26, 1873
RONALD COLEMAN—February 9, 1891
LUIS BUNUEL—February 22, 1900
JOSEPH MANKIEWICZ—February 11, 1909
HARRY BELAFONTE—March 1, 1927
JACK CASSIDY—March 5, 1927
BURT REYNOLDS—February 11, 1936
BOB MARLEY—February 5, 1945
MIA FARROW—February 9, 1945
PATTY HEARST—February 20, 1954

MARCH 1-7-8

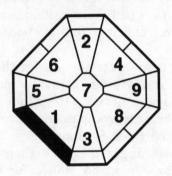

DATES THE MONTHS CHANGE

MARCH 6–APRIL 4, 1900	MARCH 6–APRIL 4, 1954
MARCH 6–APRIL 4, 1909	MARCH 6–APRIL 4, 1963
MARCH 6–APRIL 5, 1918	MARCH 5–APRIL 4, 1972
MARCH 6–APRIL 5, 1927	MARCH 6–APRIL 5, 1981
MARCH 6–APRIL 4, 1936	MARCH 6–APRIL 4, 1990
MARCH 6–APRIL 4, 1945	MARCH 6–APRIL 4, 1999

SELF-ASSERTIVE   *DEFENSIVE*
DISCRIMINATING   *HYPERSENSITIVE*
HARDWORKING   *DETAIL-MINDED*
INDEPENDENT   *SELF-CONSCIOUS*

This type of person is very independent and self-motivated, with a mind dedicated to detail. They are usually hardworking and, because of this, are often successful in their jobs or businesses. They can be lucky about money.

They are methodical and as such are not apt to "pull out all the stops." They are not distracted easily and are capable of directing their lives very independently. They are discriminating and make definite decisions. However, they sometimes become anxious about their decisions afterward.

They combine self-assertiveness with hypersensitivity and are shrewdly observant at the same time. They are self-conscious and very concerned about what others think in close relationships. Sometimes this can disrupt their social life.

They are patient and yet can seem too strong and direct. This is especially true of the women, who can be straightforward to the point of meanness. The men are outwardly more tender in this respect, although they can still be tough on the inside, where it doesn't show as much. Both the men and the women need to be aware of how their hypersensitivity contributes to the way they express themselves to others.

If they cannot find lasting work that satisfies them, they will change jobs or shift positions until they do. They have a good sense of organization. Businesswise, they are often lucky in finding a good assistant. The kind of staff or group surrounding the men of this type is the key to their success. Women of this type usually want to take care of whatever situation comes up themselves. How they handle their staff or coworkers is often very important to them.

These people are good family types. By nature they tend to be very family-oriented, enjoying a quiet home life. Yet sometimes they are fickle and susceptible to seduction. They need the right mate to be successful and are often lucky in finding one. The women make good homemakers, who love to take care of the family (in their own way!). They are attracted to self-motivated, hardworking men.

HENRIK IBSEN—March 30, 1828
GROVER CLEVELAND—March 18, 1837
SPENCER TRACY—April 5, 1900
MICKEY SPILLANE—March 9, 1918
PEARL BAILEY—March 29, 1918
URSULA ANDRESS—March 19, 1936
WALT FRAZIER—March 29, 1945
ERIC CLAPTON—March 30, 1945

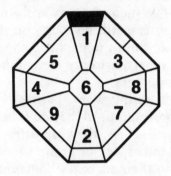

DATES THE MONTHS CHANGE

APRIL 5–MAY 5, 1900	APRIL 5–MAY 5, 1954
APRIL 5–MAY 5, 1909	APRIL 5–MAY 5, 1963
APRIL 6–MAY 5, 1918	APRIL 5–MAY 4, 1972
APRIL 6–MAY 5, 1927	APRIL 5–MAY 4, 1981
APRIL 5–MAY 5, 1936	APRIL 5–MAY 5, 1990
APRIL 5–MAY 5, 1945	APRIL 5–MAY 5, 1999

COOL, OBJECTIVE　　　　*IMPATIENT*
INTUITIVE　　　　　　　　*UNADAPTABLE*
CHARISMATIC　　　　　　*HAUGHTY*
DIGNIFIED　　　　　　　　*FASTIDIOUS*

Many people of this type deal with life through their intuition, and very often their activities are the results of their feelings or instincts. On the other hand, their nature is to look at things objectively. This can make other people think them cold, but it's just that their actions are very honest. As the balance in their life tips from intuitive to objective, the course of their life changes.

They are not the type of people to do a lot of explaining about themselves or their feelings. So for them, communication always takes time to develop. When they make decisions, they give much thought to the process. They are always conscious of whether or not their decisions are right for their purpose. They are afraid of being thought of as stupid. In fact, their way of thinking is very proud and dignified—a trait that makes them look down on others at times.

Most of these people are distant from their parents, especially the father. From an early age, they develop independently. Their lives are better if they are in a leadership position, for they are natural leaders. They are fastidious, yet impatient, and this can cause difficulties. It may be hard for others to get along with them.

Compromise is very difficult for these people. If they instinctively believe that something is right, they allow themselves to proceed "full speed ahead." Once they focus on their own chosen path, they have tremendous powers of concentration. In work or business their movement is guided mostly by their own hunches. Their weakness is that they are not good explainers, making understanding them hard for the people around them. However, once everyone gets better acquainted, this is less of a problem.

Since they are not easily adaptable, they must find work that is self-satisfying. If they do, they can usually stay in one field or career, taking it to a very deep level of understanding or high achievement.

Socially, they need to be the center of attention. If they are not, they may have trouble getting along with others. They tend to make very clear distinctions between friends and enemies, so their circle may be somewhat limited.

Most of the men are not family types, so if they must adapt to a domestic situation, marriage can become problematic. The women, who are extremely independent, rarely find it easy to have a cooperative relationship. Even if they do marry, they may find it difficult to be dependent upon their husbands. These women do better if they learn to share their lives, in a community sense, as part of the whole.

LEOPOLD STOKOWSKI—April 18, 1882
WILLIAM HOLDEN—April 17, 1918
ELLA FITZGERALD—April 25, 1918
KENNETH (Kenneth E. Battelle)—April 19, 1927
GLEN CAMPBELL—April 10, 1936
ROY ORBISON—April 23, 1936
JULIAN LENNON—April 8, 1963

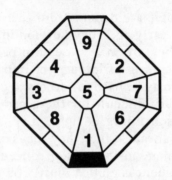

DATES THE MONTHS CHANGE

MAY 6–JUNE 5, 1900	MAY 6–JUNE 5, 1954
MAY 6–JUNE 5, 1909	MAY 6–JUNE 5, 1963
MAY 6–JUNE 5, 1918	MAY 5–JUNE 4, 1972
MAY 6–JUNE 6, 1927	MAY 5–JUNE 5, 1981
MAY 6–JUNE 5, 1936	MAY 6–JUNE 5, 1990
MAY 6–JUNE 5, 1945	MAY 6–JUNE 5, 1999

AMBITIOUS   *WORRIER*
TALENTED   *SELF-PROTECTIVE*
CONSERVATIVE   *INSECURE*
CREATIVE   *INTIMATE*

Most of this type have a basically independent nature, but are also insecure. They have great patience, but need a long time to make plans because they take everything very seriously. Sometimes their "overemphasis" about the future makes them worry because they want things to happen exactly the way they have planned them.

Their sense of self-protection is very strong, and they are often afraid to take complete responsibility for their actions. They may require someone else's approval or agreement in order to gain the conviction they need for themselves. They frequently have a need for attention and positive reinforcement from others. Although they usually have good family connections, many of them choose to remain apart. Often they are distant from their fathers.

In business they are usually flexible and ambitious. They work well in group situations, which often leads them to money and success. They can persevere and be creative. They are hardworking, talented, and intelligent, yet they may still feel insecure about being completely independent. Although they may at times have difficulties with their boss or superior, when they have to face or negotiate a difficult situation, their perseverance and easy social nature usually carry them through.

They have great sexual desire. Their love life often encompasses more than one person, and they rarely sever connections with anyone completely. They need to keep in contact with all who have loved them. Because of their self-protective nature, they are attracted to people who can make them feel needed, strong, respectable, and self-confident.

Their needs, when extreme, can make them insecure and worried. Often their personal satisfaction at these times is at the expense of someone else's, as they tend not to consider the other person enough. Marriage for both men and women of this type, unless it is to a really understanding partner, is usually not very happy.

In general, these people are independent and patient, and they will persevere in overcoming difficulty.

AYATOLLAH KHOMEINI—May 6, 1900
JAMES MASON—May 15, 1909
ALDO GUCCI—May 26, 1909
BENNY GOODMAN—May 30, 1909
MICHAEL TODD—June 2, 1909
BIRGIT NILSSON—May 17, 1918
CLIVE BARNES—May 13, 1927
ALBERT FINNEY—May 9, 1936
BOBBY DARIN—May 14, 1936
KEIR DULLEA—May 30, 1936
PETER TOWNSHEND—May 19, 1945

JUNE 1-4-2

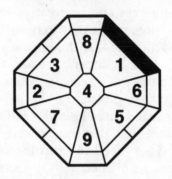

DATES THE MONTHS CHANGE

JUNE 6–JULY 7, 1900	JUNE 6–JULY 7, 1954
JUNE 6–JULY 7, 1909	JUNE 6–JULY 7, 1963
JUNE 6–JULY 7, 1918	JUNE 5–JULY 6, 1972
JUNE 7–JULY 7, 1927	JUNE 6–JULY 6, 1981
JUNE 6–JULY 6, 1936	JUNE 6–JULY 6, 1990
JUNE 6–JULY 6, 1945	JUNE 6–JULY 6, 1999

INDEPENDENT   *SELF-MOTIVATED*
STEADY   *CONSERVATIVE*
SOCIAL   *SELF-IMPORTANT*
RELIABLE   *EMOTIONAL*

These people are hardworking and serious-minded. They develop their lives very steadily. They appear soft-touching and quiet, but mentally they can be quite self-centered and opinionated. Actionwise, they are strongly self-assertive, very independent, yet emotional.

Most of them had quite a bit of affection when young from their parent of the opposite sex. As a result, the men often prefer to control things in the area of affection. Although most of the men tend to present a quiet, tender attitude, they are frequently rather emotional. The women, who usually have strong maternal instincts, have difficulty following or being in a secondary position. They may not be completely satisfied with a solely domestic life, because they have the ability to do more, but they are happy if they have control at home.

They are intelligent people. Socially, they often have problems if their expectations become too self-centered. Their minds are indeed self-motivated, and this can make it difficult for people around them to understand their way of thinking.

They are steady and reliable, yet if they desire to be leaders, they need to explain what they are thinking more clearly to those around them. They can express their talents in work or business especially well when they are in an associate position. Their dependability enables them to stay in one job for a long period of time.

In general, these people appear to have a conservative approach, yet can be extremely self-assertive and opinionated. They must learn to express themselves better and become less self-centered socially, if they want to connect more genuinely with other people.

LOUIS ARMSTRONG—July 4, 1900
ERROL FLYNN—June 20, 1909
ANDREI GROMYKO—July 6, 1909
BOB FOSSE—June 23, 1927
CAPTAIN KANGAROO (Bob Keeshan)—June 27, 1927
KEN RUSSELL—July 3, 1927
NEIL SIMON—July 4, 1927
KRIS KRISTOFFERSON—June 22, 1936
RICHARD BACH—June 23, 1936
CARLY SIMON—June 25, 1945

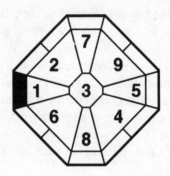

DATES THE MONTHS CHANGE

JULY 8–AUGUST 7, 1900	JULY 8–AUGUST 7, 1954
JULY 8–AUGUST 7, 1909	JULY 8–AUGUST 7, 1963
JULY 8–AUGUST 7, 1918	JULY 7–AUGUST 6, 1972
JULY 8–AUGUST 7, 1927	JULY 7–AUGUST 6, 1981
JULY 7–AUGUST 7, 1936	JULY 7–AUGUST 7, 1990
JULY 7–AUGUST 7, 1945	JULY 7–AUGUST 7, 1999

SELF-ASSERTIVE   *SENSITIVE*
INSIGHTFUL   *IMPATIENT, IMPRUDENT*
STRAIGHTFORWARD, FRANK   *OVERBEARING*
INDIVIDUALISTIC   *OPINIONATED*

This type of person is usually self-assertive and individualistic, often expressing him- or herself in a frank, straightforward manner. With their insight and frankness, they often have a strong effect on people and situations. Some people find this type overbearing, because their everyday expression is so direct and to the point.

Although these people sometimes have great strength and awareness, they are also very sensitive. Although this sensitivity is one of the factors that drive them, it can be a weakness for them too. Other people often do not see the sensitivity that lies just beneath their strong appearance, and so this type can be easily hurt if others fail to recognize their sensitive side. For this reason, they often break off with others once they have been hurt. They tend to hold their feelings inside.

Socially, they usually like to take care of people, often doing so in an individualistic manner. They are hardworking and usually hate doing anything halfway. They can become obsessive about the things they really want. Their strong self-assertion may lead them to have very clear likes and dislikes, and they can be impatient. They often expect things to turn out the way they want and so may be disappointed. Their lives may be up and down quite a bit, depending upon whether or not they can control their sensitivity. These people benefit from finding a good manager or trusted friend who can be a sounding board for their ideas and help them make wise decisions.

They usually have a good business sense and can think carefully about their options, often choosing the right ones. Although their minds are adaptable and they are able to consider most circumstances fairly, they can be opinionated. Their sensitivity can interfere with their flexibility.

Their sexual desires are strong and they tend to have a great need for self-satisfaction. The men need to be careful about becoming too self-assertive. They must learn to control themselves, and using prudence is the key to their success.

The women often have too strong a desire to control or impose their will on others. They must be aware of their tendency to be disturbingly frank in social situations.

Most of these people had a strong influence from their mothers. If they were overprotected when young, they may have difficulty making decisions later in life. Often, their decision-making process depends largely on circumstance and the way they make use of their insight and sensitivity.

HAILE SELASSIE—July 17, 1891
HARDY AMIES—July 17, 1909
INGMAR BERGMAN—July 14, 1918
ANDY WARHOL—August 7, 1927
YVES ST. LAURENT—August 1, 1936
JAN-MICHAEL VINCENT—July 15, 1945

AUGUST **1**-2-4

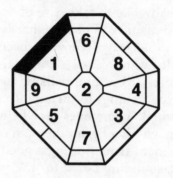

DATES THE MONTHS CHANGE

AUGUST 8–SEPT. 7, 1900	AUGUST 8–SEPT. 7, 1954
AUGUST 8–SEPT. 7, 1909	AUGUST 8–SEPT. 7, 1963
AUGUST 8–SEPT. 7, 1918	AUGUST 7–SEPT. 6, 1972
AUGUST 8–SEPT. 8, 1927	AUGUST 7–SEPT. 7, 1981
AUGUST 8–SEPT. 7, 1936	AUGUST 8–SEPT. 7, 1990
AUGUST 8–SEPT. 7, 1945	AUGUST 8–SEPT. 7, 1999

INDEPENDENT	*EVASIVE*
TENDER-TOUCHING	*EASYGOING*
HARDWORKING	*STUBBORN*
STEADY	*DETAIL-MINDED*

Most of these people are hardworking and steady, striving to build a safe, secure future. It may be hard to get to know them, because their independent, calm appearance can keep people at a distance. They are detail-minded and are usually well organized, although they may be influenced by their emotions much of the time. Because their focus is usually on their own views, many of them are less interested in or less capable of understanding others. As such, they may frequently find themselves taking care of people, yet receiving little or nothing in return.

Socially they can be good mixers if comfortable enough with the people around them. They appear easygoing, tender-touching, and serious-minded, always looking ahead to a successful, positive future.

Moneywise, they often work very hard when young. By middle age, most of them are in full bloom financially.

Their decisions are usually final. Once they make up their minds, they stubbornly refuse to give up—for good or bad.

In love, they are quite flowery and romantic and have lofty ideals about marriage. However, they tend to be dependent emotionally, and this may conflict with their independent approach to most other matters. Once they get serious, they need a great deal of attention and affection in order to feel secure, and this need can leave them quite vulnerable. If they are faced with a serious problem related to their emotional life, they often become disoriented and distraught.

The men are capable of deep affection, more than people would think from their calm appearance. Emotionally they tend to be extreme and can be moved to great anger or jealousy, as well as love and kindness, if their feelings are aroused.

The women, if married, usually take on quite a bit of responsibility for the home and the future of the family.

In general, these people are independent and have rational minds. They tend to be evasive, and although this may be the cause of difficulty, their independent attitude and clarity of mind often help them carry through.

SAMUEL GOLDWYN—August 27, 1882
ELIA KAZAN—September 7, 1909
DINO DE LAURENTIS—August 8, 1918
LEONARD BERNSTEIN—August 25, 1918
ALAN JAY LERNER—August 31, 1918
TED WILLIAMS—August 31, 1918
ROBERT SHAW—August 9, 1927
ROSALYN CARTER—August 15, 1927
JAMES COBURN—August 31, 1927
WILT CHAMBERLAIN—August 21, 1936
BUDDY HOLLY—September 7, 1936
STEVE MARTIN—August 14, 1945
VAN MORRISON—August 31, 1945

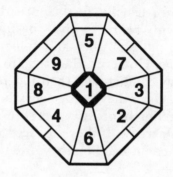

DATES THE MONTHS CHANGE

SEPTEMBER 8–OCTOBER 8, 1900	SEPTEMBER 8–OCTOBER 8, 1954
SEPTEMBER 8–OCTOBER 8, 1909	SEPTEMBER 8–OCTOBER 8, 1963
SEPTEMBER 8–OCTOBER 8, 1918	SEPTEMBER 7–OCTOBER 7, 1972
SEPTEMBER 9–OCTOBER 8, 1927	SEPTEMBER 8–OCTOBER 7, 1981
SEPTEMBER 8–OCTOBER 7, 1936	SEPTEMBER 8–OCTOBER 8, 1990
SEPTEMBER 8–OCTOBER 8, 1945	SEPTEMBER 8–OCTOBER 8, 1999

INDEPENDENT　　　*PERFECTIONIST*
SERIOUS　　　*SECRETIVE*
DIPLOMATIC　　　*SNOBBISH*
SOCIAL　　　*DETAIL-MINDED*

This type of person is bright, serious, and very independent. They tend to be very concerned with details. Their perfectionism can make it hard for them to distinguish between their ideas and reality. Often they do not care to become involved in other people's problems, and they may have a tendency to look down on others.

When they hold a leadership position in business, they expect perfection and give much attention to detail, making it difficult for their staff to follow them. Yet they can also be quite diplomatic, contributing sharp ideas and exercising calm judgment.

They are often distant from their parents or tend to have a physical weakness since childhood. They may face a serious illness once or twice in life, but they have a strong sense of survival and usually manage to pull through. Many of them have uneven emotional periods in their lives, alternating extremely happy times with equally sad or serious ones.

In love, most have a great longing for love itself. Their shyness has a certain sex appeal, and it attracts people, even if they are not handsome or beautiful. They know how to control this. Basically, their passion is easily aroused, but it fades easily as well. Yet they are very serious when they are in love. They may fall in love with two people at the same time or be attracted to a person in an uncommon position: a married person, for example, or a person of unusual character. Even though they have a good family life, they are often looking for something else. They are very good at keeping their actions secret.

Socially they function well and have a talent for diplomacy, although they don't really open their minds easily. They tend to build up very independent ideas inside and to proceed cautiously. If their expression is too opinionated, it may interfere in their relationships. It is hard for them to find and maintain close friendships.

Moneywise, they seem to have a passive kind of luck. For example, someone may recommend that they buy a certain stock; they do, and it goes up. The men and women of this type are very similar in their approach to problems.

Most of these people have high expectations for success in their jobs or businesses. Because of their independent thinking and inability to open their minds easily, there is always the possibility of loneliness in their future. This is somewhat true of all Number 1s, but especially of this type.

LEO TOLSTOY—September 9, 1828
STEPHEN D. BECHTEL—September 24, 1900
PETER FALK—September 16, 1927
R. D. LAING—October 7, 1927
JIM HENSON—September 24, 1936
JOSE FELICIANO—September 10, 1945
JESSYE NORMAN—September 15, 1945
DON MCLEAN—October 2, 1945

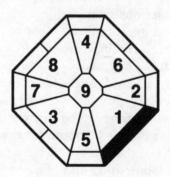

DATES THE MONTHS CHANGE

OCTOBER 9–NOVEMBER 7, 1900	OCTOBER 9–NOVEMBER 7, 1954
OCTOBER 9–NOVEMBER 7, 1909	OCTOBER 9–NOVEMBER 7, 1963
OCTOBER 9–NOVEMBER 7, 1918	OCTOBER 8–NOVEMBER 6, 1972
OCTOBER 9–NOVEMBER 7, 1927	OCTOBER 8–NOVEMBER 6, 1981
OCTOBER 8–NOVEMBER 7, 1936	OCTOBER 9–NOVEMBER 7, 1990
OCTOBER 9–NOVEMBER 7, 1945	OCTOBER 9–NOVEMBER 7, 1999

INDEPENDENT *MOODY*
CHARISMATIC *STUBBORN*
AFFECTIONATE *VAIN*
PRUDENT *CHANGEABLE*

These people tend to be in positions of leadership. They are prudent but stubborn. They can be quite persuasive and are often convincing speakers. However, if they do not get compliance right away, they rarely compromise and thus make enemies quickly. They have strong, independent characters, yet are also very affectionate and give a great amount of time to romance.

They can be vain and conceited and therefore sometimes remain at a distance socially. In social situations, they give the impression of being "on" even if they are not feeling great personally. Inside they are not as strong as they would lead people to believe. They may even appear to be flamboyant about money although in fact they are really quite conservative.

They have creative minds but are moody. As a result, their

decisions are subject to their moods—sometimes quick and impulsive, sometimes slow and ponderous. They express themselves well, but sometimes they overdo it, exaggerating what they really feel about a particular subject. Once they reveal their feelings, if they don't get the response they expect, they become very upset.

Sometimes the women appear too strong, because of their independent natures. It is not easy for them to choose the right mate. Tender people, perhaps younger men, would be good partners, since these women have a tendency to take on the responsibility for their families. The men usually prefer well-organized types of women.

These types often seem to be giving, when in fact they are taking affection. Their ability to give depends greatly on the kind of affection they get from others.

FANNY BRICE—October 29, 1891
HELEN HAYES—October 10, 1900
MERVIN LEROY—October 15, 1900
JEROME ROBBINS—October 11, 1918
ART CARNEY—November 4, 1918
GEORGE C. SCOTT—October 18, 1927
CLEO LAINE—October 27, 1927
LEE GRANT—October 31, 1927
BILL WYMAN—October 24, 1936
RICHARD CARPENTER—October 15, 1936
HENRY WINKLER—October 30, 1936

NOVEMBER 1-8-7

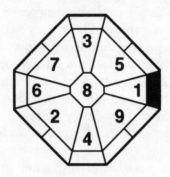

DATES THE MONTHS CHANGE

NOVEMBER 8–DECEMBER 6, 1900	NOVEMBER 8–DECEMBER 7, 1954
NOVEMBER 8–DECEMBER 7, 1909	NOVEMBER 8–DECEMBER 7, 1963
NOVEMBER 8–DECEMBER 7, 1918	NOVEMBER 7–DECEMBER 6, 1972
NOVEMBER 8–DECEMBER 7, 1927	NOVEMBER 7–DECEMBER 6, 1981
NOVEMBER 8–DECEMBER 6, 1936	NOVEMBER 8–DECEMBER 6, 1990
NOVEMBER 8–DECEMBER 6, 1945	NOVEMBER 8–DECEMBER 6, 1999

AMBITIOUS   *PROUD*
HARDWORKING   *WILLFUL*
INDEPENDENT   *WEAK-DECISION MAKER*
EASYGOING   *DISCRIMINATING*

This type is usually ambitious and has a very strong, forceful attitude. Like the February Number 1, they are independent and easygoing, have sharp minds, and are very positive and active.

They are more willful than the February Number 1. They come across as somewhat childish and spoiled but can be quite charming once you get to know them. They are very social, but a situation has to be under their control. They need to be the center of attention.

Their attitude, which is extremely important to them, takes on a dignified air. They are very conscious of their manner, and pride plays an important role in their sense of well-being. They try very hard not to "lose face" and are careful not to let people damage their reputation or hurt their feelings.

Although they may seem dignified on the outside, they are very delicate at heart. They love one person at a time and always try to possess that person completely.

This type of person expects everything to happen the way he wants and often expects to organize life around his desires. It is better for these individuals to choose a job or business that is flexible in nature because their minds are always attracted to new things.

This type of Number 1 is less easygoing than the February type, because of difficulty controlling their sensitivity. They like a flamboyant lifestyle and are often lucky about money. They work hard but may squander their earnings by not planning well.

Because it is hard for them to lose face, they can be weak decision-makers and need to choose spouses or coworkers who can help them in this area. Few of them stay in their first marriage. Marriage for them is better after a long period of friendship. The women find it difficult to be in control, although they would like to be. They stay very much in their own world, and because they are easygoing, being alone doesn't bother them. Whatever their problems, they do not stay worried long.

TOULOUSE-LAUTREC—November 24, 1864
BILLY GRAHAM—November 17, 1918
SPIRO AGNEW—November 9, 1918
DICK CAVETT—November 9, 1936
GARY HART—November 28, 1936
NEIL YOUNG—November 12, 1945
GOLDIE HAWN—November 21, 1945
BETTE MIDLER—December 1, 1945

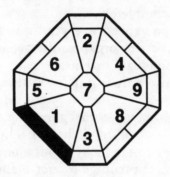

DATES THE MONTHS CHANGE

DEC. 7, 1900–JANUARY 5, 1901	DEC. 8, 1954–JANUARY 5, 1955
DEC. 8, 1909–JANUARY 5, 1910	DEC. 8, 1963–JANUARY 5, 1964
DEC. 8, 1918–JANUARY 5, 1919	DEC. 7, 1972–JANUARY 4, 1973
DEC. 8, 1927–JANUARY 5, 1928	DEC. 7, 1981–JANUARY 5, 1982
DEC. 7, 1936–JANUARY 5, 1937	DEC. 7, 1990–JANUARY 5, 1991
DEC. 7, 1945–JANUARY 5, 1946	DEC. 7, 1999–JANUARY 5, 2000

HARDWORKING   *SELF-CONSCIOUS*
TALENTED   *SENSITIVE*
INTENSE   *DETAIL-MINDED*
ORGANIZED   *SELF-INDULGENT*

These people are hard workers. They develop projects steadily with much effort. Also, they give great attention to detail, seldom compromising along the way. They have a strong sense of commitment and develop deep attachments. Their actions are tender-hearted.

By nature, they are usually quiet. People sometimes misjudge them as indecisive or negative because they may appear self-conscious in relationships with other people. They have organizational talent and can concentrate on a task well but may be too conscious of the judgment of others. They tend to change their minds quite a bit if their feelings get out of control. Because of their sensitive nature, they may adopt a straightforward attitude to try to protect themselves, yet they remain vulnerable inside.

Women of this type have luck in meeting men but often find it difficult to maintain the relationship when they become too self-indulgent. Men of this type often appear tender but can also be quite self-indulgent. Both may have difficulty expressing affection.

Their organizational ability and tendency to have luck in business is even greater than those of the March Number 1 type. It is not uncommon for them to receive an inheritance.

Once this type decides to do something, they are independent and ambitious enough to carry it through.

HENRY MILLER—December 26, 1891
J. R. R. TOLKIEN—January 3, 1892
DOUGLAS FAIRBANKS, JR.—December 9, 1909
JOSE GRECO—December 22, 1918
ANWAR SADAT—December 25, 1918
CHRISTOPHER PLUMMER—December 13, 1927
ALAN KING—December 26, 1927
WALTER MONDALE—January 5, 1928
DIANE KEATON—January 5, 1946
ALICE COOPER—December 25, 1945

JANUARY 1-6-9

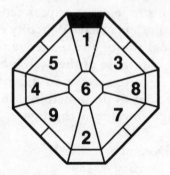

DATES THE MONTHS CHANGE

JANUARY 6–FEBRUARY 3, 1901	JANUARY 6–FEBRUARY 4, 1955
JANUARY 6–FEBRUARY 4, 1910	JANUARY 6–FEBRUARY 4, 1964
JANUARY 6–FEBRUARY 4, 1919	JANUARY 5–FEBRUARY 3, 1973
JANUARY 6–FEBRUARY 4, 1928	JANUARY 6–FEBRUARY 3, 1982
JANUARY 6–FEBRUARY 3, 1937	JANUARY 6–FEBRUARY 3, 1991
JANUARY 6–FEBRUARY 3, 1946	JANUARY 6–FEBRUARY 3, 2000

CHARISMATIC	*IMPATIENT*
DIGNIFIED	*UNADAPTABLE*
INTUITIVE	*PROUD*
INDEPENDENT	*INTENSE*

These people have a strong intuitive sense. They have the ability to move very independently, according to their feelings. Once they make a decision, they give tremendous energy to pursuing it and are not easily swayed by outside circumstance. They have a great ability to concentrate on something that interests them. However, because they tend to judge situations in their own way and move in such an independent manner, others may find them unyielding at times.

Their pride and independence contribute to their persistence. They are especially ambitious about building up and developing their financial opportunities, giving enormous energy to doing so. Once they are focused on a particular project, they become so intensely involved that they may lose their flexibility of thought. This can cause both personal and financial problems. Often, however, their intuitive sense, attention to detail, and persistence can really pay off, and they can become quite successful. Yet if they are not careful to explain their plan of action to those around them, and to consider other people's feelings and ideas, they may find themselves isolated.

Socially, they usually like to maintain a wide range of contacts and give great energy to keeping up good relationships. They have remarkable powers of persuasion and may appear at times to be manipulating people. This type usually dislikes people who try to control them.

Once they find something that interests them, they become very enthusiastic and persistent, as they move intuitively toward their goal. At times they can be too impatient, rushing into things recklessly and having to justify themselves later on.

They need to be admired, and in love they appear dignified yet are also tender. They are very positive about love and affection but may not be able to develop the proper atmosphere or feeling.

The men, depending on their efforts, can often expect to achieve a high position in life. The women are good in business, but married life may always be difficult because they are so strongly independent.

In general, these people are very good leaders and tend to see themselves in that role. They like to take care of other people in their own way and often expect others to follow their lead. However, if they remain inflexible, judging situations and moving too strongly according to their feelings, they can experience much difficulty in relationships. They need to develop patience and adaptability if they are to succeed.

W. SOMERSET MAUGHAM—January 25, 1874
CLARK GABLE—February 1, 1901
JACKIE ROBINSON—January 31, 1919
VIDAL SASSOON—January 17, 1928
ROGER VADIM—January 26, 1928
HAROLD PRINCE—January 30, 1928
JOAN RIVERS—January 20, 1937
JOSEPH WAMBAUGH—January 22, 1937
VANESSA REDGRAVE—January 30, 1937
DON EVERLY—February 1, 1937
ROBERTA FLACK—February 2, 1937
DOLLY PARTON—January 19, 1946

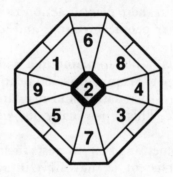

DATES THE MONTHS CHANGE

FEBRUARY 4–MARCH 5, 1899	FEBRUARY 4–MARCH 5, 1953
FEBRUARY 5–MARCH 5, 1908	FEBRUARY 4–MARCH 5, 1962
FEBRUARY 4–MARCH 5, 1917	FEBRUARY 4–MARCH 5, 1971
FEBRUARY 4–MARCH 5, 1926	FEBRUARY 5–MARCH 4, 1980
FEBRUARY 5–MARCH 5, 1935	FEBRUARY 4–MARCH 4, 1989
FEBRUARY 5–MARCH 5, 1944	FEBRUARY 4–MARCH 5, 1998

STEADY   *FASTIDIOUS*
DELICATE   *STUBBORN*
CONSERVATIVE   *SHREWDLY OBSERVANT*
SUPPORTIVE   *SELF-PROTECTIVE*

These people are steady, delicate, supportive, and conservative, but they also have a strong desire to control circumstances. They do not always have enough energy to accomplish this, even though they can be obstinate. These contradictory traits make life difficult for them.

They are often shrewd observers and can be fastidious; therefore, they are strict in criticizing themselves and others. Sometimes they express their self-interest unexpectedly, damaging their reputation.

Most of them are clear-headed and have a self-protective nature. Often they are too deliberate in doing things and may take an overly cautious attitude. Whatever they want, they do not give up easily. Their dependent nature needs strong support to help them in making decisions. Their steadiness and diligence usually help them find good advisers or partners.

They have strong confidence in themselves and are persistent. Socially they often stay within their own circle, and so they become conceited easily. Sometimes they confront others with trifling matters, because they always want to take control.

The women are mentally sensitive but quite stubborn. They want to be independent, yet their basic nature makes it difficult for them to develop their lives alone. What they need is to be adaptable, and if they are, their lives will run more smoothly. Men have a kind of feminine need to rely on someone even though they may act masculine. Both the men and the women need much attention and affection in order to fulfill their desires.

Faced with a serious decision, they may waver, even if they know definitely what they want. In order to act decisively, they need the support of strong, faithful people. When they find understanding and support, their success is assured.

Socially, most of the men appear reliable and magnanimous. This is deceptive: When an emergency arises, they are often not strong enough to take responsibility. They are not the types who can please everybody. Once they have chosen friends, they need and expect deep attachment. In love, they are self-motivated and change their minds quite often. The women are very serious and expect great attention.

They have luck with money when they are able to keep cool and detached. Any circumstance will be greatly influenced by how much and what kind of attention they get.

WILLIAM HENRY HARRISON—February 9, 1773
ABRAHAM LINCOLN—February 12, 1809
CHARLES DARWIN—February 12, 1809
ADOLPHE MENJOU—February 18, 1890
REX HARRISON—March 5, 1908
DINAH SHORE—March 1, 1917
ARTHUR O. SULZBERGER—February 5, 1926
SONNY BONO—February 16, 1935
ROGER DALTREY—March 1, 1944

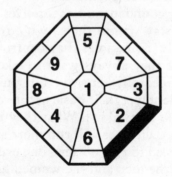

DATES THE MONTHS CHANGE

MARCH 6–APRIL 4, 1899	MARCH 6–APRIL 4, 1953
MARCH 6–APRIL 4, 1908	MARCH 6–APRIL 4, 1962
MARCH 6–APRIL 4, 1917	MARCH 6–APRIL 4, 1971
MARCH 6–APRIL 4, 1926	MARCH 5–APRIL 3, 1980
MARCH 6–APRIL 5, 1935	MARCH 5–APRIL 4, 1989
MARCH 6–APRIL 4, 1944	MARCH 6–APRIL 4, 1998

INSIGHTFUL *INFLEXIBLE*
CONSERVATIVE *CAUTIOUS*
DIGNIFIED *DEPENDENT*
PROUD *METHODICAL*

These people are often insightful but can be inflexible in situations necessitating taking a wide view of things. They usually have a proud attitude. At the same time, they are basically conservative with dependent natures. In reality, this makes it difficult for them to be independent.

Sometimes these people put themselves under the influence of more powerful persons. They want to feel secure. They have a cautiousness about keeping their dignity that may produce a good result. Sometimes this can bring a reverse effect, because the need for security is a kind of contradiction of their basic pride.

Their cautious, sacrificing nature combined with an often excellent mind helps them to exercise diplomatic skill. It helps them to develop their reputation in the social community.

Most men of this type feel a lack of responsibility for domestic duties. Sometimes overdoing this tendency makes them lose consideration for others. Their attention to detail in money matters often causes them to be stingy.

They are usually good in social situations but cannot express affection easily because they cannot be frank. If they become involved in a secret affair, they are apt to disrupt their lives severely.

They are lucky about money. Usually their financial luck comes to them indirectly: through a good partnership or a position someone gave them, through growth in benefits from an investment someone recommended, and so on.

Women of this type have the power to be quite independent and responsible. If they are to get satisfaction in marriage, they often need to be in a dominant position.

Most of the men seem to be lucky about finding wives who support them, though they never seem to be free from other cares.

It is most important for both men and women of this type to establish a relationship with an understanding lifelong partner. If not, they may have to expect a solitary future.

FRANCISCO GOYA—March 30, 1746
GLORIA SWANSON—March 27, 1899
MICHAEL REDGRAVE—March 20, 1908
DAVID LEAN—March 25, 1908
NAT KING COLE—March 17, 1917
JERRY LEWIS—March 16, 1926
JOHN FOWLES—March 31, 1926
HERB ALPERT—March 31, 1935
RICHARD CHAMBERLAIN—March 31, 1935
TONY ORLANDO—April 3, 1935
SLY STONE—March 15, 1944
JOHN SEBASTIAN—March 17, 1944
DIANA ROSS—March 26, 1944

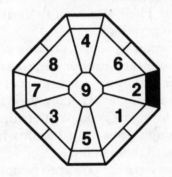

DATES THE MONTHS CHANGE

APRIL 5–MAY 5, 1899	APRIL 5–MAY 5, 1953
APRIL 5–MAY 5, 1908	APRIL 5–MAY 5, 1962
APRIL 5–MAY 5, 1917	APRIL 5–MAY 5, 1971
APRIL 5–MAY 5, 1926	APRIL 4–MAY 4, 1980
APRIL 6–MAY 5, 1935	APRIL 5–MAY 4, 1989
APRIL 5–MAY 5, 1944	APRIL 5–MAY 5, 1998

FORESIGHTFUL   *MOODY*
PERSUASIVE   *CONSERVATIVE*
CREATIVE   *DEPENDENT*
SHREWD   *SOCIAL*

These people tend to be shrewd and creative. They have a longing for the beautiful and the intellectual. They are often persuasive. Their weakness to indulge in their own interests can be impractical at times.

They usually love a social life and, as such, are often not domestic types. They have the ability to associate with many different kinds of people. They create an intellectual atmosphere and are often foresighted. They seem to read other people's minds. This helps them to be accepted and prized in social situations.

They are persuasive speakers, often offering logical comment and cheerful activity. However, at times they can be moody and too quick to comment, "leaking" a secret, their own or someone else's.

They usually give much energy to social and business dealings. They often need a place to rest or someone to treat them comfortably.

They have difficulties in love because they coolly consider what is to their benefit or what fits their sometimes hasty conclusions. When in love, they want to be loved very seriously but not restrained in their freedom. This attitude does not usually lead to easy satisfaction in marriage.

They are conservative in planning about money but may at times show off and become spendthrifts. They are good at making plans but take much time to actualize them. They are often lucky in finding others who help do this for them.

Their futures lie in their own hands and they usually move in their own way. They need to find the right person or power, however, to assist their dependent nature in developing a successful future. Their liberty to act depends upon whether or not they can find and use this person or power wisely.

*JAMES BUCHANAN—*April 23, 1791
*WILLIAM RANDOLPH HEARST—*April 29, 1863
*DUKE ELLINGTON—*April 29, 1899
*BETTE DAVIS—*April 5, 1908
*HUGH HEFNER—*April 9, 1926
*QUEEN ELIZABETH II—*April 26, 1926
*CLORIS LEACHMAN—*April 30, 1926
*BOBBY VINTON—*April 16, 1935
*DUDLEY MOORE—*April 19, 1935
*RITA COOLIDGE—*May 1, 1944

MAY 2-8-8

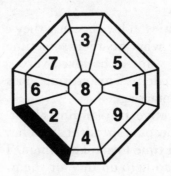

DATES THE MONTHS CHANGE

MAY 6–JUNE 5, 1899	MAY 6–JUNE 5, 1953
MAY 6–JUNE 5, 1908	MAY 6–JUNE 5, 1962
MAY 6–JUNE 5, 1917	MAY 6–JUNE 5, 1971
MAY 6–JUNE 5, 1926	MAY 5–JUNE 4, 1980
MAY 6–JUNE 6, 1935	MAY 5–JUNE 5, 1989
MAY 6–JUNE 5, 1944	MAY 6–JUNE 5, 1998

SERIOUS *AMBITIOUS*
DEPENDENT *HAUGHTY*
SHY *STUBBORN*
SELF-MOTIVATED *IMPULSIVE*

Most of these people have a somewhat contradictory nature: They are basically dependent, yet self-motivated. When they find something they want to do, they rush into it, not taking the necessary preliminary steps. This makes it hard to dispose of matters properly. As a result, someone else often has to make an appropriate settlement of matters.

They are serious and ambitious about their interests, but they are impulsive and change their minds easily.

They are delicate and shy, yet stubborn. Often they cannot judge situations clearly; this trait causes trouble when they misjudge appraisals of themselves.

They are self-motivated, yet lack firmness. They are influenced by others' speech and behavior. This results in their losing chances to develop their careers. They hesitate, though they are ready to go.

Their outward attitude is often one of haughtiness, which is the result of their efforts to mask their shy dependence.

They have sharp minds and short tempers. They have trouble putting their ideas into actions, so when they face trouble they cannot always deal with it properly.

They concentrate more on their own interests, sometimes causing them to lose consideration for others and an understanding of the whole picture. They are kind but suspicious, often having unstable relationships with associates as a result. They have a desire for exclusive possession and often seem childish. They need strong attachments but want others to go their way. They need to realize how willful they are.

Women of this type have to be careful that their expectations do not grow larger and larger, leading to frustration and dissatisfaction in love and life. They should not always expect others to make them satisfied. They often look for men of fame, yet they want to control things, finding it difficult for them to reach happiness.

Men of this type are often sensitive and emotional but are afraid to show it. Most of them like women with strong personalities. They do not usually like women to control them, however, because they want to retain their freedom.

This type has luck with money. They have ambition, but little patience. The key for their future success is patience and respect for others' needs.

HO CHI MINH—May 19, 1890
FRED ASTAIRE—May 10, 1899
JAMES STEWART—May 20, 1908
DON AMECHE—May 31, 1908
JOHN F. KENNEDY—May 29, 1917
BEATRICE ARTHUR—May 13, 1926
MILES DAVIS—May 25, 1926
MARILYN MONROE—June 1, 1926
ALLEN GINSBERG—June 3, 1926
GEORGE LUCAS—May 14, 1944
JOE COCKER—May 20, 1944
GLADYS KNIGHT—May 28, 1944

JUNE **2**–7–9

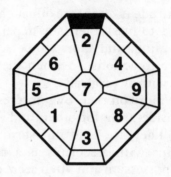

DATES THE MONTHS CHANGE

JUNE 6–JULY 6, 1899	JUNE 6–JULY 6, 1953
JUNE 6–JULY 6, 1908	JUNE 6–JULY 6, 1962
JUNE 6–JULY 7, 1917	JUNE 6–JULY 7, 1971
JUNE 6–JULY 7, 1926	JUNE 5–JULY 6, 1980
JUNE 7–JULY 7, 1935	JUNE 6–JULY 6, 1989
JUNE 6–JULY 6, 1944	JUNE 6–JULY 6, 1998

PROUD   *SELF-CONSCIOUS*
FLEXIBLE   *DETAIL-MINDED*
FORESIGHTFUL   *DELICATE*
RESOURCEFUL   *SOCIAL*

These people are often resourceful and pay close attention to detail. They have the ability to control or influence leaders while remaining in the background.

Many of this type are good judges of taste. They often have the ability to modernize and to make ideas popular.

They do not like to follow the instructions of others. They usually find satisfaction in fields of their own choice. However, they may have difficulty staying in one job or developing one career.

They are detail-minded and have organizational talents but can be somewhat careless. They can create ideas easily but cannot always make progress to actualize them. This leads people to misjudge them, since their acts are not consistent with their words.

They have good money sense but often spend it to show off. This can cause financial difficulties not apparent to others.

They are foresighted and have the power to resolve difficult problems with their soft touch. Sometimes these problems become their own, and they lose their balance, reacting so strongly that they hurt people.

Their pride is often stronger than it appears. They are usually attentive to people who follow them, but they can be suspicious of those who do not. They are often self-protective and sometimes self-conscious as well.

Most women of this type like men who have a distinct individuality, but often they cannot last in such a relationship. Men of this type like tender and tactile women, but somehow they tend to end up with just the opposite.

They can be flexible and impressionable, having traits that help them in their relationships and social life. Their tender and open attitude plus their sociability usually earns them a positive reputation with those around them.

*CALVIN COOLIDGE—*July 4, 1872
*DEAN MARTIN—*June 17, 1917
*RICHARD BOONE—*June 18, 1917
*KLAUS TENNSTEDT—*June 6, 1926
*FRANÇOISE SAGAN—*June 21, 1935
*BOZ SCAGGS—*June 8, 1944
*RAY DAVIES—*June 21, 1944
*JEFF BECK—*June 24, 1944

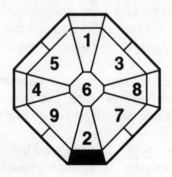

DATES THE MONTHS CHANGE

JULY 7–AUGUST 7, 1899	JULY 7–AUGUST 7, 1953
JULY 7–AUGUST 7, 1908	JULY 7–AUGUST 7, 1962
JULY 8–AUGUST 7, 1917	JULY 8–AUGUST 7, 1971
JULY 8–AUGUST 7, 1926	JULY 7–AUGUST 6, 1980
JULY 8–AUGUST 7, 1935	JULY 7–AUGUST 6, 1989
JULY 7–AUGUST 7, 1944	JULY 7–AUGUST 7, 1998

TENDER, AFFECTIONATE	*SELF-PROTECTIVE*
DELICATE	*DEPENDENT*
STYLISH	*METICULOUS*
STEADY	*INSECURE*

Most people of this type are distant in some way from their fathers. Their affectionate, delicate nature helps them find others who can help or look after them.

Their dependent and tender qualities make people feel close to them, but actually they find it hard to open up because they are self-protective and sometimes suspicious. Therefore, it is difficult for them to sustain close relationships.

They are sometimes insecure and quick to defend themselves, before they know what all the facts are. When problems become serious, they fight stubbornly until someone having authority in the situation arrives to negotiate. To this they are agreeable.

They often have style and can be show-offs. They can be tight with money and so may find it hard to command respect.

The men, because they are often shy and dependent, appear sexy. These qualities may give them an inferiority complex. Women of this type need more attention and are less dependent, having a more pretentious manner.

These people tend to be overly cautious, lacking self-reliance and leadership ability, but they can reach positions of authority by taking advantage of their steady, meticulous qualities to develop skills, techniques, and experience in professional fields.

They are shrewd and insightful, but a timidity may interfere with their ambition. They have a tendency to look to people who can help them and who will give them free rein. It is not easy for them to keep a relationship going if they are the leaders. The same can be said in matters of love. They are afraid of getting hurt but are very affectionate.

They often have interests outside their field and associate with people of power, in relationships that can bring them success. This gives them security and relief from anxiety.

GEORGE EASTMAN—July 12, 1854
HENRY FORD I—July 30, 1863
GEORGE D. CUKOR—July 7, 1899
JAMES CAGNEY—July 17, 1899
ERNEST HEMINGWAY—July 21, 1899
NELSON ROCKEFELLER—July 8, 1908
MILTON BERLE—July 12, 1908
PHYLLIS DILLER—July 17, 1917
ROBERT MITCHUM—August 6, 1917
STEVE LAWRENCE—July 8, 1935
DIAHANN CARROLL—July 17, 1935
DONALD SUTHERLAND—July 17, 1935
GERALDINE CHAPLIN—July 31, 1944

AUGUST 2-5-2

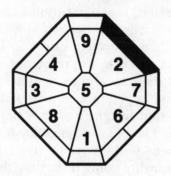

DATES THE MONTHS CHANGE

AUGUST 8–SEPTEMBER 7, 1899	AUGUST 8–SEPTEMBER 7, 1953
AUGUST 8–SEPTEMBER 7, 1908	AUGUST 8–SEPTEMBER 7, 1962
AUGUST 8–SEPTEMBER 7, 1917	AUGUST 8–SEPTEMBER 7, 1971
AUGUST 8–SEPTEMBER 7, 1926	AUGUST 7–SEPTEMBER 6, 1980
AUGUST 8–SEPTEMBER 8, 1935	AUGUST 7–SEPTEMBER 7, 1989
AUGUST 8–SEPTEMBER 7, 1944	AUGUST 8–SEPTEMBER 7, 1998

DILIGENT   *METICULOUS*
CONSERVATIVE   *STUBBORN*
FORESIGHTFUL   *SERIOUS*
STEADY   *DEPENDENT*

These people often have a conservative and stubborn nature. Most are diligent workers who build a career with steadiness. They are usually tenderhearted but pursue their objectives with strong persistence, even when they do not appear to be doing so.

Their serious, steady nature often makes them too devoted to others, and they may lose focus on what comes first. This can cause them to lose respect even though their intentions are good. They need to control the giving part of their nature because they cannot be a best friend or helpmate to everyone.

Basically they are dependent. They need a good leader to bring out their own best qualities and help them develop their careers. They have good foresight, but they are meticulous, so it takes them time to deal with matters.

Women can ask for help from others more easily than men because this type of man tends to be overly proud, even though he may know who might make things easier for him.

The women are very feminine, yet stubborn. They give great attention to whatever or whomever belongs to them, but matters have to be under their control. They see their position of mother or wife as very important. Their weakness is that they cannot control their ambition, which usually depends upon the people they are dealing with.

Men of this type are good at taking the time necessary to develop their careers successfully. Once they decide the way for their future, they give full energy to their purpose. As a result, they may not give enough attention to others. They are not adept at managing their energy. To be successful, they need to depend on their energy's being refilled by those close to them.

In love these people seldom find their ideal. They are often influenced by first impressions and physical appearance, even though they would like to be drawn to higher qualities.

CECIL B. DEMILLE—August 12, 1881
ALFRED HITCHCOCK—August 13, 1899
CHARLES BOYER—August 28, 1899
BILLY ROSE—September 6, 1899
LYNDON B. JOHNSON—August 27, 1908
FRED MACMURRAY—August 30, 1908
MEL FERRER—August 25, 1917
HENRY FORD II—September 4, 1917
JOHN DEREK—August 12, 1926
FIDEL CASTRO—August 13, 1926
SEIJI OZAWA—September 1, 1935
JACKIE DESHANNON—August 21, 1944

SEPTEMBER 2-4-3

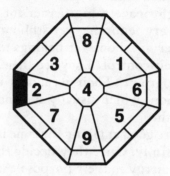

DATES THE MONTHS CHANGE

SEPTEMBER 8–OCTOBER 7, 1899	SEPTEMBER 8–OCTOBER 8, 1953
SEPTEMBER 8–OCTOBER 8, 1908	SEPTEMBER 8–OCTOBER 8, 1962
SEPTEMBER 8–OCTOBER 8, 1917	SEPTEMBER 8–OCTOBER 8, 1971
SEPTEMBER 8–OCTOBER 8, 1926	SEPTEMBER 7–OCTOBER 7, 1980
SEPTEMBER 9–OCTOBER 8, 1935	SEPTEMBER 8–OCTOBER 7, 1989
SEPTEMBER 8–OCTOBER 7, 1944	SEPTEMBER 8–OCTOBER 7, 1998

AGGRESSIVE   *SELF-INDULGENT*
SELF-MOTIVATED   *IMPATIENT*
EMOTIONAL   *DEPENDENT*
RESOURCEFUL   *DELICATE; DETAIL-MINDED*

The men and women of this type express these traits differently. The men tend to appear more tenderhearted, and the women appear more active and impatient. Inside, however, the men are usually aggressive and dependent at the same time; the women are more emotional and self-indulgent.

These people are usually good in social situations, since they have attentive attitudes. They are, however, self-indulgent and, although wanting to be the center of attention, tend to avoid serious responsibility. When forced to accept responsibility, they become very self-protective.

Because these people are aggressive but dependent, they tend to act on ideas too quickly. They lack the patience to carry through in the long run. They can, however, give full energy to the short run.

Often these people need someone to help them execute their ideas. Yet they are resourceful and strongly assertive, so they have good possibilities.

Many of this type long for sophistication, but it is basically their provincial nature that attracts people. They often have emotional ups and downs, which they find hard to control, even though these conditions usually don't last long.

In love, the women seek a great romance but usually choose conservatively to play it safe. Their adventures often lead to frustration, and they may have complications because of the conflict between their aggression and dependency. The men of this type appeal to women's motherly instincts by exhibiting a provincial, soft-touching dependency.

Their lives are often changeable because they have difficulty controlling their energy. They are not always considerate of others. They are alert to chances for improving their finances and are usually lucky in this respect.

AGATHA CHRISTIE—September 15, 1890
JOSHUA LOGAN—October 5, 1908
CAROLE LOMBARD—October 6, 1908
JERRY LEE LEWIS—September 29, 1935
JOHNNY MATHIS—September 30, 1935
JULIE ANDREWS—October 1, 1935
JACQUELINE BISSET—September 13, 1944
JULIO IGLESIAS—September 23, 1944
PATTI LABELLE—October 4, 1944

OCTOBER 2-3-4

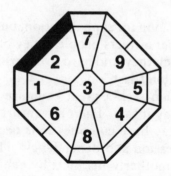

DATES THE MONTHS CHANGE

OCTOBER 8–NOVEMBER 7, 1899	OCTOBER 9–NOVEMBER 7, 1953
OCTOBER 9–NOVEMBER 7, 1908	OCTOBER 9–NOVEMBER 7, 1962
OCTOBER 9–NOVEMBER 7, 1917	OCTOBER 9–NOVEMBER 7, 1971
OCTOBER 9–NOVEMBER 7, 1926	OCTOBER 8–NOVEMBER 6, 1980
OCTOBER 9–NOVEMBER 7, 1935	OCTOBER 8–NOVEMBER 6, 1989
OCTOBER 8–NOVEMBER 6, 1944	OCTOBER 8–NOVEMBER 6, 1998

INSIGHTFUL   *DEPENDENT*
SHREWD   *SENSITIVE*
CONSERVATIVE   *IMPULSIVE*
INTENSE   *METICULOUS*

This type of person is often insightful, intense, and shrewd. They also have a tendency to be dependent and sensitive. It is difficult for them to attain power, something they really want. When they do gain power, they often have difficulty managing it.

Most of this type are good in business ventures. They can shrewdly grasp good opportunities, often through social situations rather than through their own ideas.

People of this type usually have much influence from strong mothers. They tend to give great attention to blood relations but do not usually get much in return.

They have clear likes and dislikes in their relationships that can lead them to lose clear focus on people's capabilities. They tend to depend on their emotional likes and dislikes and may have problems when they mix their personal and business relationships.

130

Because they tend to be impulsive, they do not find it easy to sustain their conservative, insightful behavior. If they can depend on a strong associate, they usually have a better chance at success.

Men of this type are not usually very domestic. They often lean on their partners for strength. Women of this type are somewhat more responsible in domestic situations than the men. They give more energy to family life but do not often get much in return.

Because they are sensitive and dependent, they have a self-protective nature that can cause problems for them. They will sometimes impulsively attack an enemy, but if the enemy exhibits strong power, they will usually give in.

Where money is concerned, this type seems to sense good possibilities instinctively. They need to be careful in managing their finances because of their impulsive nature.

In general, these people are insightful and shrewd. Their dependency makes it important that they find a strong power to lean on. They have to be careful not to let their emotional way of seeing people interfere with their ability to make a realistic evaluation.

OSCAR WILDE—October 16, 1854
PABLO PICASSO—October 25, 1881
DWIGHT D. EISENHOWER—October 14, 1890
JOAN FONTAINE—October 22, 1914
CHUCK BERRY—October 18, 1926
LUCIANO PAVAROTTI—October 12, 1935
PETER TOSH—October 19, 1944
JON ANDERSON—October 25, 1944

NOVEMBER **2**-2-5

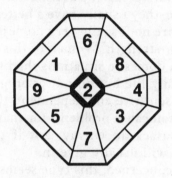

DATES THE MONTHS CHANGE

NOVEMBER 8–DECEMBER 6, 1899	NOVEMBER 8–DECEMBER 6, 1953
NOVEMBER 8–DECEMBER 6, 1908	NOVEMBER 8–DECEMBER 7, 1962
NOVEMBER 8–DECEMBER 7, 1917	NOVEMBER 8–DECEMBER 7, 1971
NOVEMBER 8–DECEMBER 7, 1926	NOVEMBER 7–DECEMBER 6, 1980
NOVEMBER 8–DECEMBER 7, 1935	NOVEMBER 7–DECEMBER 6, 1989
NOVEMBER 7–DECEMBER 6, 1944	NOVEMBER 7–DECEMBER 6, 1998

CONFIDENT　　　　　　*DELICATE*
CONSERVATIVE　　　　*STUBBORN*
RATIONAL　　　　　　　*DEPENDENT*
CONTROLLING　　　　　*CHANGEABLE*

This type often has the ability to organize matters rationally. They are usually confident and give great consideration to their appearance, which attracts people.

They are often conservative but have a sense of rivalry that can interfere with smooth relationships. They sometimes are quite stubborn and may try to push their will on others.

They are usually quite bright and long to be independent but often need help and attention to gain self-confidence. They can be easily influenced by the words and behavior of others, however, and so must guard against changing their minds too easily.

Socially this type can appear moderate and conservative, yet at the same time they may expect others to recognize their superiority.

Their rational organizational ability helps them in business and money matters. They are usually good savers.

Because these people can often be changeable and dependent, they may vacillate between different courses of action.

Men of this type are sometimes very conservative, leading people to think they are indecisive. This can make them lose good opportunities. Sometimes the men try to cover their moderate natures by overexaggerating their masculinity. They often like ambitious women but may have difficulty following another's lead. Women of this type are usually very maternal. They give much attention to family matters.

In general, this type has a way of getting an opinion across, and using this influence to their best advantage. They can be rather steady if they make an effort to control their somewhat changeable nature.

Since these people often lack the strength to be independent, they should minimize their desire to be in complete control of situations. They should accept the help of sincere persons around them in order to get the most out of life.

MARTIN VAN BUREN—December 5, 1782
EUGENE ORMANDY—November 18, 1899
ALISTAIR COOKE—November 20, 1908
INDIRA GANDHI—November 19, 1917
WOODY ALLEN—December 1, 1935
TOM SEAVER—November 17, 1944
JODIE FOSTER—November 19, 1962

DECEMBER 2-1-6

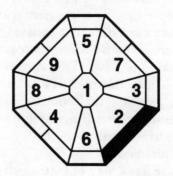

DATES THE MONTHS CHANGE

DEC. 7, 1899–JANUARY 5, 1900	DEC. 7, 1953–JANUARY 5, 1954
DEC. 7, 1908–JANUARY 5, 1909	DEC. 8, 1962–JANUARY 5, 1963
DEC. 8, 1917–JANUARY 5, 1918	DEC. 8, 1971–JANUARY 5, 1972
DEC. 8, 1926–JANUARY 5, 1927	DEC. 7, 1980–JANUARY 4, 1981
DEC. 8, 1935–JANUARY 5, 1936	DEC. 7, 1989–JANUARY 4, 1990
DEC. 7, 1944–JANUARY 5, 1945	DEC. 7, 1998–JANUARY 4, 1999

STEADY   *METICULOUS*
INDUSTRIOUS   *SELF-PROTECTIVE*
CAUTIOUS   *INFLEXIBLE*
BRIGHT   *DEPENDENT*

Although these people are often bright, steady, and industrious, they usually want to control matters. This can complicate their lives.

They are often meticulous and expect perfection. This slows down their forward movement. They usually try to be rational, but their determined nature can cause them to lose flexibility. This tendency complicates things and makes it difficult for others to follow their thinking.

Many of this type are longing for large-scale recognition, but more often they build reputation in a steady, gradual way. They usually succeed when they can lean on a stronger power. It is often difficult, however, for them to adapt to other people's ways of thinking and doing things.

In making decisions, these people can be somewhat inefficient or slow because of their caution. They have a dependent nature yet are independent in spirit.

Men of this type are serious and emotionally sensitive. They may be afraid to show their sensitive, delicate side. They would rather appear dignified. Many of them are self-protective.

Women tend to be more independent, proud, and obstinate. They like to control. They can be very cautious in keeping their leadership.

This type of person often spends money on vanity or on gaining fame, but they do better financially when they cooperate with a partner or take advice from associates.

In general, these people are not afraid to work hard for a living. If they apply their tendency to be cautious and avoid seeking more recognition than necessary, they can succeed more easily. Their steady, industrious nature helps them to reach goals even though reaching them may take time.

NOEL COWARD—December 16, 1899
LEW AYRES—December 28, 1908
BARRY GOLDWATER—January 1, 1909
LEE REMICK—December 14, 1935
TRACY AUSTIN—December 12, 1962

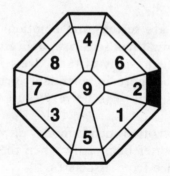

DATES THE MONTHS CHANGE

JANUARY 6–FEBRUARY 3, 1900	JANUARY 6–FEBRUARY 3, 1954
JANUARY 6–FEBRUARY 3, 1909	JANUARY 6–FEBRUARY 3, 1963
JANUARY 6–FEBRUARY 4, 1918	JANUARY 6–FEBRUARY 4, 1972
JANUARY 6–FEBRUARY 4, 1927	JANUARY 5–FEBRUARY 3, 1981
JANUARY 6–FEBRUARY 4, 1936	JANUARY 5–FEBRUARY 3, 1990
JANUARY 6–FEBRUARY 3, 1945	JANUARY 5–FEBRUARY 3, 1999

BRIGHT   *MOODY*
EXPRESSIVE   *DEPENDENT*
PERSUASIVE   *VAIN*
EASYGOING   *IMPULSIVE*

These people are often bright and expressive. They can be very persuasive and convincing. They are often easygoing and social but tend also to be vain, moody, and impulsive.

They are usually accepted and praised by others, but their moodiness makes them seem evasive sometimes, and people may question their reliability.

Because this type can be vain, they usually strive for attention or recognition. They plan well, but often need others to actualize their plans. As a result, they devote much energy expressly to attracting others.

Moneywise, they must be careful not to become spendthrifts, since their vanity can lead them to use money to show off. They plan well, if slowly, so they can usually spend more wisely if they listen to the advice of honest people.

Women of this type want to be loved very deeply, but because they tend to want to control matters, they may encounter problems. Men of this type seem able to bring out the maternal instinct in women, yet they have a strong urge to retain their freedom.

When it comes to making decisions, this type can sometimes have problems. They often want to deal quickly with situations, but their dependent, moody nature can lead to impulsive or confused solutions.

These people especially need the right partner, mate, or staff to be successful. Patiently listening to the ideas of others and including them in their planning will help much. Since they are capable of establishing the better part of their plans quite well, they need only exert this extra energy to find, listen to, and work with others to complete a well-planned life.

WOLFGANG AMADEUS MOZART—January 27, 1756
ADOLPH ZUKOR—January 7, 1873
FRANKLIN DELANO ROOSEVELT—January 30, 1882
GENE KRUPA—January 15, 1909
ETHEL MERMAN—January 16, 1909
JOHNNY RAY—January 10, 1927
ALAN ALDA—January 28, 1936
ROD STEWART—January 10, 1945
TOM SELLECK—January 29, 1945
MARTY BALIN—January 30, 1945
STEPHEN STILLS—January 30, 1945

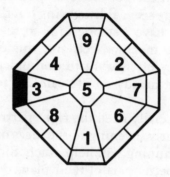

DATES THE MONTHS CHANGE

FEBRUARY 4–MARCH 4, 1898	FEBRUARY 5–MARCH 5, 1952
FEBRUARY 5–MARCH 6, 1907	FEBRUARY 4–MARCH 5, 1961
FEBRUARY 5–MARCH 5, 1916	FEBRUARY 4–MARCH 5, 1970
FEBRUARY 4–MARCH 5, 1925	FEBRUARY 4–MARCH 5, 1979
FEBRUARY 4–MARCH 4, 1934	FEBRUARY 4–MARCH 4, 1988
FEBRUARY 5–MARCH 5, 1943	FEBRUARY 4–MARCH 4, 1997

FORCEFUL	*RASH, HASTY*
DECISIVE	*SELF-ASSERTIVE*
FORESIGHTFUL	*IMPATIENT*
INTELLIGENT	*SENSITIVE*

When these people are young, their activity and enthusiastic energy often bring them early success. Their decisive spirit, foresight, intelligence, and shrewdness help them to find success very quickly. Many gain acceptance in the world in this manner, even though their actions may be rough and lacking in polish.

They are sharp, positive, and talented, but their self-assertiveness can lead them into playing "King of the Mountain," which can cause a tarnishing of their reputation. Their impatience and haste make them quick to act, and the energy their enthusiasm requires can wear them down. So, if they are planning a long-distance run in life, they must learn how to control their energy now.

They are fluent talkers, well reasoned and persuasive, but they are also impatient and find it easy to change their loyalties if that is to their benefit. When they are young, these traits give them a kind of premature charm. When they reach middle age, these charms may begin to look like bluffing and buck-passing. Lack of responsibility and overprotective actions can lead them into much difficulty.

Most of them have sharp, shrewd minds for foresighted financial planning that brings good luck in money matters.

In love, the enthusiastic side of their nature leads them to become involved, lose interest, and change partners quickly for their own benefit, whether it be politically or sexually. Their sensitivity leads them here and there, so it is difficult for them to get full satisfaction. Loneliness can be a problem for them.

Because of their sensitivity and tendency to make sudden changes, many experience periodic ups and downs in life. If they are enthusiastic when their spirits are high, they can reach success very early. Many find success in their field before or by their early thirties.

BERTOLT BRECHT—February 10, 1898
W. H. AUDEN—February 21, 1907
JACKIE GLEASON—February 26, 1916
JACK LEMMON—February 8, 1925
ROBERT ALTMAN—February 20, 1925
SAM PECKINPAH—February 21, 1925
HANK AARON—February 5, 1934
ALAN BATES—February 17, 1934
DAVID GEFFEN—February 21, 1943
GEORGE HARRISON—February 25, 1943

MARCH 3-4-4

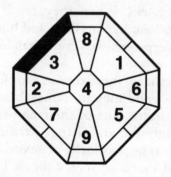

DATES THE MONTHS CHANGE

MARCH 5–APRIL 4, 1898	MARCH 6–APRIL 4, 1952
MARCH 7–APRIL 5, 1907	MARCH 6–APRIL 4, 1961
MARCH 6–APRIL 4, 1916	MARCH 6–APRIL 4, 1970
MARCH 6–APRIL 4, 1925	MARCH 6–APRIL 4, 1979
MARCH 6–APRIL 4, 1934	MARCH 5–APRIL 3, 1988
MARCH 6–APRIL 5, 1943	MARCH 5–APRIL 4, 1997

FORESIGHTFUL   *SENSITIVE*
TENDER   *EVASIVE*
CREATIVE   *IMPATIENT*
CONFIDENT   *EMOTIONAL*

These people are usually foresighted and affable, but inside they are often quite sensitive. Though they do not always show it, this trait occasionally comes out and causes them trouble. If they keep their feelings inside, they become frustrated and may lash out at someone close.

Most grew up with great affection from their parent of the opposite sex. Usually the men are tender and gregarious, good in social and business situations. They often use up their energy outside the family, so wives should not expect constant attention at home. Women of this type are very independent, and their expectations of male affection are often excessive. They have strong maternal instincts but don't like to be controlled by men, even though powerful men attract them.

Their confident attitude often adds to their reputation, and although they take time to make decisions, their choices are usually wise. Because they lack patience and tenacity, these people sometimes fail to reach their goals. Usually, their lives move smoothly and successfully, but sometimes this easy flow is disrupted by divorce or loss of position.

They often gain praise for their intelligence and original ideas, yet, in the beginning, people around them may have difficulty understanding the way their minds work. These people tend to be evasive and need to explain themselves in detail to give others a better grasp of their thoughts.

In love, the men usually quickly and easily choose someone who is to their benefit. They want to possess their loved one entirely. When they are in love, they are very serious; they want only one love at a time. The women of this type have the ability to love more freely and without constraints.

Many of this type can develop successful businesses but are weak about organizing their home life. If they have an understanding mate, they remain young in spirit. They do not do well alone.

MICHELANGELO—March 6, 1475
JOHN TYLER—March 29, 1790
VINCENT VAN GOGH—March 30, 1853
HARRY JAMES—March 15, 1916
EUGENE MCCARTHY—March 29, 1916
GREGORY PECK—April 5, 1916
SHIRLEY JONES—March 31, 1934
ALAN ARKIN—March 26, 1934
LYNN REDGRAVE—March 8, 1943
EDDIE MURPHY—April 3, 1961

APRIL **3**-3-5

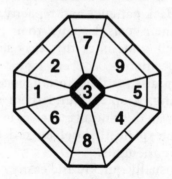

DATES THE MONTHS CHANGE

APRIL 5–MAY 4, 1898	APRIL 5–MAY 5, 1952
APRIL 6–MAY 6, 1907	APRIL 5–MAY 5, 1961
APRIL 5–MAY 5, 1916	APRIL 5–MAY 5, 1970
APRIL 5–MAY 5, 1925	APRIL 5–MAY 5, 1979
APRIL 5–MAY 5, 1934	APRIL 4–MAY 4, 1988
APRIL 6–MAY 5, 1943	APRIL 5–MAY 4, 1997

CURIOUS   *RASH*
HARDWORKING   *SHREWD*
SELF-ASSERTIVE   *SENSITIVE*
STRAIGHTFORWARD   *STUBBORN*

These people are usually very sensitive and stubborn, even though they appear softhearted and tender. They make a clear distinction between likes and dislikes in their human relationships, often as a means of protecting themselves. Most have been strongly influenced by their mothers.

They have the power to lead, but are not always strong enough to completely control the situations that would give them full satisfaction. They are often lucky to be surrounded by good staff or followers who assist them and respect their position. The actions and attitudes of the men are very straightforward. If they have real ability, it will be admired; if not, they may lose their reputation. The women are also straightforward but appear more sensitive emotionally.

They have a spirit of inquiry, foresighted intelligence, and the good sense to adapt themselves well to most circumstances. These powers produce the marketable ideas that often bring them beneficial opportunities.

Sometimes their high level of sensitivity and freshness leads them to seek new concepts and presentations, but their rashness and stubbornness can make it difficult for them to complete their projects.

They are passionate lovers but are impatient. Relationships often depend on the tilt of their passions. Many have difficulty staying in their first marriage. Their key to success depends upon their courage, and whether or not they can attract good people who can help them. For the most part, people will follow them because of their charm and talent.

CHARLIE CHAPLIN—April 16, 1889
ADOLF HITLER—April 20, 1889
FRED ZINNEMANN—April 29, 1907
KATE SMITH—May 1, 1907
ALFRED BLOOMINGDALE—April 15, 1916
YEHUDI MENUHIN—April 22, 1916
GLENN FORD—May 1, 1916
ROD STEIGER—April 14, 1925
SHIRLEY MACLAINE—April 24, 1934
MICHAEL BENNETT—April 8, 1943

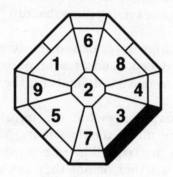

DATES THE MONTHS CHANGE

MAY 5–JUNE 5, 1898	MAY 6–JUNE 5, 1952
MAY 7–JUNE 6, 1907	MAY 6–JUNE 5, 1961
MAY 6–JUNE 5, 1916	MAY 6–JUNE 5, 1970
MAY 6–JUNE 5, 1925	MAY 6–JUNE 5, 1979
MAY 6–JUNE 5, 1934	MAY 5–JUNE 4, 1988
MAY 6–JUNE 6, 1943	MAY 5–JUNE 5, 1997

DIGNIFIED	*SENSITIVE*
DELICATE	*INFLEXIBLE*
RATIONAL	*IMPATIENT*
PROUD	*RASH*

These people are usually proud and dignified. They often appear shy, and people may think they are indecisive. This is not true. They can be very stubborn about making their own decisions. At times, their pride can lead them to feel a sense of superiority to others.

They can be rash and sometimes inflexible of opinion, but they usually know what they have to do or want to do. Many get their opportunities for success at an early age. Much of their success is based on these early foundations.

They are weak in cooperative relationships. The reason for this is that their impatient nature is often hard for people to follow. They may act too proud or self-important, causing difficulty with colleagues.

The men have problems finding satisfaction in marriage. The women tend to be more sensitive and are usually more showy than the men. They act very decisively and independently. Sometimes their attitude is too strong for people, especially other women, and they may provoke negative reactions if they are not careful.

In love, both men and women have a sense of self-importance and pride. They like to be in the spotlight and want attention. Even when they part with someone, they try to retain a social relationship. For them, the most important thing is that "somebody loves them," for they are usually romantic and are easily hurt. Once hurt, they find it difficult to keep up the relationship because of their sensitivity and pride. Still, they cannot cut off ties completely.

If they have enough attention and affection, they can solve their problems, using their rational, well-adjusted minds. They are well organized in planning about money.

LAURENCE OLIVIER—May 22, 1907
JOHN WAYNE—May 26, 1907
JOHNNY WEISSMULLER—June 2, 1907
YOGI BERRA—May 19, 1925
MALCOLM X—May 19, 1925
TONY CURTIS—June 3, 1925
PETER NERO—May 22, 1934
PAT BOONE—June 1, 1934
JACK BRUCE—May 14, 1943
JOE NAMATH—May 31, 1943

JUNE 3-1-7

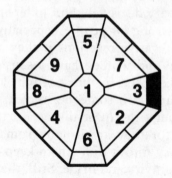

DATES THE MONTHS CHANGE

JUNE 6–JULY 6, 1898	JUNE 6–JULY 6, 1952
JUNE 7–JULY 7, 1907	JUNE 6–JULY 6, 1961
JUNE 6–JULY 6, 1916	JUNE 7–JULY 7, 1970
JUNE 6–JULY 7, 1925	JUNE 6–JULY 7, 1979
JUNE 6–JULY 7, 1934	JUNE 5–JULY 6, 1988
JUNE 7–JULY 7, 1943	JUNE 6–JULY 6, 1997

INSIGHTFUL   *SENSITIVE*
HARDWORKING   *SELF-PROTECTIVE*
INTENSE   *SOCIAL*
STRAIGHTFORWARD   *EASYGOING*

These people are insightful, but their approach to life is easygoing. They are often able to protect themselves from great failure but may find it difficult to reach full success because of their laidback approach.

Most of them are bright and determined. They can concentrate well but often have an inflexible view. Their family relationships and traditions are very important to them, yet they can be quite objective when evaluating relatives.

They have a straightforward attitude but are very sensitive when dealing with their own serious problems: in confessing their love, for example, or when receiving criticism. Socially, the women often take the lead. The men need to express what is on their minds more clearly, since they can have such definite ideas.

Most are hard workers, with a positive way of looking at life. They know what they want. They give great energy to achieving what they want. If they cannot find satisfaction in a work situation, however, they may sometimes quit a job or position rather suddenly.

Most are able to gain money passively. For example, someone in the same company may recommend buying stock instead of taking a bonus. The stock may rise and they may make a big profit. They can benefit from good partnerships since they are sometimes weak at planning or managing their money.

They often expend great energy in their social life. Because of a self-protective nature, they strictly choose associates with whom they are comfortable before they open up.

They usually seek a strong love to counteract their insecurity. They often expect perfect love, and it is not easy for them to compromise in marriage. Many are attracted to a person in an uncommon condition: a married person, for example, or a person of unique character, or a person in an unusual position. Their natural self-protectiveness often guards them from hurt in these situations, but once free again they tend to repeat this pattern of attraction.

When they take a more flexible view of life, their insightful and straightforward nature helps them to reach their goals more easily.

ALICE A. BAILEY—June 16, 1880
HELEN KELLER—June 27, 1880
JEAN COCTEAU—July 5, 1889
ERICH MARIA REMARQUE—June 22, 1898
PAUL MELLON—June 11, 1907
ROBERT MCNAMARA—June 9, 1916
OLIVIA DEHAVILAND—July 1, 1916
MAUREEN STAPLETON—June 21, 1925
GENE WILDER—June 11, 1934
XAVIERA HOLLANDER—June 15, 1934
JAMES LEVINE—June 23, 1943
GERALDO RIVERA—July 4, 1943
DAN AYKROYD—July 1, 1952
PRINCESS DIANA—July 1, 1961

JULY **3**-9-8

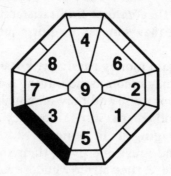

DATES THE MONTHS CHANGE

JULY 7–AUGUST 6, 1898	JULY 7–AUGUST 7, 1952
JULY 8–AUGUST 8, 1907	JULY 7–AUGUST 7, 1961
JULY 7–AUGUST 7, 1916	JULY 7–AUGUST 7, 1970
JULY 8–AUGUST 7, 1925	JULY 8–AUGUST 7, 1979
JULY 8–AUGUST 7, 1934	JULY 7–AUGUST 6, 1988
JULY 8–AUGUST 7, 1943	JULY 7–AUGUST 6, 1997

INTELLIGENT   *IMPATIENT*
AMBITIOUS   *SENSITIVE*
SHOWY   *TALKATIVE*
SELF-MOTIVATED   *VAIN*

These people are often ambitious and intelligent. They can be impatient and moody, having qualities that often interfere with attaining their lofty goals. They are often persuasive and are able to speak convincingly. They may appear stronger than they really are. Though their attitude can seem haughty and vain, they actually are quite sensitive.

They sometimes have a difficult time making decisions because of their excessive sensitivity. Their moody actions can sometimes lead to failure. Usually they need to look before they leap. They need enough time to make decisions if they are not to miss their opportunities.

Besides being moody, these people are often impatient and sensitive, so that life is a series of ups and downs for them. Their actions can be quite contradictory, depending upon their emotional state. They expend much energy in their social life, and they alternate showiness with timidity. This affects their love life, which also has intervals of jagged highs and lows.

They are usually very concerned about money and often find ways to put enough aside. They try to find assistance or know someone who can help them.

Most people of this type have good relationships with their families. The women appear more independent than the men. Men more often outwardly express the sensitive side of their natures. Both, however, are usually self-motivated.

They are often ambitious, yet their sensitive nature is in control. Many of these people need the backing of another person in order to be a success; however, they tend to follow what satisfies them. They can profit by opening their minds to a wider view of life.

MARCEL PROUST—July 10, 1871
ERLE STANLEY GARDNER—July 17, 1889
ALEXANDER CALDER—July 22, 1898
AMELIA EARHART—July 24, 1898
HENRI MOORE—July 30, 1898
BARBARA STANWYCK—July 16, 1907
KEENAN WYNN—July 27, 1916
JACQUES D'AMBOISE—July 28, 1934
MICK JAGGER—July 26, 1943

AUGUST **3**-8-9

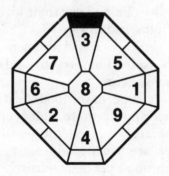

DATES THE MONTHS CHANGE

AUGUST 7–SEPTEMBER 7, 1898	AUGUST 8–SEPTEMBER 7, 1952
AUGUST 9–SEPTEMBER 8, 1907	AUGUST 8–SEPTEMBER 7, 1961
AUGUST 8–SEPTEMBER 7, 1916	AUGUST 8–SEPTEMBER 7, 1970
AUGUST 8–SEPTEMBER 7, 1925	AUGUST 8–SEPTEMBER 7, 1979
AUGUST 8–SEPTEMBER 7, 1934	AUGUST 7–SEPTEMBER 6, 1988
AUGUST 8–SEPTEMBER 7, 1943	AUGUST 7–SEPTEMBER 6, 1997

PROUD
INTELLIGENT
INSIGHTFUL
AMBITIOUS

SENSITIVE
OPINIONATED
IMPULSIVE
WILLFUL

These people usually are intelligent and have good insight. They generally have leadership qualities that make for easy success, but they often find it hard to follow orders.

They are proud but gentle-mannered, and they are good in social situations. They crave attention, and if they do not get it, they are hurt. They are responsible people, but often they are disappointed because of their misunderstanding of others. Their ideas develop out of projects that would be to their own benefit.

They are impulsive and therefore should take extra time for decision making. If they have to decide on something right away, they can become very nervous. When making important decisions, they should sometimes depend on another's advice.

They are conscientious about money and are also lucky in that respect. In love, the men are often attracted to women with strong personalities, and the women are attracted to fame. They are opinionated, so love must move their way. Problems are often caused by the influence of financial situations. They can be especially opinionated in their human relationships. If they like someone, they can accept almost anything that person does; if not, they find fault with any transgression.

These types are often ambitious and their active minds lead them to seek new things to conquer. They are good in business planning and also in sales.

In general, these people have somewhat childish minds. This might cause them to act immaturely. Their brains are usually very active, however, and they tend to stay spiritually young. This quality gives them the ambition to face new ideas and fields of endeavor.

CLAUDE DEBUSSY—August 22, 1862
LILLIAN CARTER—August 15, 1898
MARTHA RAYE—August 27, 1916
MIKE DOUGLAS—August 11, 1925
OSCAR PETERSON—August 15, 1925
DONALD O'CONNOR—August 30, 1925
ROBERT DENIRO—August 17, 1943
VALERIE PERRINE—September 3, 1943
JIMMY CONNORS—September 2, 1952

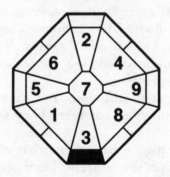

DATES THE MONTHS CHANGE

SEPTEMBER 8–OCTOBER 7, 1898	SEPTEMBER 8–OCTOBER 7, 1952
SEPTEMBER 9–OCTOBER 8, 1907	SEPTEMBER 8–OCTOBER 7, 1961
SEPTEMBER 8–OCTOBER 8, 1916	SEPTEMBER 8–OCTOBER 8, 1970
SEPTEMBER 8–OCTOBER 8, 1925	SEPTEMBER 8–OCTOBER 8, 1979
SEPTEMBER 8–OCTOBER 8, 1934	SEPTEMBER 7–OCTOBER 7, 1988
SEPTEMBER 8–OCTOBER 8, 1943	SEPTEMBER 7–OCTOBER 7, 1997

DECISIVE	*INSECURE*
ORGANIZED	*NERVOUS*
EXPRESSIVE	*DELICATE*
PATIENT	*SELF-CONSCIOUS*

Most of these people are hard workers, and they always seek possible new fields. They give up quickly if they find negativity. During childhood their life seems easy and positive when they have their parents' support, but they actually need to expend a great deal of effort to develop their own success.

Their attention to detail, sensitivity, and insecurity make them overly expressive in social situations. They use great energy for this purpose and need to refill the well somewhere, and most choose to do so in their homes. Those they live with should be informed of their needs to avoid misunderstanding. Communication may be difficult unless those concerned are aware of the problem.

They are very conscious of personal criticism. A bad reputation is very upsetting to them, making them insecure and hurt.

Most are interested in their social lives, and are initially open-hearted even before they get to know people well. Because of their insecurity, they may be a bit overbearing. They act this way to protect themselves, though others find their behavior difficult to accept. This can lead them to be hurt easily. Their wariness sometimes makes them self-conscious and suspicious, resulting in loneliness.

They have the energy to organize, but are somewhat careless. Most of them make good money by hard work. They also have the energy to overcome difficulty and often gain the opportunity to make substantial money.

Women of this type appear stronger than the men; however, they are always looking for security. The men often need someone with stronger character to agree with what they do before they do it.

They are usually dream chasers, but many of them give up on the way to reaching their goals, only to regret it later. One or two dreams can be good for them, but too many can lead to failure.

GEORGE GERSHWIN—September 26, 1898
PETER SELLERS—September 8, 1925
B. B. KING—September 16, 1925
BRIAN EPSTEIN—September 19, 1934
SOPHIA LOREN—September 20, 1934
BRIGITTE BARDOT—September 28, 1934
"MAMA" CASS ELLIOTT—September 19, 1943
CHRISTOPHER REEVE—September 25, 1952

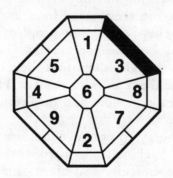

DATES THE MONTHS CHANGE

OCTOBER 8–NOVEMBER 6, 1898	OCTOBER 8–NOVEMBER 6, 1952
OCTOBER 9–NOVEMBER 7, 1907	OCTOBER 8–NOVEMBER 7, 1961
OCTOBER 9–NOVEMBER 7, 1916	OCTOBER 9–NOVEMBER 7, 1970
OCTOBER 9–NOVEMBER 7, 1925	OCTOBER 9–NOVEMBER 7, 1979
OCTOBER 9–NOVEMBER 7, 1934	OCTOBER 8–NOVEMBER 6, 1988
OCTOBER 9–NOVEMBER 7, 1943	OCTOBER 8–NOVEMBER 6, 1997

INSIGHTFUL	*INFLEXIBLE*
DEDICATED	*STUBBORN*
HARDWORKING	*HAUGHTY*
CONSERVATIVE	*SENSITIVE*

Most people of this type develop their lives independently. They are often sensitive and conservative in attitude. Basically they are dedicated and hardworking.

They usually move through their lives with strong intuition, though they cannot easily adapt to different situations. They need to work with people or things they like or agree with. In this fashion, they steadily accumulate experience, and this helps them become proficient in their field and usually brings them financial gain.

Women of this type express themselves much more sharply than the men and they often have the ability to lead. They usually have some specific type of their own in mind when it comes to love. Many of the men are shy but stubborn, making it difficult for people to approach them. For their own happiness, they need to be more passionate.

Both the men and women are usually conservative but impatient. When they are in control of their energy and feelings, they appear calm. If they face disturbing situations or if someone hurts them, they can be very caustic in order to hide their vulnerability.

They usually have a strong will to carry through their goals. Once they are interested in something, they give great energy to it. They are often, however, inflexible, so it is difficult for them to maintain control of these situations. They are, usually, insightful and have strong intuition, qualities that help them to break through most difficulties.

WALTER CRONKITE—November 4, 1916
LENNY BRUCE—October 13, 1925
ANGELA LANSBURY—October 16, 1925
JOHNNY CARSON—October 23, 1925
MARGARET THATCHER—October 13, 1925
CATHERINE DENEUVE—October 22, 1943
JONI MITCHELL—November 7, 1943

NOVEMBER 3-5-3

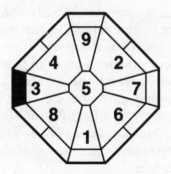

DATES THE MONTHS CHANGE

NOVEMBER 7–DECEMBER 6, 1898	NOVEMBER 7–DECEMBER 6, 1952
NOVEMBER 8–DECEMBER 7, 1907	NOVEMBER 8–DECEMBER 6, 1961
NOVEMBER 8–DECEMBER 6, 1916	NOVEMBER 8–DECEMBER 6, 1970
NOVEMBER 8–DECEMBER 7, 1925	NOVEMBER 8–DECEMBER 7, 1979
NOVEMBER 8–DECEMBER 7, 1934	NOVEMBER 7–DECEMBER 6, 1988
NOVEMBER 8–DECEMBER 7, 1943	NOVEMBER 7–DECEMBER 6, 1997

SELF-CONFIDENT　　　　*IMPATIENT*
FRANK　　　　　　　　　*STUBBORN*
CREATIVE　　　　　　　*RASH*
INTELLIGENT　　　　　　*DIPLOMATIC*

This type of person has many similarities with the February-born Number 3. Most of these people have good family connections, but difficulties can occur that may cause terminal breakups of relationships.

They are strongly self-confident. They usually talk very sharply and often have little self-control. Sometimes their vehement self-assertion can hurt people and make enemies.

They are very open-minded but stubborn in making and carrying out their decisions. This can lead to failure sometimes, because as soon as they get an idea, they rush out to translate it into action without any further consideration or research.

They need to be more deliberate and thoughtful in their affairs. They may fall quickly into very passionate love. But because they often choose a partner on the basis of a first impression, they are disappointed when their passion fades easily.

Moneywise they are conscious about financial planning, and they work hard. They also love to spend money for pleasure.

Women of this type are usually very sensitive and self-assertive. Men tend to want control of any circumstance that comes up. Both the men and women have difficulty agreeing with others' opinions. This may cause them to lose friends and acquaintances.

Most are insightful and talented. When they keep an open mind and learn to compromise with others, they save energy and can attain their goals more easily, although they may get somewhat less in overall satisfaction.

MARK TWAIN (Samuel Clemens)—November 30, 1835
RENE CLAIR—November 11, 1898
RICHARD BURTON—November 10, 1925
ROCK HUDSON—November 17, 1925
ROBERT F. KENNEDY—November 20, 1925
JULIE HARRIS—December 2, 1925
CARL SAGAN—November 9, 1934
LAUREN HUTTON—November 17, 1943
RANDY NEWMAN—November 29, 1943
NADIA COMANECI—November 12, 1963

DECEMBER **3**-4-4

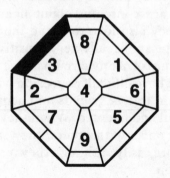

DATES THE MONTHS CHANGE

DEC. 7, 1898–JANUARY 4, 1899	DEC. 7, 1952–JANUARY 6, 1953
DEC. 8, 1907–JANUARY 6, 1908	DEC. 7, 1961–JANUARY 5, 1962
DEC. 7, 1916–JANUARY 5, 1917	DEC. 6, 1970–JANUARY 5, 1971
DEC. 8, 1925–JANUARY 5, 1926	DEC. 8, 1979–JANUARY 5, 1980
DEC. 7, 1934–JANUARY 5, 1935	DEC. 7, 1988–JANUARY 4, 1989
DEC. 8, 1943–JANUARY 5, 1944	DEC. 7, 1997–JANUARY 4, 1998

FORESIGHTFUL　　　　*EMOTIONAL*
TENDER　　　　*SELF-PROTECTIVE*
SOCIAL　　　　*IMPULSIVE*
CONFIDENT　　　　*SENSITIVE*

This type of person has many similarities with the March Number 3. Most are very sensitive and emotional. Usually the men are soft-hearted and confident. Their external appearance charms people in business and in social life, but they are somewhat hard-grained in their hearts. The women are more sharply outspoken than the men.

They usually have high ideals, though they sometimes may seem to lack sincerity because they do not care to consider what others think.

They often have shrewd minds but are impulsive. They have the ability to actualize foresighted ideas, but their need for respect makes them afraid of making mistakes. Making decisions is also difficult. Once a decision is made, they may find it is not the right one and have to choose another alternative.

They have strong emotions and are optimistic but impatient. If their emotions become unbalanced, their actions are erratic. Because of this weakness, they may lose the respect of other people.

In love, they are serious and self-protective, but tender in speech and behavior. They are good mixers in social life and make a wide circle of relationships. Most of the men of this type do not express themselves clearly; even though they love someone, their actions may seem indecisive to the other person. Most of them grow up with affection from members of the opposite sex in their family.

Most of the men expect to be respected by their partner and the women have strong maternal instincts. The women like men who have distinct personalities, but they do not like to be controlled.

Most of these people are very active. Their view of life is always to look outside the home. It is not easy for them to develop their home life satisfactorily; they need an understanding mate for marriage to be successful.

Financially, most of them make good money with a superior's backing. Also, they know how to save. But they have to be careful to exercise control in their social life, which might involve excess expenditures.

ANDREW JOHNSON—December 29, 1808
KIRK DOUGLAS—December 9, 1916
SAMMY DAVIS, JR.—December 8, 1925
DICK VAN DYKE—December 13, 1925
GEORGE MARTIN—January 3, 1926
JIM MORRISON—December 8, 1943
KEITH RICHARDS—December 18, 1943
JOHN DENVER—December 31, 1943

JANUARY 3-3-5

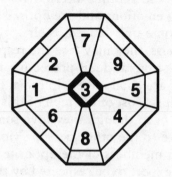

DATES THE MONTHS CHANGE

JANUARY 5–FEBRUARY 3, 1899	JANUARY 6–FEBRUARY 3, 1953
JANUARY 7–FEBRUARY 4, 1908	JANUARY 6–FEBRUARY 3, 1962
JANUARY 6–FEBRUARY 3, 1917	JANUARY 6–FEBRUARY 3, 1971
JANUARY 6–FEBRUARY 3, 1926	JANUARY 6–FEBRUARY 4, 1980
JANUARY 6–FEBRUARY 4, 1935	JANUARY 5–FEBRUARY 3, 1989
JANUARY 6–FEBRUARY 4, 1944	JANUARY 5–FEBRUARY 3, 1998

SELF-ASSERTIVE   *SENSITIVE*
HARDWORKING   *STUBBORN*
PASSIONATE   *IMPATIENT*
TALENTED   *EXPLOSIVE*

This type of person has many similarities with the April-born Number 3. They are usually influenced by strong mothers. They are self-assertive and stubborn outwardly, but sensitive and less confident inside. This sometimes gives them difficult decisions to make. They can be hurt easily.

Most of them are business-minded and are hard workers. They are good in the fields of planning and sales but have less ability to carry plans into execution. They often have good connections with superiors who play a big part in their careers. If they have their own business, they should think "action before words" in pursuing success and security.

They can be intense and rash, having qualities that can lead them to make big mistakes, though some deliberation and foresight can counteract these weaknesses.

They often have to face business difficulties even though they work very hard. They are good talkers, but their penchant for frankness can lead them to point out other people's flaws too accurately, resulting in enemies.

Because they have definite likes and dislikes, their opinions may or may not be accepted depending upon whether people agree with them.

In love they are passionate but impatient. If they find satisfaction, they may stay longer but often this is not the case. They expect perfect and continuous satisfaction, a goal that is difficult and perhaps impossible to achieve.

Financially, they are very conscientious in planning, and their reputation for being business-minded and hardworking brings them luck in money matters.

Most of these people are talented and able to become successful when young. They give explosive energy in an effort to gain complete satisfaction. This and their sensitivity to others' words and actions may cause them difficulty later as they age and are less able to expend the energy necessary for high-pressure living. If they can control these energies, they can expect an easier life when they're older.

MILLARD FILLMORE—January 7, 1800
EDGAR ALLEN POE—January 19, 1809
NIJINSKY—January 12, 1890
HUMPHREY BOGART—January 23, 1899
JOSÉ LIMON—January 12, 1908
SOUPY SALES—January 8, 1926
PATRICIA NEAL—January 20, 1926
ELVIS PRESLEY—January 8, 1935
SHERRIL MILNES—January 10, 1935
A. J. FOYT—January 16, 1935
JIMMY PAGE—January 8, 1944

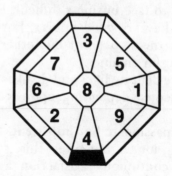

DATES THE MONTHS CHANGE

FEBRUARY 3–MARCH 4, 1897	FEBRUARY 5–MARCH 5, 1951
FEBRUARY 5–MARCH 5, 1906	FEBRUARY 5–MARCH 4, 1960
FEBRUARY 5–MARCH 6, 1915	FEBRUARY 4–MARCH 5, 1969
FEBRUARY 5–MARCH 5, 1924	FEBRUARY 4–MARCH 5, 1978
FEBRUARY 4–MARCH 5, 1933	FEBRUARY 4–MARCH 5, 1987
FEBRUARY 4–MARCH 5, 1942	FEBRUARY 4–MARCH 4, 1996

EMOTIONAL	*MANIPULATIVE*
AMBITIOUS	*POOR DECISION-MAKER*
INDEPENDENT	*CAUTIOUS*
CLEAR-MINDED	*MONEY-CONSCIOUS*

These people have active minds and catch on to things quickly. They are often fluent conversationalists and good speakers with a proven ability to persuade. They can be cautious, and tend to be self-protective. Sometimes they tend to manipulate others.

They are afraid of being hurt, losing anything, or making decisions. They fight hard against anything that will make them lose self-confidence.

They are often slow to open up and show that they have strong sexual feelings. When they do, they can be very tender and loving with their partners. Sex can be an outlet for their insecurity.

Compromise can be difficult for them.

They need to be active since they are apt to be cautious and worry when not enough is happening. They have a strong desire for material things.

They tend to be ambitious, steady workers, and good at handling money.

Men and women of this type are very similar, though the women are more self-protective and want more control over others. The men are more likely to look for a strong ally to lean on while controlling others. These people may have some difficult period to break through. If they can learn to consider other people more during this time, their lives improve greatly.

LON CHANEY—February 10, 1906
LORNE GREENE—February 12, 1915
ZERO MOSTEL—February 18, 1915
LEE MARVIN—February 19, 1924
SIDNEY POITIER—February 20, 1924
GLORIA VANDERBILT—February 20, 1924
YOKO ONO—February 18, 1933
PRINCE ANDREW—February 19, 1960

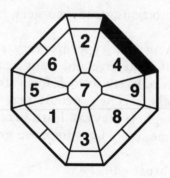

DATES THE MONTHS CHANGE

MARCH 5–APRIL 3, 1897	MARCH 6–APRIL 5, 1951
MARCH 6–APRIL 5, 1906	MARCH 5–APRIL 4, 1960
MARCH 7–APRIL 5, 1915	MARCH 6–APRIL 4, 1969
MARCH 6–APRIL 4, 1924	MARCH 6–APRIL 4, 1978
MARCH 6–APRIL 4, 1933	MARCH 6–APRIL 4, 1987
MARCH 6–APRIL 4, 1942	MARCH 5–APRIL 3, 1996

EMOTIONAL   *SELF-CONSCIOUS*
SENSITIVE   *ORGANIZED*
CONSERVATIVE   *DETAIL-MINDED*
TENDER   *METICULOUS*

Most of these people are tender-hearted and have highly sensitive natures. Though they have an innate grasp of art and can understand artistic fields of endeavor very well, they tend to be quite conservative.

They have quick minds but spend too much time with minor details. This trait sometimes interferes with their natural ability to organize.

Their sensitive, emotional natures make them prey to the opinions and judgments of others. If they are hurt or misjudged, they retaliate strongly.

Faced with difficulty, they make their own decisions, though they often worry about these decisions afterward.

Men of this type are especially cautious and conservative when they are young. Their attention to detail can be extreme, and they expect perfection even in unimportant things. People tend to find them picky. Men generally improve with age, relaxing their preoccupation with minutiae. Women seem to know exactly what they want in terms of family and their position in it. They are strongly self-assertive. Both women and men are self-conscious and sometimes overreact as a result. They are likely also to change their minds suddenly. If they are unable to express their own ideas in an effective way, they get very upset, frustrated by the inability to clearly communicate.

They find it hard to carry out their own ideas unless someone offers them a hand, though they become strong and forceful when they near the attainment of a goal.

Although they are tender and good to others, the critical judgment of friends and colleagues can become a sore point with them. People are surprised to see someone so understanding react so forcefully when threatened. They need to learn how to express themselves and not be so easily influenced by the opinions of others.

SARAH VAUGHAN—March 27, 1924
MARLON BRANDO—April 3, 1924
DORIS DAY—April 3, 1924
MICHAEL CAINE—March 14, 1933
MARSHA MASON—April 3, 1942

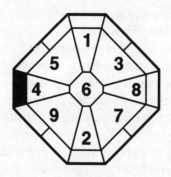

DATES THE MONTHS CHANGE

APRIL 4–MAY 4, 1897	APRIL 6–MAY 5, 1951
APRIL 6–MAY 5, 1906	APRIL 5–MAY 4, 1960
APRIL 6–MAY 6, 1915	APRIL 5–MAY 5, 1969
APRIL 5–MAY 5, 1924	APRIL 5–MAY 5, 1978
APRIL 5–MAY 5, 1933	APRIL 5–MAY 5, 1987
APRIL 5–MAY 5, 1942	APRIL 4–MAY 4, 1996

EMOTIONAL   *ENTHUSIASTIC*
ACTIVE   *INFLEXIBLE*
STUBBORN   *IMPATIENT*
CONTROLLED   *GOOD CONCENTRATION*

The actions of this type person are controlled by their emotions. The success or failure of students, for example, will often depend on whether or not they like the teacher. When confronted with fears or suspicions, they become thoroughly depressed. However, once they recover, it is easy for them to forget the focus of their anxieties.

They are impatient as well as emotional, so their actions can be self-indulgent, even spoiled. In their dealings with other people, they are often too honest and proud, being cheated or used by others. By nature, if they are interested in something, they can concentrate intensely, sometimes to the point of exhaustion. On the other hand, they can be impatient and give up easily if they must do things that they really do not like. It is important that they be involved with projects that give them a sense of personal fulfillment.

Once they manage to focus on something they really want to do, they become very enthusiastic and single-minded. This leads them to explore their interests more fully and professionally.

They appear easygoing but are actually all in a flurry. They are tender-hearted outwardly but stormy and impatient inside. Their minds do not adapt well or easily to new situations, and they are moved by feelings and emotions. Their judgments and intuitions are often correct, but because they are controlled by emotion, they have difficulty adjusting a calculation or insight once it has been made. They are often talented in the negotiation of large-scale business exchanges but, because they are impatient, tend to have difficulty in small-scale calculations.

They find it hard to consider others' needs because they are so concerned with their own. This preoccupation results in a bluntly candid frankness that many people perceive as snobbishness. They need to be more considerate of others and more deliberate in their decision making.

SOL HUROK—April 9, 1888
THORNTON WILDER—April 17, 1897
ANTHONY QUINN—April 21, 1915
ORSON WELLES—May 6, 1915
CAROL BURNETT—April 26, 1933
BARBRA STREISAND—April 24, 1942

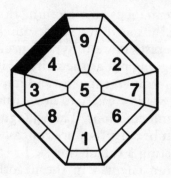

DATES THE MONTHS CHANGE

MAY 5–JUNE 4, 1897	MAY 6–JUNE 5, 1951
MAY 6–JUNE 6, 1906	MAY 5–JUNE 5, 1960
MAY 7–JUNE 6, 1915	MAY 6–JUNE 5, 1969
MAY 6–JUNE 5, 1924	MAY 6–JUNE 5, 1978
MAY 6–JUNE 5, 1933	MAY 6–JUNE 5, 1987
MAY 6–JUNE 5, 1942	MAY 5–JUNE 4, 1996

CONFIDENT   *INDECISIVE*
HARMONIOUS   *DETERMINED*
ADAPTABLE   *EVASIVE*
EMOTIONAL   *CHANGEABLE*

These people are determined. They can be strong-willed, bordering on rude, but don't often show this harsh side of their personality. Their confidence and creativity often help them get ahead.

They have a strong sense of justice and a wiseness that draw people to them. It is their nature to take care of others, and this characteristic often results in a leadership position in social situations. People are attracted by these qualities, and yet, because this type tends to be evasive, it is not easy for others to really be sure what is going on in their minds.

It is their luck to have good connections in human relationships, which in turn bring them material rewards. In business, however, their impulsive, changeable nature interferes with their leadership potential; they are more likely to be successful in an activity initiated by someone else. They are not, however, followers, and their opportunities lie in assisting and taking care of others.

Marriage can be a problem for this type because they change their minds and have difficulty keeping their promises. They have the ability to make money but do not always manage it wisely.

IRVING BERLIN—May 11, 1888
FRANK CAPRA—May 19, 1897
ROBERTO ROSSELLINI—May 8, 1906
JOSEPHINE BAKER—June 3, 1906
ROSS HUNTER—May 6, 1924

JUNE 4-4-5

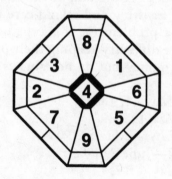

DATES THE MONTHS CHANGE

JUNE 5–JULY 6, 1897	JUNE 6–JULY 7, 1951
JUNE 7–JULY 7, 1906	JUNE 6–JULY 6, 1960
JUNE 7–JULY 7, 1915	JUNE 6–JULY 6, 1969
JUNE 6–JULY 6, 1924	JUNE 6–JULY 6, 1978
JUNE 6–JULY 7, 1933	JUNE 6–JULY 7, 1987
JUNE 6–JULY 7, 1942	JUNE 5–JULY 6, 1996

EMOTIONAL   *STUBBORN*
TENDER   *EVASIVE*
PERSISTENT   *CHANGEABLE*
SELF-MOTIVATED   *SMOOTH-MANNERED*

These people are very emotional and stubborn. They are tender yet opinionated. Though they are self-motivated, they need admiration for what they do or they become very disappointed. Most are bright and quick to change their opinions, making it hard for people to know what they are thinking. Since their evasive, emotional nature can distance people, for their own happiness they need to explain themselves more.

Because they change their minds often and are always looking for new interests, a very specialized job that really holds their interest is best for them. The only way they can achieve success is to keep their interests stable; only then will they be able to develop career goals.

They have their own ideas and seldom consider their effect on others. They appear easygoing but are really overanxious because of their erratic emotional nature. They need someone with a sympathetic ear to give them good advice, as it is difficult for them to make firm decisions.

They love to be admired. Their self-motivated actions, however, make acceptance by others difficult, even though they can be smooth-mannered.

Men and women of this type are much the same. They both need to control their emotions. The women have strong maternal instincts, and the men need someone who can help them keep their self-confidence.

Because these people tend to have an erratic kind of life, they need patience and firm faith that their basic warmth and kindness will attract other people who will help them reach their goals.

BILLY WILDER—June 22, 1906
GEORGE SANDERS—July 3, 1906
DAVID ROCKEFELLER—June 12, 1915
GEORGE BUSH—June 12, 1924
SIDNEY LUMET—June 25, 1924
PAUL MCCARTNEY—June 18, 1942

JULY **4**-3-6

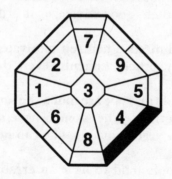

DATES THE MONTHS CHANGE

JULY 7–AUGUST 6, 1897	JULY 8–AUGUST 7, 1951
JULY 8–AUGUST 7, 1906	JULY 7–AUGUST 6, 1960
JULY 8–AUGUST 8, 1915	JULY 7–AUGUST 7, 1969
JULY 7–AUGUST 7, 1924	JULY 7–AUGUST 7, 1978
JULY 8–AUGUST 7, 1933	JULY 8–AUGUST 7, 1987
JULY 8–AUGUST 7, 1942	JULY 7–AUGUST 6, 1996

EMOTIONAL   *DIGNIFIED*
TENDER   *PROUD*
SENSITIVE   *INTENSE*
FAITHFUL   *CAUTIOUS*

Most people of this type have been strongly influenced by their mothers. They are very sensitive and cautious, tending to be perfectionists. Because they are proud, they find it hard to change their attitudes easily.

Men of this type have a natural strength and determination of will. Women often have problems because they appear too forceful and proud. Both need to control this strong attitude.

When they become emotionally involved, they lose perspective and can become very jealous. They have very strong likes and dislikes that can often cloud their judgment.

Although they are by nature dignified and proud, they are very sensitive inside. The men find this difficult to control and can become vulnerable.

172

They strongly desire affection but are proud and possessive too.

This type can best develop success within a big organization or system. If it requires an extended time investment, they have the faith and patience necessary to accomplish their goals. It is very important to this type that whatever they are doing has meaning for them within the framework of their own existence.

JOHN HUSTON—August 5, 1906
JOSEPH KENNEDY, JR.—July 25, 1915
VINCENT SARDI, JR.—July 23, 1915
JAMES BALDWIN—August 2, 1924
PETER O'TOOLE—August 2, 1933
HARRISON FORD—July 13, 1942
MARGARET COURT—July 16, 1942
LUCIE ARNAZ—July 17, 1951

AUGUST 4-2-7

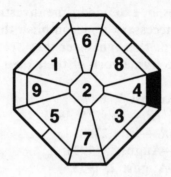

DATES THE MONTHS CHANGE

AUGUST 7–SEPTEMBER 6, 1897	AUGUST 8–SEPTEMBER 7, 1951
AUGUST 8–SEPTEMBER 8, 1906	AUGUST 7–SEPTEMBER 7, 1960
AUGUST 9–SEPTEMBER 8, 1915	AUGUST 8–SEPTEMBER 7, 1969
AUGUST 8–SEPTEMBER 7, 1924	AUGUST 8–SEPTEMBER 7, 1978
AUGUST 8–SEPTEMBER 7, 1933	AUGUST 8–SEPTEMBER 7, 1987
AUGUST 8–SEPTEMBER 7, 1942	AUGUST 7–SEPTEMBER 6, 1996

EMOTIONAL　　　　　　　*CALCULATING*
HYPERSENSITIVE　　　　 *CONSERVATIVE*
TENDER　　　　　　　　 *SELF-CENTERED*
FORESIGHTFUL　　　　　 *DELICATE*

These people tend to be conservative yet foresightful. They seem to be easygoing and calm. Actually they are hypersensitive and emotional inside. While they seem to be listening to the opinions of others, they are really quite self-centered and unlikely to be persuaded.

They have a great sense of beauty, and by cultivating their esthetic sense, they can improve the quality of their lives. If they want to make money, they need to control their emotional nature to carry through. They have to balance the two strong sides of their nature, emotion and calculation, if they are to achieve success.

Fortunately the self-centered part of their nature does not show much on the outside, due to their tender-hearted expression. However, their self-assertion is quite strong and can make others resentful or hostile.

Men of this type have a kind of feminine or delicate quality. They tend to judge situations by emotional rather than rational considerations. Their nature is to take first, give second. Women's minds tend to be clearer, and they can deal independently with facts. Both men and women expect a lot of attention. Once they fall in love, they are very emotional. They often have problems with one-sided love relationships.

In business, they are detail-minded and use calm judgment to achieve their purpose. By being conservative early in life, they often make money later. They are not the type to make a fortune in a single stroke.

In general, they need to consider others more and should not expect to receive before they give.

ETHEL BARRYMORE—August 15, 1879
T. E. LAWRENCE (OF ARABIA)—August 15, 1888
INGRID BERGMAN—August 29, 1915
REGINA RESNIK—August 30,1924
BUDDY HACKETT—August 31, 1924
ROMAN POLANSKI—August 18, 1933
ISAAC HAYES—August 20, 1942

SEPTEMBER 4-1-8

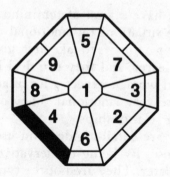

DATES THE MONTHS CHANGE

SEPTEMBER 7–OCTOBER 7, 1897	SEPTEMBER 8–OCTOBER 8, 1951
SEPTEMBER 9–OCTOBER 8, 1906	SEPTEMBER 8–OCTOBER 7, 1960
SEPTEMBER 9–OCTOBER 8, 1915	SEPTEMBER 8–OCTOBER 7, 1969
SEPTEMBER 8–OCTOBER 7, 1924	SEPTEMBER 8–OCTOBER 8, 1978
SEPTEMBER 8–OCTOBER 8, 1933	SEPTEMBER 8–OCTOBER 8, 1987
SEPTEMBER 8–OCTOBER 8, 1942	SEPTEMBER 7–OCTOBER 7, 1996

SERIOUS	*EMOTIONAL*
INDEPENDENT	*IMPRACTICAL*
TENACIOUS	*STUBBORN*
SELF-MOTIVATED	*SELF-PROTECTIVE*

These people take a serious, sincere approach to situations. They do not compromise easily. It is hard for them to deal with complicated problems, but often, when faced with a serious change in life, this type is blessed with good luck or timely assistance from others to see them through.

They are bright but not practical. They can be downright stubborn about their ideas. They have high ideals and sufficient intelligence to be realistic in almost everything they do if they can control their inflexibility.

They are social-minded and can develop a good circle of acquaintances. Yet they often try to control people, although they would actually derive more benefit from letting those around them help, advise, and support them.

176

They can isolate themselves in several ways. Their emotional erraticness can be off-putting to acquaintances. Secondly, they sometimes look down on others when they think their way is the best.

When it comes to love and affection, they are actually quite shy and do not reveal their true feelings easily. They are more likely to be receptive to the emotions of others than to actively express their own. They have high ideals about love and are drawn into dreams or fantasies full of passion and excitement. Because of their conviction that love must be like this, they often experience extreme ups and downs when real problems arise.

Men and women of this type are very similar. They share the ability to plan and execute their will, but rather than trying to control others, they should develop a greater focus in their own living and use their tenacity to achieve realistic goals.

These people have a great sense of responsibility for their blood relatives. They need to expand their responsibility to include nonrelatives and to learn to consider and respect other people's qualities and ideas.

MAURICE CHEVALIER—September 12, 1888
WILLIAM FAULKNER—September 25, 1897
LAUREN BACALL—September 16, 1924
MARCELLO MASTROIANNI—September 28, 1924
TRUMAN CAPOTE—September 30, 1924
JIMMY CARTER—October 1, 1924
CHARLTON HESTON—October 4, 1924
RICHARD HARRIS—October 1, 1933

OCTOBER 4-9-9

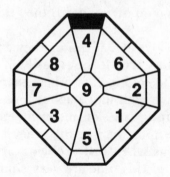

DATES THE MONTHS CHANGE

OCTOBER 8–NOVEMBER 6, 1897

OCTOBER 9–NOVEMBER 7, 1906

OCTOBER 9–NOVEMBER 7, 1915

OCTOBER 8–NOVEMBER 7, 1924

OCTOBER 9–NOVEMBER 7, 1933

OCTOBER 9–NOVEMBER 7, 1942

OCTOBER 9–NOVEMBER 7, 1951

OCTOBER 8–NOVEMBER 6, 1960

OCTOBER 8–NOVEMBER 6, 1969

OCTOBER 9–NOVEMBER 7, 1978

OCTOBER 9–NOVEMBER 7, 1987

OCTOBER 8–NOVEMBER 6, 1996

PROUD
EMOTIONAL
FORESIGHTFUL
AFFECTIONATE

MOODY
EXPRESSIVE
FICKLE
STUBBORN

These people are proud and have an expressive style that does not always come from their real feelings, but from a need to appear a certain way. Because of this trait, they may unintentionally distance people.

They have strong powers of persuasion and are expressive talkers, often able to sway others' opinions. If people don't follow their advice, they usually get very upset.

They are creative and foresightful and have a sense of beauty. Their minds are eager to explore new ideas. Often they become overextended and lose focus. This loss of control causes them much confusion.

Although they never like other people to control them, they are very dependent upon others for attention and affection. Their actions are strong and they give affection in a grand, showy manner. This display often confuses others. The actions and expressions of this type are very different from their actual feelings.

This type often has difficulty with family connections. They are intelligent but moody, the result being that although they are able to make quick, sharp decisions, those decisions are often dependent upon the mood of the moment.

The women are more proud than the men, and they try to control matters. They are unaware of the effect their stormy style has on other people. They expect and need the admiration of all. The men are also proud but more indecisive than the women. Even though they may have good ideas and ability, they can fail to capitalize on opportunities because of their inability to act quickly.

These people are very sensitive to change. They are often on top of trends. Their creative sense and ability to catch the movement of fashion are very acute because of their foresight. Their moodiness, however, can cause emotional ups and downs that may damage their reputations. When they are down emotionally, they tend to lose control.

In business, despite their foresight and creativity, indecision can interfere with opportunity. They need to subdue their pride and develop more ambition.

JOHN ADAMS—October 30, 1730
EUGENE O'NEILL—October 16, 1888
LUCIANO VISCONTI—November 2, 1906
ARTHUR MILLER—October 17, 1915
LEE IACOCCA—October 15, 1924

NOVEMBER **4**-8-1

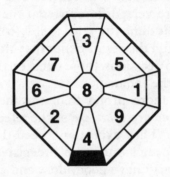

DATES THE MONTHS CHANGE

NOVEMBER 7–DECEMBER 6, 1897	NOVEMBER 8–DECEMBER 7, 1951
NOVEMBER 8–DECEMBER 7, 1906	NOVEMBER 7–DECEMBER 6, 1960
NOVEMBER 8–DECEMBER 7, 1915	NOVEMBER 7–DECEMBER 6, 1969
NOVEMBER 8–DECEMBER 6, 1924	NOVEMBER 8–DECEMBER 6, 1978
NOVEMBER 8–DECEMBER 6, 1933	NOVEMBER 8–DECEMBER 6, 1987
NOVEMBER 8–DECEMBER 7, 1942	NOVEMBER 7–DECEMBER 6, 1996

EMOTIONAL
AMBITIOUS
SHARP-MINDED
SELF-CENTERED

INSECURE
WEAK DECISION-MAKER
MONEY-CONSCIOUS
MANIPULATIVE

These people usually have active minds and appear dignified, but emotionally they are often insecure. They give much energy to accumulating financial security, but it is hard for them to hold onto their money. When their energy level decreases, their insecurity increases and they are prone to worry and frustration. They often use food, sex, or some personal indulgence as an outlet for this anxiety.

They have the power to convince other people and are often manipulative if they want something badly enough. Socially they may try to lead people for self-centered purposes.

It is very difficult for them to make decisions if they must lose or give up anything in the process. They are ambitious and industrious but must be careful to employ patience in building their future step by step.

Women of this type are not very dependent upon their mates, whom they often try to control.

Men of this type appear dignified outwardly but can be insecure inside.

In general, these people are self-protective and find compromise hard. Their attitude is usually high-minded and bright.

(See also February type Number 4)

ALFRED G. VANDERBILT—November 27, 1843
OTTO PREMINGER—December 5, 1906
ALEXANDER HAIG—December 2, 1924
MARTIN SCORCESE—November 17, 1942
CALVIN KLEIN—November 19, 1942
JIMI HENDRIX—November 27, 1942

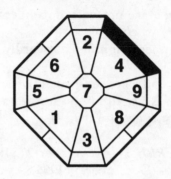

DATES THE MONTHS CHANGE

DEC. 7, 1897–JANUARY 4, 1898	DEC. 8, 1951–JANUARY 5, 1952
DEC. 8, 1906–JANUARY 5, 1907	DEC. 7, 1960–JANUARY 4, 1961
DEC. 8, 1915–JANUARY 6, 1916	DEC. 7, 1969–JANUARY 5, 1970
DEC. 7, 1924–JANUARY 5, 1925	DEC. 7, 1978–JANUARY 5, 1979
DEC. 7, 1933–JANUARY 5, 1934	DEC. 7, 1987–JANUARY 5, 1988
DEC. 8, 1942–JANUARY 5, 1943	DEC. 7, 1996–JANUARY 4, 1997

DECISIVE
ORGANIZED
EMOTIONAL
HYPERSENSITIVE

VERY DETAIL-CONSCIOUS
DEPENDENT
EXPLOSIVE
SELF-CONSCIOUS

These people often have an easy manner that other people mistake for indecision. Actually, this type can be very decisive when faced with important choices. A concern for detail sometimes makes them worry about their decisions after the fact.

They have strong organizational powers, but their obsessive pursuit of detail and persistent probing of others can become annoying. They tend to become involved too deeply with people too early in the relationship, but in general they are lucky in finding satisfying love relationships. They do have difficulty sustaining these relationships for a long period of time, however.

Women of this type try to organize family life on their terms yet still depend strongly on their husbands. The men have less energy for the home but do well in their job or business.

In general, these people make friends easily but are slack about keeping up friendships. They have a similarly loose approach to money.

They are emotional and dependent and as such are vulnerable to other people's opinions. Although they may not manifest it outwardly, they are strongly influenced by those around them.

They don't give up easily, even if they are confused emotionally. They have the ability to pursue what they want with great determination and enthusiasm.

They can expect life to develop favorably if they demonstrate their abilities in partnership, rather than leadership. Often it is through the advice or suggestions of others that this type finds access to the achievement of goals.

(See also March type Number 4)

RAY MILLAND—January 3, 1907
FRANK SINATRA—December 12, 1915
EDITH PIAF—December 19, 1915
EDWARD I. KOCH—December 12, 1924

JANUARY 4-6-3

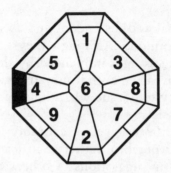

DATES THE MONTHS CHANGE

JANUARY 5–FEBRUARY 3, 1898	JANUARY 6–FEBRUARY 4, 1952
JANUARY 6–FEBRUARY 4, 1907	JANUARY 5–FEBRUARY 3, 1961
JANUARY 7–FEBRUARY 4, 1916	JANUARY 6–FEBRUARY 3, 1970
JANUARY 6–FEBRUARY 3, 1925	JANUARY 6–FEBRUARY 4, 1979
JANUARY 6–FEBRUARY 3, 1934	JANUARY 6–FEBRUARY 3, 1988
JANUARY 6–FEBRUARY 4, 1943	JANUARY 6–FEBRUARY 3, 1997

EMOTIONAL
SELF-ASSERTIVE, AGGRESSIVE
HONEST
INTENSE

INFLEXIBLE
PROUD
IMPATIENT
RECKLESS

These people are emotional, moved readily by their feelings. They are also proud and reckless, appearing to be self-assured. They tend to discriminate clearly between likes and dislikes, creating difficulty in relationships. They sometimes reject people on the basis of their first impression, which often proves to be correct.

If they are interested in a project, they can concentrate and carry it through; if not, they are unable to sustain interest. Socially they do well, making wide connections and gaining favorable business opportunities. People find their honesty refreshing and endearing. They are better, however, at negotiating large-scale rather than small-scale business exchanges, overseas rather than local, for example. They are calm in the face of serious situations, with the exception of emotional crises. Here they can appear to be calm but are quite stormy within.

Their weakness is that they move by feeling, and since they are poor explainers, others find it difficult to understand them. In general, this type expresses itself more strongly than the April type Number 4. Also, the women tend to be stronger, more active and aggressive than the men. They have problems keeping their strong emotional nature under control. It is difficult for this type to sustain a first marriage unless they find the perfect mate. The men expect strong, sensitive, active women, yet want to keep their freedom.

There is a tendency for this type to be distant from their parents, especially the father. They must be careful to focus their powers of concentration on one thing at a time or they may exhaust themselves. (See also April type Number 4)

DOUGLAS MACARTHUR—January 26, 1880
W. C. FIELDS—January 29, 1880
JAMES MICHENER—February 3, 1907
JOHN DELOREAN—January 6, 1925
GWEN VERDON—January 13, 1925
YUKIO MISHIMA—January 14, 1925
TELLY SAVALAS—January 21, 1925
PAUL NEWMAN—January 26, 1925
JANIS JOPLIN—January 19, 1943
KATHERINE ROSS—January 29, 1943

FEBRUARY **5**-2-8

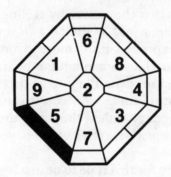

DATES THE MONTHS CHANGE

FEBRUARY 4–MARCH 4, 1896	FEBRUARY 4–MARCH 5, 1950
FEBRUARY 4–MARCH 5, 1905	FEBRUARY 4–MARCH 5, 1959
FEBRUARY 5–MARCH 5, 1914	FEBRUARY 5–MARCH 4, 1968
FEBRUARY 5–MARCH 6, 1923	FEBRUARY 4–MARCH 5, 1977
FEBRUARY 5–MARCH 5, 1932	FEBRUARY 4–MARCH 5, 1986
FEBRUARY 4–MARCH 5, 1941	FEBRUARY 4–MARCH 5, 1995

DETERMINED *STUBBORN*
SERIOUS *OSTENTATIOUS*
SELF-MOTIVATED *DELICATE*
CONTROLLING *INFLEXIBLE*

These people are usually determined idealists who possess the stubborn ambition needed to achieve their goals. Often their lack of adaptability results in great dissatisfaction when things are not going their way. They plan seriously and thoroughly for their future.

They depend on others for attention no matter what they are doing. If they are getting enough emotional support, they are very calm and can make sound judgments. When their emotional support is off-balance, they can really get themselves into trouble when faced with an important decision.

They often are ostentatious and overbearing but are actually quite preoccupied with appearances.

Their desires are strong and they tend to break off with people who interfere with their projects or goals.

Women of this type can be quite independent, but they need much attention to be satisfied. Men tend to cover up their vulnerability with the appearance of a strong exterior.

There is a delicate aspect to this type's mind that can cause complications and frustration in relationships. At the same time, they can be helpful and nice to those who become a part of their social life or who come under their control.

Others cannot usually control these people; their influence is very strong. They sometimes can lose control of themselves if they are not careful.

They often turn life to their own best interests. Many will not give up until they achieve satisfaction.

GYPSY ROSE LEE—February 9, 1914
ARTHUR KENNEDY—February 17, 1914
ZSA ZSA GABOR—February 6, 1923
ED MCMAHON—March 6, 1923
FRANÇOIS TRUFFAUT—February 6, 1932
MILOS FORMAN—February 18, 1932
EDWARD M. KENNEDY—February 22, 1932
JOHNNY CASH—February 26, 1932
ELIZABETH TAYLOR—February 27, 1932
MARK SPITZ—February 10, 1950
KAREN CARPENTER—March 2, 1950

MARCH **5**-1-9

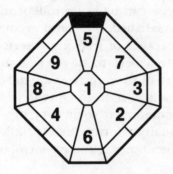

DATES THE MONTHS CHANGE

MARCH 5–APRIL 3, 1896	MARCH 6–APRIL 4, 1950
MARCH 6–APRIL 4, 1905	MARCH 6–APRIL 4, 1959
MARCH 6–APRIL 5, 1914	MARCH 5–APRIL 4, 1968
MARCH 7–APRIL 5, 1923	MARCH 6–APRIL 4, 1977
MARCH 6–APRIL 4, 1932	MARCH 6–APRIL 4, 1986
MARCH 6–APRIL 4, 1941	MARCH 6–APRIL 4, 1995

BRIGHT   *IMPRACTICAL*
DETERMINED   *STUBBORN*
INDEPENDENT   *PROUD*
HUMANE   *SELF-PROTECTIVE*

These people are especially bright when dealing with subjects that interest them. They see things their way, however, and so are not always practical. Their decisions can be quite arbitrary.

They are proud and independent. Often they try to control other people and engineer events so that they turn out to their own best liking.

They tend to be talented and have a discerning eye for art and beauty. This talent is often a good means for proving themselves.

They tend to isolate themselves but, because they are basically humane, they do not often remain isolated, as people sense this quality and are attracted to it.

Socially they are good talkers when they want to be, though they are not always comfortable with this role.

They express their love or affection poorly and are not always good at reading others' feelings. They tend to be self-protective and may find themselves in one-sided love situations more often than not.

Financially they seem to be lucky. Often in times of serious decision, positive things happen for them.

In general, these individuals can benefit from widening their view of life to include the broad world outside their somewhat narrow focus on personal concerns.

NEVILLE CHAMBERLAIN—March 18, 1869
ALBERT EINSTEIN—March 14, 1878
TENNESSEE WILLIAMS—March 26, 1914
EDMUND MUSKIE—March 28, 1914
ALEC GUINNESS—April 2, 1914
CYD CHARISSE—March 8, 1923
MARCEL MARCEAU—March 22, 1923
ARIF MARDIN—March 15, 1932
DEBBIE REYNOLDS—April 1, 1932
ANTHONY PERKINS—April 4, 1932
WAYNE NEWTON—April 3, 1941
PAUL KANTNER—March 17, 1941

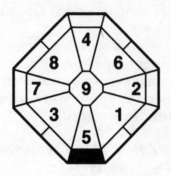

DATES THE MONTHS CHANGE

APRIL 4–MAY 4, 1896	APRIL 5–MAY 5, 1950
APRIL 5–MAY 5, 1905	APRIL 5–MAY 5, 1959
APRIL 6–MAY 5, 1914	APRIL 5–MAY 4, 1968
APRIL 6–MAY 5, 1923	APRIL 5–MAY 4, 1977
APRIL 5–MAY 5, 1932	APRIL 5–MAY 5, 1986
APRIL 5–MAY 5, 1941	APRIL 5–MAY 5, 1995

CONTROLLING	*SELF-INDULGENT*
PERSISTENT	*IMPULSIVE*
EXPRESSIVE	*INSECURE*
PROUD	*STUBBORN*

These people want to gain control in as many areas of life as they can. They expend great energy when dealing with things they want. Because they are insecure, they cannot always carry through their desires without getting help from others. Relationships become strained and sometimes impossible when they try to control the other people.

They long for success and fame and are often driven by vanity to seek levels for which they do not have the necessary talent. Actually, they tend to be conservative, even somewhat plain by nature. All aspects of their lives can be affected by the struggle between what they actually are and what they long to be.

They are often convincing speakers. They can be bright and creative, but moody. Their decision making is often colored by the mood of the moment. Although they can make decisions quickly and decisively, they tend to worry and become insecure when activity stops or slows down.

Because their success often comes after they connect with a stronger person or power, they must not betray those who help them if they want their success to continue. In their desire to control, they tend to turn their backs on those who helped them attain their position.

Most of this type are affectionate and good socially. The women are more likely to serve others. They expect much in return for doing so. Men tend to be shy outside but strong willed inside.

These types of people are usually very positive about a job or business, yet seem to develop a peculiar hesitation about going ahead full force. They need help to proceed.

These people must guard their health, because they are easily depressed by anything that interferes with their movement. Their impulsive pursuit of what they want requires all the strength they can muster to keep going.

THOMAS JEFFERSON—April 13, 1743
LIONEL BARRYMORE—April 28, 1878
JULES STEIN—April 26, 1896
WILLIAM FULBRIGHT—April 9, 1905
LIONEL HAMPTON—April 29, 1914
ELAINE MAY—April 21, 1932
HALSTON—April 23, 1932
MICHAEL MORIARTY—April 5, 1941
JULIE CHRISTIE—April 14, 1941
PETE ROSE—April 14, 1941
ANN-MARGARET—April 28, 1941
DAVID CASSIDY—April 12, 1950
PETER FRAMPTON—April 22, 1950

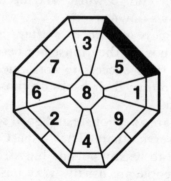

DATES THE MONTHS CHANGE

MAY 5–JUNE 4, 1896	MAY 6–JUNE 5, 1950
MAY 6–JUNE 5, 1905	MAY 6–JUNE 5, 1959
MAY 6–JUNE 5, 1914	MAY 5–JUNE 5, 1968
MAY 6–JUNE 6, 1923	MAY 5–JUNE 5, 1977
MAY 6–JUNE 5, 1932	MAY 6–JUNE 5, 1986
MAY 6–JUNE 5, 1941	MAY 6–JUNE 5, 1995

SERIOUS　　　　　　　*SELF-INDULGENT*
STEADY　　　　　　　*DEPENDENT*
CONTROLLING　　　　　*TENACIOUS*
MENTALLY ACTIVE　　　*STUBBORN*
PERSISTENT

These people tend to be serious and steady. Once they decide that they want to pursue something, be it a hobby or a personal or business goal, they go after it enthusiastically, persistently, and even recklessly at times.

Their minds are always active, occupied with a variety of subjects. Engaging in these mental gymnastics can be frustrating for them, and although they keep this frustration inside, it often shows itself in the form of a gambling habit or some other personal outlet. Fortunately, they often have luck when they do gamble.

They appear more self-contained and stronger than they really are. They actually have a dependent nature but, because they don't want people to know this, will avoid advice from others. This causes problems when they are faced with serious situations which require consultation. Decisions become difficult and require some time.

They sometimes tend to make a show of power, acting stronger than they really are. They are proud to a fault about their position and status. If they do not keep their pride in check, they can lose balance in dealing with problems. It is not easy for them to be good leaders since they sometimes tend not to want to give up anything. This makes negotiation difficult.

When social circumstances are under their control, they are quite charitable.

They have a stubbornness that can work positively for them, making them appear quite charming in a childish sort of way. This stubbornness works negatively when it appears as self-indulgence. They care a great deal about the impression they make on others.

Although the women of this type are usually trying to control their husbands or lovers, the men are busy looking after their own interests. Married life is not easy for this type.

Both the men and the women are hard workers who are strongly attached to money. Generally, even if they fail, these people have the energy necessary to rebuild themselves.

ISADORA DUNCAN—May 27, 1878
JOSEPH COTTEN—May 15, 1905
HENRY FONDA—May 16, 1905
JOE LOUIS—May 13, 1914
ANNE BAXTER—May 7, 1923
RICHARD AVEDON—May 15, 1923
VALENTINO—May 11, 1932
HENRY KISSINGER—May 27, 1932
BOB DYLAN—May 24, 1941
STACY KEACH—June 2, 1941
CHARLIE WATTS—June 2, 1941
STEVIE WONDER—May 13, 1950
BERNIE TAUPIN—May 22, 1950

JUNE 5-7-3

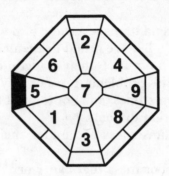

DATES THE MONTHS CHANGE

JUNE 5–JULY 6, 1896	JUNE 6–JULY 7, 1950
JUNE 6–JULY 7, 1905	JUNE 6–JULY 7, 1959
JUNE 6–JULY 7, 1914	JUNE 6–JULY 6, 1968
JUNE 7–JULY 7, 1923	JUNE 6–JULY 6, 1977
JUNE 6–JULY 6, 1932	JUNE 6–JULY 6, 1986
JUNE 6–JULY 6, 1941	JUNE 6–JULY 6, 1995

CONTROLLING   *RASH*
STRAIGHTFORWARD   *HASTY*
HYPERSENSITIVE   *STUBBORN*
DETAIL-MINDED   *IMPATIENT*
SELF-CONSCIOUS

Although these people want to control things, they are also self-conscious and sensitive to others' opinions. Their reluctance to give up whatever position they take leads to difficulty in relationships.

They approach the things they want to do with boundless energy that can lead to great success, but often their impatience results in a job that is unfinished.

They are very sensitive to details and have the ability to organize, but because they are rash and hasty, they sometimes do not successfully complete the projects they have taken on.

If they are in control of a situation, they are very reliable and understanding of others. However, if someone is dissatisfied with their work or is in control of circumstances, they tend to react forcefully and awkwardly in an attempt to assert their opinions. They stubbornly insist they are right.

They are often successful if they can have their own way about developing their careers.

Their weakness is their hypersensitive reaction to others' opinions. They need to control their rash behavior or their lives will be a series of ups and downs. If they can keep their hypersensitivity in check, the future may hold great possibilities for them.

FRANK LLOYD WRIGHT—June 8, 1869
GEORGE M. COHAN—July 4, 1878
GEORGE ABBOTT—June 23, 1887
LILLIAN HELLMAN—June 20, 1905
LES PAUL—June 9, 1923
MARIO M. CUOMO—June 15, 1932

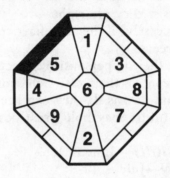

DATES THE MONTHS CHANGE

JULY 7–AUGUST 6, 1896	JULY 8–AUGUST 7, 1950
JULY 8–AUGUST 7, 1905	JULY 8–AUGUST 7, 1959
JULY 8–AUGUST 7, 1914	JULY 7–AUGUST 6, 1968
JULY 8–AUGUST 8, 1923	JULY 7–AUGUST 7, 1977
JULY 7–AUGUST 7, 1932	JULY 7–AUGUST 7, 1986
JULY 7–AUGUST 7, 1941	JULY 7–AUGUST 7, 1995

CONTROLLING	*EVASIVE*
STRONG-WILLED	*STUBBORN*
SELF-ASSERTIVE	*EMOTIONAL*
INTENSE	*INFLEXIBLE*

These people have a strong will to develop life their own way. Once interested in something, they focus their minds, concentrate fully, and give great energy to carrying through their plans. These qualities often earn them good reputations and professional success.

When forced to deal with small-scale troubles, they become evasive, and when situations do not go their way, their inflexibility will cause them grief.

They are smooth-mannered and tender in social situations. They usually associate with a wide circle of acquaintances but clearly discriminate between "friend" and "foe." They look at people very objectively and tend not to relate deeply to another's concerns unless they are really interested in a friendship. They do not often confide in others and can be detached and critical.

Many of this type are distant from their fathers. They find their greatest opportunities outside the family, using their own powers of self-assertion.

They can be very stubborn and emotional. If they don't like a situation, they tend to change it or move away from it immediately. They must learn to check this tendency if they are to finish projects.

In marriage they have high ideals and are hard to satisfy. They find it hard to compare themselves realistically to others or to see themselves as others do.

Many of these people are successful in fields that give them a strong sense of personal involvement. Their intuition is powerful, and they can develop a deep understanding of matters that interest them.

Although they appear very strong, they are emotionally vulnerable inside and need to be realistic about their view of themselves.

MARC CHAGALL—July 7, 1887
DUCHESS OF WINDSOR—July 19, 1896
MYRNA LOY—August 2, 1905
BILLY ECKSTINE—July 8, 1914
ESTHER WILLIAMS—August 8, 1932
OSCAR DE LA RENTA—July 22, 1932
RICCARDO MUTI—July 28, 1941
PAUL ANKA—July 30, 1941

AUGUST 5-5-5

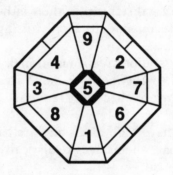

DATES THE MONTHS CHANGE

AUGUST 7–SEPTEMBER 6, 1896
AUGUST 8–SEPTEMBER 7, 1905
AUGUST 8–SEPTEMBER 7, 1914
AUGUST 9–SEPTEMBER 8, 1923
AUGUST 8–SEPTEMBER 7, 1932
AUGUST 8–SEPTEMBER 7, 1941

AUGUST 8–SEPTEMBER 7, 1950
AUGUST 8–SEPTEMBER 7, 1959
AUGUST 7–SEPTEMBER 7, 1968
AUGUST 8–SEPTEMBER 7, 1977
AUGUST 8–SEPTEMBER 7, 1986
AUGUST 8–SEPTEMBER 7, 1995

CONTROLLING
FORESIGHTFUL
DETERMINED
TALENTED

CHANGEABLE
STUBBORN
SELF-MOTIVATED
HUMANE

These people always want to be in control of situations. It is very hard for them to consider the opinions of others. They have intense energy and often talent in their fields of interest. They have remarkable self-motivation and drive. Often this leads to considerable achievement but sometimes great difficulty because it is hard for them to consider others in situations involving their self-interest.

They have strong motivation and foresight, so if they learn to control their intense energies, they can achieve high goals.

People who come under their control are often well taken care of. The women have a magnanimous attitude toward others. Men seem to express this to a lesser degree. If anyone turns against either, however, they will resist giving in to the utmost.

They are frank and straightforward, but somewhere inside is a timidity that interferes with their outward strength and causes emotional ups and downs. There is an inability to keep their attitude as consistent and positive as it appears, so their lives tend to go through many changes.

They can be stubborn yet humane if someone needs their help. In love, they get involved easily but find sustaining a relationship hard unless everything goes their way.

This type needs to accept the timidity that comes from the sensitive side of their nature. It can attract people to them and make relationships go more smoothly.

BENJAMIN HARRISON—August 20, 1833
SAM LEVENE—August 28, 1905
RHONDA FLEMING—August 10, 1923
RICHARD ADLER—August 23, 1923
RICHARD ATTENBOROUGH—August 29, 1923
DAVID CROSBY—August 14, 1941

SEPTEMBER 5-4-6

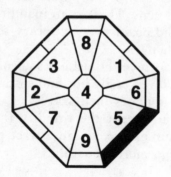

DATES THE MONTHS CHANGE

SEPTEMBER 7–OCTOBER 7, 1896	SEPTEMBER 8–OCTOBER 8, 1950
SEPTEMBER 8–OCTOBER 8, 1905	SEPTEMBER 8–OCTOBER 8, 1959
SEPTEMBER 8–OCTOBER 8, 1914	SEPTEMBER 8–OCTOBER 7, 1968
SEPTEMBER 9–OCTOBER 8, 1923	SEPTEMBER 8–OCTOBER 7, 1977
SEPTEMBER 8–OCTOBER 7, 1932	SEPTEMBER 8–OCTOBER 7, 1986
SEPTEMBER 8–OCTOBER 8, 1941	SEPTEMBER 8–OCTOBER 8, 1995

CONTROLLING   *IMPULSIVE*
DIGNIFIED   *STUBBORN*
STRONG-WILLED   *EMOTIONAL*
MAGNANIMOUS   *EVASIVE*

Like all Number 5s, these people have great ability to control. Many of this type go into speculative ventures or large-scale operations to which they devote much energy. If they lose interest, however, they lose the necessary energy to complete the task.

Most are bright and full of ideas, but they tend always to seek out something new. This makes it difficult for others to know what's going on in their minds. These people need to explain what they are thinking, feeling, or trying to accomplish.

They are stubborn yet dignified. Also, because they are not very adaptable, it is difficult for them to adjust when confronted with things that are different from what they expect.

They are emotional and magnanimous when dealing with other people's feelings. They need to control their strong wills if they are to develop their lives smoothly.

200

Most seem to have great affection from the parent of the opposite sex. This can diminish their appreciation of affection from others and can result in their having difficulty gaining emotional satisfaction from friends and lovers.

Women of this type are sometimes meticulous and generally strong and steady inside. The men tend to be more tender and emotional while still maintaining a stubborn exterior.

Most seem to have luck in finances, especially when facing a crisis or change. At these times, they can expend the tremendous effort that brings success.

In love, women find it difficult to be domestic. It is hard for them to last in a first marriage or relationship. If it endures, it is often because they take great responsibility for their own life. Men are very considerate of their families, but this can be secondary to whatever else they may be trying to do with their lives at the moment.

They need to aim for a calm, steady development of their lives instead of one hundred percent satisfaction of their wants.

MOHANDAS GANDHI—October 2, 1869
BUSTER KEATON—October 4, 1896
JOSEPH E. LEVINE—September 9, 1905
GRETA GARBO—September 18, 1905
JOHN WERNER KLUGE—September 21, 1914
WALTER MATTHAU—October 1, 1923
PATSY CLINE—September 8, 1932
RAY CHARLES—September 23, 1932
OTIS REDDING—September 9, 1941
LINDA MCCARTNEY—September 24, 1941
CHUBBY CHECKER—October 3, 1941

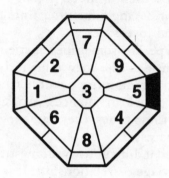

DATES THE MONTHS CHANGE

OCTOBER 8–NOVEMBER 6, 1896	OCTOBER 9–NOVEMBER 7, 1950
OCTOBER 9–NOVEMBER 7, 1905	OCTOBER 9–NOVEMBER 7, 1959
OCTOBER 9–NOVEMBER 7, 1914	OCTOBER 8–NOVEMBER 6, 1968
OCTOBER 9–NOVEMBER 7, 1923	OCTOBER 8–NOVEMBER 6, 1977
OCTOBER 8–NOVEMBER 6, 1932	OCTOBER 8–NOVEMBER 7, 1986
OCTOBER 9–NOVEMBER 7, 1941	OCTOBER 9–NOVEMBER 7, 1995

CONTROLLING *SELF-ASSERTIVE*
STRAIGHTFORWARD *STUBBORN*
EASYGOING *SENSITIVE*
SOCIAL *CALCULATING*

This type is strongly self-assertive but has great sensitivity that interferes with this quality. They express themselves in a straightforward and easygoing manner, but often become too aggressive when they really want something, causing people to doubt their sincerity. This may lead them to abandon their goals.

They usually have excellent minds for business and quite frequently find opportunities through social relationships. A friend may come up with a good idea that this type will develop and expand into a great success.

Because of the great energy they expend achieving their various goals, they are often considered greedy. In fact, the object of their energies is less important to them than the process of achievement. Because they seem to be constantly moving on to new things, they require projects that can hold their interest if they are to settle down for any length of time.

These people are often strongly influenced by their mothers, and they tend to seek out relationships that provide them with maternalistic comfort.

The men, though not generally domestic types, often seek relationships with older women. Once they have set up their family life, their interests shift outside the home. Women of this type are usually very active. They give everything their best effort, though giving up quickly if they feel something is not right for them. In love they are easily hurt by deep involvements that don't last and will become hesitant about liaisons, remaining aloof for a long period of time. In general, they look for tender, caring mates.

This type discriminates clearly between likes and dislikes. They also draw a strict line between their private and public lives, demanding respect for their privacy.

In business they tend to favor someone less competent whom they like over a more able person they do not care for. This sometimes causes difficulties with other colleagues. They give great attention to people they like but brusquely cut off those who have not earned their affection.

They love social life and spend lavishly if they have the money. When short on cash, they will unmercifully tighten the purse strings, appearing stingy to those around them.

CHIANG KAI-SHEK—October 31, 1887
LILLIAN GISH—October 14, 1896
RUTH GORDON—October 30, 1896
DYLAN THOMAS—October 27, 1914
HERSCHEL BERNARDI—October 20, 1923
JESSE JACKSON—October 8, 1941
HELEN REDDY—October 25, 1941
ART GARFUNKEL—November 5, 1941

NOVEMBER **5**-2-8

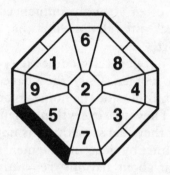

DATES THE MONTHS CHANGE

NOVEMBER 7–DECEMBER 5, 1896	NOVEMBER 8–DECEMBER 7, 1950
NOVEMBER 8–DECEMBER 7, 1905	NOVEMBER 8–DECEMBER 7, 1959
NOVEMBER 8–DECEMBER 7, 1914	NOVEMBER 7–DECEMBER 6, 1968
NOVEMBER 8–DECEMBER 7, 1923	NOVEMBER 7–DECEMBER 6, 1977
NOVEMBER 7–DECEMBER 6, 1932	NOVEMBER 8–DECEMBER 6, 1986
NOVEMBER 8–DECEMBER 6, 1941	NOVEMBER 8–DECEMBER 6, 1995

DETERMINED   *EMOTIONALLY DEPENDENT*
PROUD   *STUBBORN*
SOCIAL   *LESS ADAPTABLE*
SELF-MOTIVATED   *VAIN*

These people are often self-motivated and determined, but they sometimes encounter difficulty in their drive to be independent. They can stubbornly want to carry all their desires through to conclusion and need the attention of others to accomplish this. They need support and affection if they are to handle situations calmly and objectively.

They tend to be vain about their appearance. Outwardly sophisticated and tender, they are inwardly proud and concerned with success.

Smooth and concerned for others in social situations, they are really seldom satisfied unless in control of the people and the events around them.

They do not adapt easily to new situations, insisting they have their own way. Sometimes inconsiderate, they are very sensitive to weaker people and often try to offer assistance.

Men of this type expend great energy on their life outside the home, leaving little psychic reserve for the domestic front. The women tend to be somewhat haughty and proud, and often have difficulty expressing affection for this reason.

These people are usually more interested in a sterling reputation than in money itself.

In general, these people have a knack for solving difficult problems but must have a reason for doing it. They must be willing to use their energy and not be lazy.

ANDRE GIDE—November 22, 1869
BORIS KARLOFF—November 23, 1887
IRA GERSHWIN—December 6, 1896
TOMMY DORSEY—November 19, 1905
JOE DIMAGGIO—November 25, 1914
PETULA CLARK—November 15, 1932
ROBERT GUILLAUME—November 30, 1932
LITTLE RICHARD (PENNIMAN)—December 5, 1932
BONNIE RAITT—November 8, 1950

DECEMBER **5**-1-9

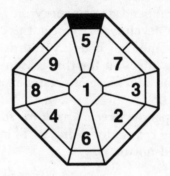

DATES THE MONTHS CHANGE

DEC. 6, 1896–JANUARY 4, 1897

DEC. 8, 1905–JANUARY 5, 1906

DEC. 8, 1914–JANUARY 5, 1915

DEC. 8, 1923–JANUARY 6, 1924

DEC. 7, 1932–JANUARY 5, 1933

DEC. 7, 1941–JANUARY 5, 1942

DEC. 8, 1950–JANUARY 5, 1951

DEC. 8, 1959–JANUARY 5, 1960

DEC. 7, 1968–JANUARY 4, 1969

DEC. 7, 1977–JANUARY 5, 1978

DEC. 7, 1986–JANUARY 5, 1987

DEC. 7, 1995–JANUARY 5, 1996

PROUD

BRIGHT

CONTROLLING

INDEPENDENT

STUBBORN

IMPRACTICAL

CAREFUL

IDEALISTIC

These people tend to be very proud. They often have high ideals regarding their own interests and wants. They tend to be bright and can focus intensely on things that intrigue them.

Their pride and narrow focus can make it difficult for them to be followers. It is usually better for all concerned for this type to assume a leadership position. If they are in control of other people, however, they need to explain clearly what they are thinking so others can follow them intelligently.

When they face situations in which they have an interest, they speak openly and clearly about them. If they lose interest, they tend to withdraw and say nothing, even in social situations.

They are independent and do not open their minds to others easily. This can distance them from friends and colleagues.

206

They are active socially, but when social relationships become serious, they often lose their ability to express themselves clearly.

When this type really wants something, they seem almost automatically able to draw the right kind of help into their lives and are able to move forward on a project quickly.

This type of Number 5 is less practical than the March type and so is not always strong enough to carry through idealistic dreams. They can compensate by using extra energy to break through and achieve their goals.

HENRI MATISSE—December 31, 1869
CONRAD HILTON—December 25, 1887
HOWARD R. HUGHES—December 24, 1905
DOROTHY LAMOUR—December 10, 1914
RICHARD WIDMARK—December 26, 1914
ELLEN BURSTYN—December 7, 1932
CICELY TYSON—December 19, 1932
DIONNE WARWICK—December 12, 1941

JANUARY 5-9-1

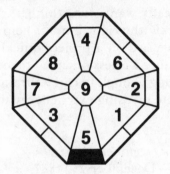

DATES THE MONTHS CHANGE

CONTROLLING   *MOODY*
PERSISTENT   *STUBBORN*
EXPRESSIVE   *PROUD*
AFFECTIONATE   *INSECURE*

This type usually tries to make their way independently in their career and life. They want to control everything and seldom give up even if it takes a long time to reach their goal.

They are often persuasive and able to speak convincingly in public. They appear bright and cheerful, but their basic nature is not to open themselves up. They are proud and fearful of being hurt. It is not easy for them to trust other people.

They are self-assertive but find it difficult to act unless they are calm and free of worry.

In a partnership, they do not usually allow the other person equal footing.

Many people of this type are sexually attractive, and often they become involved in more than one relationship. They are very affectionate but not openly so, and this contributes to their sex appeal. They can be very jealous.

Most people of this type do not rely on their family for assistance. They achieve their success independently.

They are conservative about money. They spend reasonably and wisely. When they must spend, they like to do so with great personal style.

Women of this type are patient but stubborn. When dissatisfied or frustrated by a situation, they become overbearing and obsessive about their problems. The men are especially stubborn. Once they have made up their minds, they will remain persistent to the end.

In general, these people possess a great energy that carries them through their lives. Their stubbornness may interfere with their adaptability; however, their strong will and patience will help them to ultimately reach their goals.

WILLIAM MCKINLEY—January 29, 1843
ARISTOTLE ONASSIS—January 20, 1906
ERNEST BORGNINE—January 24, 1915
DEAN JONES—January 25, 1933
MUHAMMAD ALI—January 18, 1942
MAC DAVIS—January 21, 1942
GRAHAM NASH—February 2, 1942
CRYSTAL GAYLE—January 9, 1951
PHIL COLLINS—January 31, 1951

FEBRUARY 6-5-6

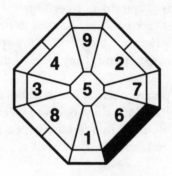

DATES THE MONTHS CHANGE

FEBRUARY 4–MARCH 5, 1895	FEBRUARY 4–MARCH 5, 1949
FEBRUARY 5–MARCH 5, 1904	FEBRUARY 4–MARCH 5, 1958
FEBRUARY 4–MARCH 5, 1913	FEBRUARY 4–MARCH 5, 1967
FEBRUARY 5–MARCH 5, 1922	FEBRUARY 5–MARCH 4, 1976
FEBRUARY 5–MARCH 5, 1931	FEBRUARY 4–MARCH 4, 1985
FEBRUARY 5–MARCH 5, 1940	FEBRUARY 4–MARCH 5, 1994

STRONG-WILLED　　　　*CONTROLLING*
FORESIGHTFUL　　　　　*STUBBORN*
STYLISH　　　　　　　　*INFLEXIBLE*
INDEPENDENT　　　　　*PROUD*

These people are usually strong and independent in spirit. They appear ambitious and self-confident and have a comforting air of reliability. They are often, however, obstinate and unadaptable.

They can usually carry through a project with a great sense of style but sometimes become too strong-willed to allow compromise.

They have leadership potential but only when made aware of their tendency to ignore the advice and needs of others. They really enjoy leadership and power. When they are not in power, however, their pride may suffer and they often have difficulty accepting a situation.

Women of this type often take on positions of heavy responsibility because of their pride and strong will. Although they are able to carry on their lives in an independent manner, domestic situations prove difficult for them unless they are aware of their obstinate nature. Men of this type tend to become overconfident before they really have sufficient energy to reach their goals.

Most of these people know how to earn and manage money. They do not always spend it wisely, however.

In general, this type tends to seek "completeness," which proves difficult unless they strive to be more adaptable. Even so, they usually have foresight and good judgment.

AUGUSTE RENOIR—February 25, 1841
BABE RUTH—February 6, 1895
JIMMY DORSEY—February 29, 1904
JAMES DEAN—February 8, 1931
CLAIRE BLOOM—February 15, 1931
TOM WOLFE—March 2, 1931
SMOKEY ROBINSON—February 19, 1940
ANDY GIBB—March 5, 1958

MARCH **6**-4-7

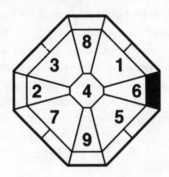

DATES THE MONTHS CHANGE

MARCH 6–APRIL 4, 1895	MARCH 6–APRIL 4, 1949
MARCH 6–APRIL 4, 1904	MARCH 6–APRIL 4, 1958
MARCH 6–APRIL 4, 1913	MARCH 6–APRIL 4, 1967
MARCH 6–APRIL 4, 1922	MARCH 5–APRIL 4, 1976
MARCH 6–APRIL 5, 1931	MARCH 5–APRIL 4, 1985
MARCH 6–APRIL 4, 1940	MARCH 6–APRIL 4, 1994

STRONG-WILLED *EASYGOING*
TENDER *EMOTIONAL*
CONFIDENT *EVASIVE*
SOCIAL *STUBBORN*

The nature of this type is rather complex, as there is a constant shifting between a strong, self-assured demeanor and one considerably more easygoing. No wonder it takes this type a long time to reach (and act on) important decisions! They usually control their lives the way they want but are often misjudged, because they cannot easily explain the complex workings of their minds to other people. They may appear evasive, shy, or afraid. This, of course, is not the case. Their determination and faith usually overcome their indecision. They may be influenced by the great affection given them by their parent of the opposite sex. This can make them expect too much when they fall in love.

They are emotional and tender, so are comfortable in social situations. It is their nature to look after others who come within their circle.

The men have pride in what they do and need to be appreciated for it. They need to construct a good foundation from which to build their self-confidence. The women have a very strong maternal instinct to take care of people in their circle, provided they can control the situation. They are happy to give in this manner but must be careful not to become possessive, demanding the exclusive love of another.

They seem able to get money but don't always know how to hold on to it. They tend to be big spenders when they do have it. The women are especially thoughtful of others when they have extra cash.

They are not always good planners because they are emotional. They find it hard to follow any path that seems contrary to their judgment or will.

They are usually able to find a mate, friend, or someone else who will assist them. They must realize the importance of this relationship, especially in times of crisis.

JAMES MADISON—March 16, 1751
EDGAR CAYCE—March 18, 1877
AL JOLSON—March 26, 1886
JACK KEROUAC—March 12, 1922
RICHARD KILEY—March 31, 1922
WILLIAM SHATNER—March 22, 1931
LORETTA LYNN—March 14, 1940

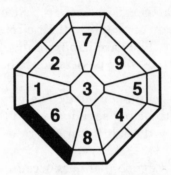

DATES THE MONTHS CHANGE

APRIL 5–MAY 5, 1895	APRIL 5–MAY 5, 1949
APRIL 5–MAY 5, 1904	APRIL 5–MAY 5, 1958
APRIL 5–MAY 5, 1913	APRIL 5–MAY 5, 1967
APRIL 5–MAY 5, 1922	APRIL 5–MAY 4, 1976
APRIL 6–MAY 5, 1931	APRIL 5–MAY 4, 1985
APRIL 5–MAY 5, 1940	APRIL 5–MAY 5, 1994

STRONG-WILLED   *CAUTIOUS*
SELF-MOTIVATED   *OPINIONATED*
INSIGHTFUL   *IMPATIENT*
STYLISH   *SENSITIVE*

This type is often kind to others but only when they can control the relationship. They appear decisive and magnanimous but are quite sensitive and afraid of losing their self-confidence. They have a strong influence from their mothers.

They are insightful and have high ideals, which leads them to expect others to accept their social and political views. Socially this causes them problems since they do not leave room for the ideas and needs of others.

Their caution can lead them to miss opportunities. Although they are quick to catch on, they get into difficulty because they may wait too long to act.

Most are ambitious and feel that their opinions are the only correct ones. They want to develop success in their own way and may lose patience. This can cause difficulties at times.

They tend to be stylish and are desirable allies in social situations. They also try to lend a hand to others if it is in their power.

Men of this type are more sensitive than the women. They often take care of relatives. Women of this type, if they have a strong family background, often lead independent or ambitious lives. Women with weaker family foundations may be unbending and driven, often using other people in the process. They seldom look back or appreciate their past. Most of the women have luck finding mates. Men of this type are luckier in finding business partners.

When these types can clearly communicate their ambitions and ideas to others, they can look forward to successful lives.

IMMANUEL KANT—April 22, 1724
HANS CHRISTIAN ANDERSEN—April 21, 1805
JOHN GIELGUD—April 14, 1904
BING CROSBY—May 2, 1904
LIONEL HAMPTON—April 20, 1913
TYRONE POWER—May 5, 1913
CHARLES MINGUS—April 22, 1922
JACK KLUGMAN—April 27, 1922
HERBIE HANCOCK—April 12, 1940
AL PACINO—April 25, 1940

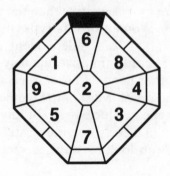

DATES THE MONTHS CHANGE

MAY 6–JUNE 5, 1895	MAY 6–JUNE 5, 1949
MAY 6–JUNE 5, 1904	MAY 6–JUNE 5, 1958
MAY 6–JUNE 5, 1913	MAY 6–JUNE 5, 1967
MAY 6–JUNE 6, 1922	MAY 5–JUNE 4, 1976
MAY 6–JUNE 6, 1931	MAY 5–JUNE 5, 1985
MAY 6–JUNE 5, 1940	MAY 6–JUNE 5, 1994

STRONG-WILLED   *PROUD*
ORGANIZED   *CAUTIOUS*
STEADY   *DELICATE*
CALM   *SELF-CONSCIOUS*

These people are proud and strong-willed. Often other people think they are conceited and difficult to approach. Actually they are quite self-conscious and need the attention of others.

They are steady workers and can organize well. They are usually considerate, a trait that enables them to gain positions of leadership. Sometimes they become overconfident, and that can become problematic. They are not always good followers and have difficulty accepting guidance or criticism. This attitude produces problems in partnerships or work situations.

They have the ability to look at matters objectively, which helps them to develop a good social life and possibilities for their future through social contacts. Sometimes this objectivity causes them to look down on certain people without quite realizing they are doing so. This trait can result in a dearth of long-time relationships.

In serious situations they tend to be too cautious and cause themselves worry.

Women of this type often have difficulty because people read their calm, proud natures and find coldness and haughtiness instead. The men tend to be self-conscious and even more cautious than the women.

Generally, these types are good leaders and hard workers, planning well for their futures.

PIERRE CURIE—May 15, 1859
RUDOLPH VALENTINO—May 6, 1895
SALVADOR DALI—May 11, 1904
STEWART GRANGER—May 6, 1913
JOSEPH PULITZER, JR.—May 13, 1913
RICK NELSON—May 8, 1940
BILLY JOEL—May 9, 1949

JUNE **6**–1–1

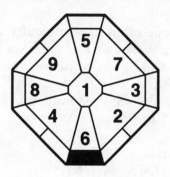

DATES THE MONTHS CHANGE

JUNE 6–JULY 6, 1895	JUNE 6–JULY 6, 1949
JUNE 6–JULY 7, 1904	JUNE 6–JULY 7, 1958
JUNE 6–JULY 7, 1913	JUNE 6–JULY 7, 1967
JUNE 6–JULY 7, 1922	JUNE 5–JULY 6, 1976
JUNE 7–JULY 7, 1931	JUNE 6–JULY 6, 1985
JUNE 6–JULY 6, 1940	JUNE 6–JULY 6, 1994

STRONG-WILLED　　　　*MAGNANIMOUS*
BRIGHT　　　　　　　　*TENACIOUS*
SELF-ASSERTIVE　　　　*INSECURE*
PERFECTIONIST　　　　　*INFLEXIBLE*

Most of this type are bright and strong-willed. They tend to be inwardly insecure; this insecurity, when combined with their tendency to be self-assertive, can result in poor communication with others. They are often brilliant but impractical. They tend to see things in their own narrow way, sometimes missing the more practical, broader view completely. They find it difficult to adapt to others' ideas when they clash with their own tenaciously held opinions.

They tend to be stylish and possess a good aesthetic sense. Their insecurity coupled with their organizational ability makes them long for perfection. They appreciate the better things in life; and have an eye for beauty, though it is usually limited to whatever field they have chosen to focus upon.

Because they are magnanimous, they give attention to people who are weaker than they. They want matters their own way, however, so people do not always appreciate their efforts.

They tend to build bridges to their goals. However, they tend to burn these bridges behind them, only to begin building new ones. They are fated to rebuild, since they are not comfortable with stable conditions.

Women of this type are more self-protective than the men. They often try to control because they cannot be good followers. The men are more magnanimous but still try to be in control. Both the men and the women find expressing love or affection very difficult, because they are afraid they may end up hurt.

Financially, if they plan in a steady, conservative manner, they can become successful.

In general, this type needs to avoid burning bridges behind them. They must learn to build up their lives conservatively and to become more comfortable in the presence of stability.

JACK DEMPSEY—June 24, 1895
JUDY GARLAND—June 10, 1922
BILL BLASS—June 22, 1922
PIERRE CARDIN—July 7, 1922
LESLIE CARON—July 1, 1931
TOM JONES—June 7, 1940
NANCY SINATRA—June 9, 1940
MERYL STREEP—June 22, 1949
LINDSAY WAGNER—June 22, 1949

JULY **6**-9-2

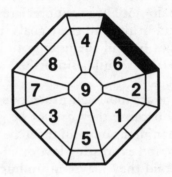

DATES THE MONTHS CHANGE

JULY 7–AUGUST 7, 1895	JULY 7–AUGUST 7, 1949
JULY 8–AUGUST 7, 1904	JULY 8–AUGUST 7, 1958
JULY 8–AUGUST 7, 1913	JULY 8–AUGUST 6, 1967
JULY 8–AUGUST 7, 1922	JULY 7–AUGUST 6, 1976
JULY 8–AUGUST 7, 1931	JULY 7–AUGUST 6, 1985
JULY 7–AUGUST 7, 1940	JULY 7–AUGUST 7, 1994

STRONG-WILLED *MILD-MANNERED*
DILIGENT *MOODY*
PRUDENT *SELF-CONCERNED*
THOUGHTFUL *VAIN*

This type has a strong will but tends to behave in a somewhat mild manner. They usually want things their way, however, and work diligently to achieve their goals. They are often prudent and can be persuasive speakers.

In social situations they are good mixers. They attract people who are then often disappointed when they find this type cannot always put their self-confident ideas into action. They sometimes are unable to sustain leadership because of their lack of concern for others.

They are diligent in their job or career, and superiors are often willing to help them. If they consider others and move practically, they can be good leaders.

The men can be quite conservative but expend a great deal of time and money to preserve a dignified appearance. They are often vain, and this tendency can interfere with their personal relationships. They need love and attention at home to help refuel their depleted psychic reserves. Women of this type are usually good talkers, faithful, and able to control a family calmly—provided things go their way. Both men and women have difficulty making clear decisions because their moods change so often. If people of this nature try hard to be more practical and realistic, they can avoid moodiness and steadily build a more stable future.

They tend to accumulate money in small increments. They have to be careful not to be wasteful because of their vanity.

In general the keys to success for this type are not to rush things and to use their prudence and diligence in achieving worthwhile lifetime goals.

GUY DE MAUPASSANT—August 5, 1850
GERALD R. FORD—July 14, 1913
RED SKELTON—July 18, 1913
BLAKE EDWARDS—July 26, 1922
RINGO STARR—July 7, 1940

AUGUST 6-8-3

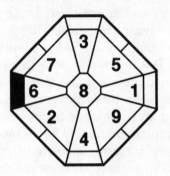

DATES THE MONTHS CHANGE

AUGUST 8–SEPTEMBER 7, 1895	AUGUST 8–SEPTEMBER 7, 1949
AUGUST 8–SEPTEMBER 7, 1904	AUGUST 8–SEPTEMBER 7, 1958
AUGUST 8–SEPTEMBER 7, 1913	AUGUST 7–SEPTEMBER 7, 1967
AUGUST 8–SEPTEMBER 7, 1922	AUGUST 7–SEPTEMBER 6, 1976
AUGUST 8–SEPTEMBER 8, 1931	AUGUST 7–SEPTEMBER 7, 1985
AUGUST 8–SEPTEMBER 7, 1940	AUGUST 8–SEPTEMBER 7, 1994

DIGNIFIED   *RASH*
MAGNANIMOUS   *SELF-MOTIVATED*
STYLISH   *WILLFUL*
PROUD   *AMBITIOUS*

These people sometimes appear larger than life because of their dignity, magnanimity, and stylishness. These qualities often attract opportunities for them in their careers and result in enormous social appeal.

They often discriminate between people they like or dislike. If they like someone, they are very considerate; if not, they prefer to avoid the person entirely.

They are proud and have high ideals. Once they set their sights on a goal, they expend great energy toward achieving it. Because they tend to be rash, they can sometimes lose their judgment or sense of balance. They need to realize the importance of taking time to let matters develop, instead of rushing ahead impatiently and ruining things.

They are ambitious and their minds are active. This leads them to expect positive development of their lives. Sometimes their minds are so active that their focus becomes very spread out, and they may have trouble juggling all the balls they've thrown into the air.

Most men of this type give great energy to their personal development, sometimes without enough caution. They rush forward without thought, resulting in tumultuous ups and downs. They often like strong women but do not like to be controlled. The women, when faced with the facts of a given situation, usually have a stronger reaction than the men. To be satisfied with events, they want to control them. Often this attitude alienates others, especially other women. Sometimes problems develop when women of this type insist on organizing the family after their own image.

In general this type seems to have luck in terms of money and recognition. Their magnanimous nature works well for them as long as they strive to include consideration for others in their plans.

NAPOLEON BONAPARTE—August 15, 1769
COUNT BASIE—August 21, 1904
JOHN MITCHELL—September 5, 1913
EYDIE GORME—August 16, 1931
VALERIE HARPER—August 22, 1940
RAQUEL WELCH—September 4, 1940
MICHAEL JACKSON—August 29, 1958

SEPTEMBER **6**–7–4

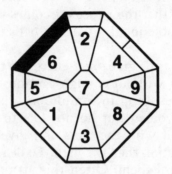

DATES THE MONTHS CHANGE

SEPTEMBER 8–OCTOBER 7, 1895

SEPTEMBER 8–OCTOBER 8, 1904

SEPTEMBER 8–OCTOBER 8, 1913

SEPTEMBER 8–OCTOBER 8, 1922

SEPTEMBER 9–OCTOBER 8, 1931

SEPTEMBER 8–OCTOBER 7, 1940

SEPTEMBER 8–OCTOBER 8, 1949

SEPTEMBER 8–OCTOBER 8, 1958

SEPTEMBER 8–OCTOBER 8, 1967

SEPTEMBER 7–OCTOBER 7, 1976

SEPTEMBER 8–OCTOBER 7, 1985

SEPTEMBER 8–OCTOBER 7, 1994

PROUD
STRONG-WILLED
EASYGOING
STYLISH

HYPERSENSITIVE
EMOTIONAL
SELF-CONSCIOUS
DETAIL-MINDED

These people are usually proud and hardworking. They often make good leaders. They are detail-oriented and have a strong desire to control circumstances in their own way.

They are easygoing when dealing with people in their own circle, but in situations where outsiders are involved, their willfulness can make them act pushy, even inconsiderate.

They are often very good socially as this allows them an outlet for their stylish, magnanimous nature. However, they can be hypersensitive and self-conscious, tending to overreact to the opinions and attitudes of others. If someone turns against them, they are easily hurt, and their affable manner changes to a more forceful, retaliatory one. Their hypersensitivity leaves them vulnerable, and they need to become aware of this point to learn how to control it.

They are usually reliable, and once they have a goal, they give much positive energy to its attainment. They are sometimes gifted intellectually and have a good grasp of politics.

Women of this type don't usually get deeply involved emotionally unless they find someone who will guarantee them success or security. A secure future is often more important to them than love. Once they have found the right person, they will devote themselves to helping him or her succeed. The men tend to be more stylish and give more energy to their life outside the home. Emotionally, however, they need much attention and affection.

This type of person is usually lucky with money and position, especially in a leadership position. However, they must develop the ability to consider other people and learn to control their hypersensitivity. If they do, their reputation will grow and greatly increase their capacity for leadership and their potential for personal achievement.

GROUCHO MARX—October 2, 1895
STANLEY KRAMER—September 29, 1913
ARTHUR PENN—September 27, 1922
ANNE BANCROFT—September 17, 1931
LARRY HAGMAN—September 21, 1931
BARBARA WALTERS—September 25, 1931
TWIGGY (LESLIE HORNBY)—September 19, 1949
BRUCE SPRINGSTEEN—September 23, 1949

OCTOBER 6–6–5

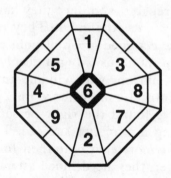

DATES THE MONTHS CHANGE

OCTOBER 8–NOVEMBER 7, 1895	OCTOBER 9–NOVEMBER 7, 1949
OCTOBER 9–NOVEMBER 7, 1904	OCTOBER 9–NOVEMBER 7, 1958
OCTOBER 9–NOVEMBER 7, 1913	OCTOBER 9–NOVEMBER 7, 1967
OCTOBER 9–NOVEMBER 7, 1922	OCTOBER 8–NOVEMBER 6, 1976
OCTOBER 9–NOVEMBER 7, 1931	OCTOBER 8–NOVEMBER 6, 1985
OCTOBER 8–NOVEMBER 6, 1940	OCTOBER 8–NOVEMBER 6, 1994

STYLISH   *SELF-ASSERTIVE*
DIGNIFIED APPEARANCE   *STUBBORN*
ORGANIZED   *CAUTIOUS*
PERSISTENT   *INFLEXIBLE*

These people tend to appear dignified and stylish. They are self-assertive and find it difficult to obey others. Inside they are more sensitive than they appear. They can organize well but, at the same time, find it difficult to explain their actions. They would rather get someone else to do their explaining.

In general their persistence leads them to investigate matters of interest thoroughly. They cannot change their focus until they have satisfied themselves in some way.

Socially both the men and the women tend to excel, but sometimes they get into trouble if they are too proud to obey or follow others' ideas. This can affect the women more seriously than the men. They have the nature to take care of others but are not good at letting others lead. Usually they are not domestic and function better in situations and jobs where they can use their intuitiveness to follow their ideas through to satisfaction. If worries come their way, they suffer because they concentrate too long and hard, wasting great energy.

Financially they seem to do better when they can use their sense of style in such a way as to impress people. If they can learn to accept others' ideas and control their stubborn streak, they can earn much money and respect. Once they are able to use their energies in well-organized projects and to overcome their tendency to be inflexible and overly persistent, they can usually find success.

BURT LANCASTER—November 2, 1913
VIVIEN LEIGH—November 5, 1913
BARBARA BEL GEDDES—October 31, 1922
CHARLES BRONSON—November 3, 1922
DAN RATHER—October 31, 1931
IKE TURNER—November 5, 1931
MIKE NICHOLS—November 6, 1931
JOHN LENNON—October 9, 1940

NOVEMBER 6-5-6

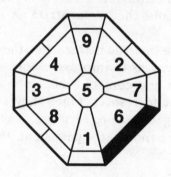

DATES THE MONTHS CHANGE

NOVEMBER 8–DECEMBER 6, 1895	NOVEMBER 8–DECEMBER 6, 1949
NOVEMBER 8–DECEMBER 6, 1904	NOVEMBER 8–DECEMBER 6, 1958
NOVEMBER 8–DECEMBER 7, 1913	NOVEMBER 8–DECEMBER 7, 1967
NOVEMBER 8–DECEMBER 7, 1922	NOVEMBER 7–DECEMBER 6, 1976
NOVEMBER 8–DECEMBER 7, 1931	NOVEMBER 7–DECEMBER 6, 1985
NOVEMBER 7–DECEMBER 6, 1940	NOVEMBER 7–DECEMBER 6, 1994

STRONG-WILLED	*STUBBORN*
PROUD	*HAUGHTY*
FAITHFUL	*EGOISTIC*
MAGNANIMOUS	*UNADAPTABLE*

These people tend to be interested in life on a large scale. They are not afraid to take chances and don't like wasting energy in matters of small concern.

They like to have things their way and are not good followers. Once they have made up their minds, they tend to block out the opinions and ideas of others. Usually they are late-maturing, having been unable to follow the guidance of others in youth.

They have the ability to organize but would be more successful if they weren't so insistent upon having their own way. Because they do not adapt easily and insist on orchestrating everything, they take longer to be successful or reach their goals. They expend great energy that can be adjusted to more efficient use when they recognize their stubbornness and listen to the opinions of others.

Although the men take more time to reach a leading position, when they do, they are often good at it. The women are often the leaders in the family. Because they tend to be overly proud and very strong-willed, they need to be careful not to overpower other family members. They like to take care of others, but when they insist on having their own way about it, the recipients often lack appreciation.

Financially these types are magnanimous. When they have money, they are not afraid to use it to help others, usually in their own way.

In general, although very often strong-willed, these people can be faithful and humane in social and family life. However, they need time to polish themselves so that they can develop the life-style best for them.

ROBERT LOUIS STEVENSON—November 13, 1850
SCOTT JOPLIN—November 24, 1868
BUSBY BERKELEY—November 29, 1895
ALGER HISS—November 11, 1904
ROBERT RYAN—November 11, 1913
ELEANOR POWELL—November 21, 1913
MARY MARTIN—December 1, 1913
NATALIA MAKAROVA—November 21, 1940
RICHARD PRYOR—December 1, 1940

DECEMBER 6–4–7

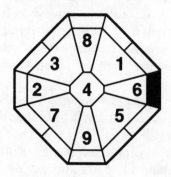

DATES THE MONTHS CHANGE

DEC. 7, 1895–JANUARY 5, 1896	DEC. 7, 1949–JANUARY 5, 1950
DEC. 7, 1904–JANUARY 5, 1905	DEC. 7, 1958–JANUARY 5, 1959
DEC. 8, 1913–JANUARY 5, 1914	DEC. 8, 1967–JANUARY 5, 1968
DEC. 8, 1922–JANUARY 5, 1923	DEC. 7, 1976–JANUARY 4, 1977
DEC. 8, 1931–JANUARY 5, 1932	DEC. 7, 1985–JANUARY 4, 1986
DEC. 7, 1940–JANUARY 5, 1941	DEC. 7, 1994–JANUARY 5, 1995

EASYGOING　　　　　*EVASIVE*
STYLISH　　　　　　*SENSITIVE*
EMOTIONAL　　　　　*WILLFUL*
CREATIVE　　　　　　*CAUTIOUS*

Because these people are often stylish and easygoing, they enjoy entertaining. Their attitudes are controlled by their emotions, making them appear evasive to others, who cannot understand what they are thinking. They are bright and have actively wandering minds.

Most of them are influenced by the strong affection of their parent of the opposite sex. This often leads them to expect too much when they fall in love.

Women of this type have strong maternal instincts. They want to take care of those people who come into their lives; however, they do not often go out of their way for people outside their circle. Men might be apt to go outside their circle.

Outwardly these people appear to have a soft touch, but actually they are quite willful and cautious. One cannot always be sure about their motives since their minds are controlled by their emotions. Generally they do not like to be controlled by others, instead preferring to take charge.

Financially they are magnanimous and seem able to make money, loving to spend it. But they must be careful not to be too easygoing in their spending, especially in social life.

Their easygoing attitude can be valuable when dealing with worrisome situations, but when a situation requires a strong carry-through, this type may fail to provide themselves with enough energy or may opt for an easier solution.

MARLENE DIETRICH—December 27, 1904
CARLO PONTI—December 11, 1913
JANE WYMAN—January 4, 1914
RITA MORENO—December 12, 1931
FRANK ZAPPA—December 21, 1940
ROBIN AND MAURICE GIBB—December 22, 1949
SISSY SPACEK—December 25, 1949

JANUARY 6-3-8

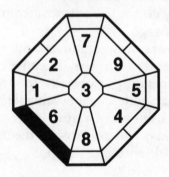

DATES THE MONTHS CHANGE

JANUARY 6–FEBRUARY 3, 1896	JANUARY 6–FEBRUARY 3, 1950
JANUARY 6–FEBRUARY 3, 1905	JANUARY 6–FEBRUARY 3, 1959
JANUARY 6–FEBRUARY 4, 1914	JANUARY 6–FEBRUARY 4, 1968
JANUARY 6–FEBRUARY 4, 1923	JANUARY 5–FEBRUARY 3, 1977
JANUARY 6–FEBRUARY 4, 1932	JANUARY 5–FEBRUARY 3, 1986
JANUARY 6–FEBRUARY 3, 1941	JANUARY 6–FEBRUARY 3, 1995

SELF-MOTIVATED   *SENSITIVE*
ORGANIZED   *CAUTIOUS*
PERFECTIONISTS   *SELF-PROTECTIVE*
MAGNANIMOUS   *THRIFTY*

The actions of these people are usually self-motivated. They like to organize matters their way. They often have been strongly influenced by their mothers.

They tend to be cautious and sensitive, so it is difficult for them to be decisive, even when they know what they should do.

They are good organizers, especially when things can be done their way. They tend to be perfectionists and to discriminate when it comes to food or hobbies or people. This can limit their circle of communication with people in general. They are magnanimous with people who follow their lead and tend to be inconsiderate of those who don't.

Because they are self-protective, they are afraid to be told they are wrong. They express their views as the right views. They are often very good at building up wealth.

Usually they are domestic-minded, especially the men. The women sometimes isolate themselves because they want to control their own lives completely. They really need others to help them develop in the best way.

In general, these types are ambitious, and this helps them to look ahead when the going gets rough. This ability to be positive through difficult times prepares them well for the future.

They take their perfectionism seriously, even more than the April type, and do not like having another person in a superior position. When this type begins to look at situations from viewpoints other than their own, they often find more successful solutions to their problems.

GEORGE BURNS—January 20, 1896
JEAN STAPLETON—January 19, 1923
CAROL CHANNING—January 31, 1923
NORMAN MAILER—January 31, 1923
RICHARD LESTER—January 19, 1932
YVETTE MIMIEUX—January 8, 1941
FAYE DUNAWAY—January 14, 1941
SUSANNAH YORK—January 9, 1941
PLACIDO DOMINGO—January 21, 1941
NEIL DIAMOND—January 24, 1941
LINDA BLAIR—January 22, 1959

FEBRUARY 7-8-4

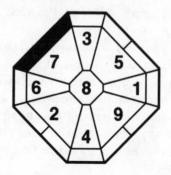

DATES THE MONTHS CHANGE

FEBRUARY 4–MARCH 4, 1894
FEBRUARY 5–MARCH 6, 1903
FEBRUARY 5–MARCH 5, 1912
FEBRUARY 4–MARCH 5, 1921
FEBRUARY 4–MARCH 5, 1930
FEBRUARY 5–MARCH 5, 1948

FEBRUARY 5–MARCH 5, 1948
FEBRUARY 4–MARCH 5, 1957
FEBRUARY 4–MARCH 5, 1966
FEBRUARY 4–MARCH 5, 1975
FEBRUARY 4–MARCH 4, 1984
FEBRUARY 4–MARCH 4, 1993

EASYGOING
FLEXIBLE
ENTERTAINING
SOCIABLE

HYPERSENSITIVE
SELF-CENTERED
NERVOUS
CALCULATING

These people have an entertaining nature and are sociable. This gives them many opportunities to meet people and explore future possibilities. They appear polished and are good talkers, attracting people easily, yet they are sensitive and always try to protect themselves. Most of them are calculating; this quality contributes to their flexibility since they are always considering and weighing choices. They must take care not to allow their flexibility to lapse into insincerity.

Most have an affable nature, yet their strong self-motivation makes them ambitious in structuring their lives. Because of this unusual combination of easygoing personality and strong drive toward achievement, they may at times be self-centered in an almost childish way.

Their flexibility also enables them to deal with most situations

234

that come up, but when they have to face a serious personal problem, they must watch their hypersensitivity as it springs into action. This makes them very nervous and they are often too easily influenced by the type of situation they may face. They become especially upset if their financial situation falls out of balance, although they are usually pretty lucky about money.

Most have sharp minds that are always actively seeking fulfillment. They have high ideals and expect much but are afraid of losing anything. This tendency explains why they often take so long to reach an important decision. They hate to give up one thing in order to gain something else; they would like to "have it all."

They give great energy to building up their own self-confidence. Although their attitude toward others may be very open and frank, they are often too busy with their own pursuits to consider deeply what other people think or want. However, they have an intrinsic sense of duty to take care of others, and if they learn to understand other people's needs, they will be able to develop their own lives more easily.

Men of this type are more easygoing than the women, often expecting to find a strong mate. However, they also enjoy their freedom and cannot be held too closely. Women of this type do not fall in love easily, but once they have found a man who can provide a secure future, their love follows. They are very protective of their families.

These people have very good luck with money and position and have great energy to build up a successful future. Their easygoing nature sometimes gets in the way of their strong ambition. Most important for them to learn is how to control their hypersensitivity so that it does not interfere with their ability to face and deal with situations.

GEORGE WASHINGTON—February 22, 1732
JACK BENNY—February 14, 1894
ROBERT WAGNER—February 10, 1930
JOHN FRANKENHEIMER—February 19, 1930
JOANNE WOODWARD—February 27, 1930
PETER FONDA—February 23, 1939
TOMMY TUNE—February 28, 1939
JENNIFER O'NEILL—February 20, 1948
BERNADETTE PETERS—February 28, 1948

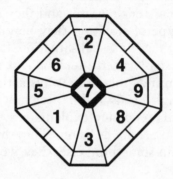

DATES THE MONTHS CHANGE

MARCH 5–APRIL 4, 1894	MARCH 6–APRIL 4, 1948
MARCH 7–APRIL 5, 1903	MARCH 6–APRIL 4, 1957
MARCH 6–APRIL 4, 1912	MARCH 6–APRIL 4, 1966
MARCH 6–APRIL 4, 1921	MARCH 6–APRIL 6, 1975
MARCH 6–APRIL 4, 1930	MARCH 5–APRIL 3, 1984
MARCH 6–APRIL 5, 1939	MARCH 5–APRIL 4, 1993

HARDWORKING	*STUBBORN*
ENTERTAINING	*DETAIL-MINDED*
FORCEFUL	*NERVOUS*
GOOD ORGANIZERS	*SELF-CONSCIOUS*

Most of these people are very hard workers, who invest a great deal of energy in carrying projects they like to completion. They have good organizational abilities, yet they can be too detail-minded, often giving enormous amounts of attention or importance to small things. On the positive side, their talent and efforts earn them good reputations; on the other hand, too much attention to detail can interfere with their natural abilities to organize and complete projects in ways they may never realize.

Although they display considerable self-confidence, inside they can be nervous and hypersensitive. They are often easily influenced by circumstance. If they are criticized, their self-confidence may collapse. Stubbornly they strive for consistency and never give up their drive toward completeness. They are afraid of criticism and the hurt it causes them. Damage of any kind to their reputation can be unbearable.

Their sensitivity and strong self-consciousness give them a good manner and appearance. Socially they tend to be charming, with a naturally entertaining spirit. If they know that people like them, they will open up. However, if someone is against them, they become hurt first, then respond very forcefully. Social life is not easy for them. They expend great amounts of energy, and they need quiet time to psychically refuel themselves and an understanding partner who will give them the room to do it. They are intensely private at these times, refusing to allow people deeper access to their feelings. But once their energies are renewed, they can devote much attention to other people.

They are very perceptive, almost possessing a "sixth sense." Artistic and often spiritually inclined, they catch on very quickly. Their hypersensitivity can cause them to change their mind easily, yet they make their decisions independently most of the time. However, decision making is often a worrisome process for them, as they always wonder afterward whether they made the right choice. Whatever may happen, this type should not hold feelings back. If they do not express themselves, it can affect their physical condition.

The men of this type have greater individuality than the women. The women have a very positive attitude and an ability to take care of their families.

These people need to be in a safe, positive, loving environment that enables them to grow and flourish while keeping outside influences at a minimum. They should seek to build such an atmosphere for themselves as a preliminary step to success if they are not born into it naturally. Although they must often struggle with an inferiority complex, they are usually lucky about finding an understanding helpmate, wife or husband, or favorable business associate who can help them progress and shield them from undesirable situations. In this way, these people can achieve greatness.

EMILE ZOLA—April 2, 1840
LAWRENCE WELK—March 11, 1903
SIMONE SIGNORET—March 25, 1921
DIRK BOGARDE—March 29, 1921
STEPHEN SONDHEIM—March 22, 1930
STEVE MCQUEEN—March 24, 1930

DAVID JANSSEN—March 27, 1930
NEIL SEDAKA—March 13, 1939
ALI MCGRAW—April 1, 1939
MARVIN GAYE—April 2, 1939
STEPHEN L. SCHWARTZ—March 6, 1948
JAMES TAYLOR—March 12, 1948
ANDREW LLOYD WEBBER—March 22, 1948

APRIL 7-6-6

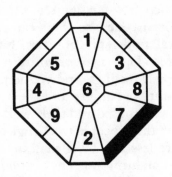

DATES THE MONTHS CHANGE

APRIL 5–MAY 4, 1894	APRIL 5–MAY 5, 1948
APRIL 6–MAY 6, 1903	APRIL 5–MAY 5, 1957
APRIL 5–MAY 5, 1912	APRIL 5–MAY 5, 1966
APRIL 5–MAY 5, 1921	APRIL 7–MAY 5, 1975
APRIL 5–MAY 5, 1930	APRIL 4–MAY 4, 1984
APRIL 6–MAY 5, 1939	APRIL 5–MAY 4, 1993

GOOD ORGANIZERS	*INFLEXIBLE*
STRONG-WILLED	*STUBBORN*
CONFIDENT	*HYPERSENSITIVE*
DIGNIFIED	*STORMY*

This type of Number 7 can be somewhat unbalanced. On the one hand, they are dignified and proud, with great faith in themselves. On the other hand, they are hypersensitive, moving along according to their feelings. So this type is up and down a great deal, depending upon their reactions to different situations. The most important thing for them is to learn to control their sensitivity.

This type is greatly influenced by their feelings because they possess strong intuition, unlike most Number 7s, who are more affected by outside forces. They tend to see life on a grand scale, setting lofty goals for themselves and expecting a high degree of perfection as they set out to achieve them. They usually possess the necessary energy to see their desires through. Once they have found something that pleases them, they become very enthusiastic about developing it. This kind of positive energy and enthusiasm helps them complete projects. However, their concentration and efforts at this point may become so intense that they are unable to consider anything or anyone else. This can cause problems.

They have natural leadership abilities, but their hypersensitivity often interferes. They may organize matters in their own style, according to their feelings, and yet be prone to lose control of both their organizational ability and their considerable energy once their sensitivity is aroused and their well-being is threatened.

It is never easy for these people to change their mind or adjust their plans. They are less adaptable than many because they like to follow their powerful intuition. They cannot hold their passionate feelings inside easily. If what they think happens to coincide with what others think, things develop smoothly. If not, they can create quite a distance between themselves and others by stubbornly refusing to compromise. It is often difficult for others to follow this type for these reasons.

In love, once they become emotionally involved, they are very affectionate. The men of this type use more energy for life outside the home and are not naturally domestic. The women are more independent and tend to organize life their own way, which can be both good and bad. Their attitudes are rather dignified, and so they are often misjudged by others as being haughty or proud. They enjoy leadership and have the power and energy to take on much responsibility at work and at home.

Balancing their sensitivity is the key to developing success for this type. If they can bring this under control, and learn to adapt themselves to situations, they have the potential for both leadership and high achievement.

IMMANUEL KANT—April 22, 1724
ULYSSES S. GRANT—April 27, 1822
CLEMENTINE CHURCHILL—April 8, 1885
HAROLD LLOYD—April 20, 1894
RUDOLF HESS—April 26, 1894
DR. BENJAMIN SPOCK—May 2, 1903
DAVID FROST—April 7, 1939
FRANCIS FORD COPPOLA—April 7, 1939
DUSTY SPRINGFIELD—April 16, 1939
JUDY COLLINS—May 1, 1939
GIORGIO DISANT'ANGELO—May 5, 1939

MAY 7-5-7

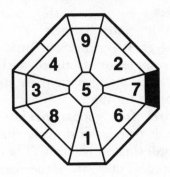

DATES THE MONTHS CHANGE

MAY 5–JUNE 5, 1894	MAY 6–JUNE 5, 1948
MAY 7–JUNE 6, 1903	MAY 6–JUNE 5, 1957
MAY 6–JUNE 5, 1912	MAY 6–JUNE 5, 1966
MAY 6–JUNE 5, 1921	MAY 6–JUNE 5, 1975
MAY 6–JUNE 5, 1930	MAY 5–JUNE 4, 1984
MAY 6–JUNE 5, 1939	MAY 5–JUNE 5, 1993

HYPERSENSITIVE   *CALCULATING*
EASYGOING   *STUBBORN*
SOCIABLE   *SELF-ASSERTIVE*
TALENTED   *PERSISTENT*

Most of these people are naturally blessed with the energy necessary to construct fulfilling lives. Rather than attempting to "fit in," to existing frameworks, this type usually seeks to find or create situations that fit them. They can accomplish much more working on their own than working as part of a group in which they cannot set their own pace.

They possess an interesting combination of personality traits. On the one hand, they are hypersensitive, very easily influenced, and self-protective. On the other hand, they are gregarious, entertaining, and very sociable. It is in learning to balance these complicated traits that they can gain the greatest understanding of themselves. If they can control their sensitivity, they have a good chance of attaining whatever they desire.

Although they can be easygoing, they are also strongly self-assertive and can be very calculating. They can use this trait positively, giving projects their all once they become involved. They dislike doing something only halfway. They prefer to proceed cautiously and with great seriousness, until they can see their project through to completion. Coupled with their sensitivity is great foresight, and this, along with their stubborn persistence, helps them carry things through.

In public, they are often good conversationalists. Their approach to other people or relationships is one of wide-eyed innocence, sometimes bordering on idealism. They can be easily taken advantage of or cheated if not aware of the dual edge of these traits.

Their naturally entertaining natures often lead them to love (and to expect!) a life of luxury. They are usually lucky about money, spending it freely on their own pleasures and enjoyments. They need someone who can restrain them financially and help them mind their spending, without taking the fun out of it. This type also has the ability to create good family relationships.

The men may allow their sensitivity to interfere with their powers of organization. They tend to prefer great freedom of movement and a relaxed, unstructured mode of living. The women have the energy and determination necessary to organize their lives and don't like being controlled by their husbands.

These people are usually very sociable, giving great importance to their social life. They love entertaining and good food. They often focus their talents on a variety of artistic pursuits. They expend much energy in this way, so they need time to relax and refuel themselves.

DOLLY MADISON—May 20, 1768
RICHARD WAGNER—May 22, 1813
MARTHA GRAHAM—May 11, 1894
DASHIELL HAMMETT—May 27, 1894
BOB HOPE—May 29, 1903
PHIL SILVERS—May 11, 1912
PERRY COMO—May 18, 1912
SAM SNEAD—May 27, 1912
DANIEL BERRIGAN—May 9, 1921
NELSON RIDDLE—June 1, 1921
CLINT EASTWOOD—May 31, 1930

JUNE 7-4-8

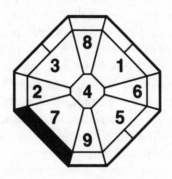

DATES THE MONTHS CHANGE

JUNE 6–JULY 6, 1894	JUNE 6–JULY 6, 1948
JUNE 7–JULY 7, 1903	JUNE 6–JULY 6, 1957
JUNE 6–JULY 6, 1912	JUNE 6–JULY 6, 1966
JUNE 6–JULY 7, 1921	JUNE 6–JULY 7, 1975
JUNE 6–JULY 7, 1930	JUNE 5–JULY 6, 1984
JUNE 6–JULY 7, 1939	JUNE 6–JULY 6, 1993

RESOURCEFUL   *TENACIOUS*
TENDER   *HYPERSENSITIVE*
SOCIAL   *EMOTIONAL*
CAUTIOUS   *WILLFUL*

These people appear lively, cheerful, and tender. This gives them an easy, natural expression in their social life, which they pursue actively. Inside, however, they are often willful and unbending. They dislike having to obey.

Most of them are very bright and resourceful, keeping their minds on what seems logical to them. In their day-to-day lives, they do not necessarily appear logical. This is because they are powerfully influenced by their feelings and sensitivity. They change their mind quite often. Even so, they try to stick to their own ideas and follow their own way whenever possible.

They are usually cautious and prudent, so they take time to clear their minds and make a decision. Once they have something firmly in hand, however, their tenacity of purpose is quite strong indeed. This makes them the type who will "never give up."

Their thinking can be very much controlled by their emotional, hypersensitive nature. This accounts for their occasional lack of consistency, which can become a problem. It may take them some time to reach a point in life where they are satisfied, because they change their minds at will, but they always have the potential to achieve and never lose hope. In fact, even if they plummet into the depths of despair, this type can break through their difficulties by using their strong will and great determination.

Most of these people had much attention from their parent of the opposite sex. This greatly influences their requirements for affection in their adult lives.

Although the men of this type have their own strong, definite ideas about developing their lives, the women seek to ally themselves with powerful men who possess a powerful appearance or presence.

These people tend to judge everything by their own standards, making it difficult for people around them to understand their ideas. However, they do have the nature to take care of people who come within their circle of influence. At first, they give much attention and consideration to others, but eventually they want to control the situation themselves.

With their unbending nature and high sensitivity, they are often alienated from powerful or influential people because they find it difficult to follow a stronger lead. This may leave them isolated, not knowing how to make good use of their lives. At these times, they rely on their charm, easy self-confidence, and resourcefulness to see them through.

LOU GEHRIG—June 19, 1903
DUKE OF EDINBURGH—June 10, 1921
JANE RUSSELL—June 21, 1921
JOSEPH PAPP—June 22, 1921
NANCY REAGAN—July 6, 1921
ROBERT EVANS—June 29, 1930
TODD RUNDGREN—June 22, 1948

JULY **7**-3-9

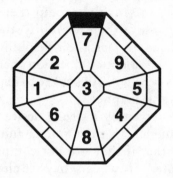

DATES THE MONTHS CHANGE

JULY 7–AUGUST 6, 1894	JULY 7–AUGUST 6, 1948
JULY 8–AUGUST 8, 1903	JULY 7–AUGUST 7, 1957
JULY 7–AUGUST 7, 1912	JULY 7–AUGUST 7, 1966
JULY 8–AUGUST 7, 1921	JULY 8–AUGUST 7, 1975
JULY 8–AUGUST 7, 1930	JULY 7–AUGUST 6, 1984
JULY 8–AUGUST 7, 1939	JULY 7–AUGUST 6, 1993

FLEXIBLE   *HYPERSENSITIVE*
PROUD   *SELF-RIGHTEOUS*
BRIGHT   *IMPATIENT*
RESOURCEFUL   *HASTY*

These people are quick-witted and flexible, adapting themselves easily to most circumstances. Their resourceful minds bring forth fresh, often brilliant, ideas that other people are willing to accept. Their foresight, good conversational abilities, and intelligent expression in social situations attract people who may be interested in following their ideas or taking part in their projects. They are especially good at seeking out interesting, profitable financial prospects.

They are proud and hypersensitive, and when faced with an important situation, they are compelled by a strong sense of justice to deal with it fairly, honestly, and straightforwardly. It is impossible for these people to hide their feelings. Once they feel some-

245

thing strongly, they will not compromise themselves or try to fool themselves into thinking or acting differently.

Their brightness and sensitivity help them to read other people's minds. Yet, in spite of their flexibility, they are self-righteous about likes and dislikes. In fact, their flexibility can at times be so excessive that other people may question their sincerity or think them fickle. But this type will always try to express what's on their minds in a clear, frank manner.

These people are driven by a strong desire for affection, which has a powerful influence on their minds and hearts. Sometimes, they need so much that if they are not completely satisfied, they become very frustrated. However, they are clever enough to reveal that frustration only to those people who can understand it or help them.

Their hypersensitivity can interfere with their naturally flexible, resourceful minds. They may make hasty decisions before they really organize their thinking on a subject. They feel compelled to do something as soon as the situation presents itself, and this impatience can be their undoing if they don't think things through.

Women of this type are very proud and quite frank. They want to be fully satisfied and need great affection or they become frustrated.

The men of this type have strong desires, but their energy is not always strong enough to match, usually because of their sensitivity. Their decisions may be weak, because they change their minds often and tend to lose their chance to act. They need to get their desires under control and to learn to consider others more.

The men are sometimes gamblers but, when faced with a serious choice, do not act decisively. Both the men and the women of this type are strongly influenced by their mothers, and this has considerable bearing on their needs. In the area of affection, their flexibility can interfere with their commitment to a relationship. However, it provides much energy for other areas of life.

In love, this type may give up easily. Their passions burn brightly and may cool down over time. Once this happens, these sensitive people have to face frustration until they find the attention and affection they need.

REMBRANDT—July 15, 1606
ALDOUS HUXLEY—July 26, 1894

WOODY GUTHRIE—July 14, 1912
JOHN GLENN—July 18, 1921
NEIL ARMSTRONG—August 5, 1930
ELEANOR SMEAL—July 30, 1939
PETER BOGDANOVICH—July 30, 1939
PEGGY FLEMING—July 27, 1948

AUGUST 7-2-1

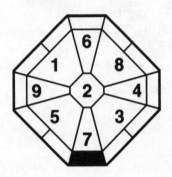

DATES THE MONTHS CHANGE

AUGUST 7–SEPTEMBER 7, 1894	AUGUST 7–SEPTEMBER 7, 1948
AUGUST 9–SEPTEMBER 8, 1903	AUGUST 8–SEPTEMBER 7, 1957
AUGUST 8–SEPTEMBER 7, 1912	AUGUST 8–SEPTEMBER 7, 1966
AUGUST 8–SEPTEMBER 7, 1921	AUGUST 8–SEPTEMBER 7, 1975
AUGUST 8–SEPTEMBER 7, 1930	AUGUST 7–SEPTEMBER 6, 1984
AUGUST 8–SEPTEMBER 7, 1939	AUGUST 7–SEPTEMBER 7, 1993

STEADY   *HYPERSENSITIVE*
CAREFUL   *SELF-PROTECTIVE*
RESOURCEFUL   *CALCULATING*
SOCIAL   *INSECURE*

Most of this type are resourceful and have the steadiness to develop their lives successfully. This gives them the ability to judge complicated situations calmly.

These people are always seeking attention; it is essential to their sense of well-being. Since they tend to be hypersensitive and self-protective, they can be easily influenced by others in such a way as to make them insecure. They are aware of their own emotional vulnerability and so try to hide or minimize their insecurities to the outside world. Although outwardly they may appear one way, inside they are often feeling something entirely different. They need and expect others to understand and sympathize with their inner feelings, whether they express them or not.

Generally they are good socially, because it affords them an opportunity to get to know what is in others' minds. When they receive enough attention from other people, they are good listeners and good conversationalists. Even so, they are extremely cautious and do not trust easily.

Once this type knows what they want to do, they make strong decisions. Because they are so careful, they often need more time to make up their minds, and other people mistakenly think them poor decision makers. At times, their insecurities can interfere with their ability to carry a project through to completion.

Although they are attracted to bright, showy appearances, their caution can inhibit their natural enthusiasm. Yet they always long for excitement and the fine things in life and keep a positive long-range outlook.

Many of these people have difficulty in love, because they do not trust easily and are very self-protective. They may be too careful and take so much time to commit themselves that their lovers will tire of waiting and give up.

In business, these people have great potential to develop future success because of their steady, resourceful nature. However, they must not put too much emphasis on money. If they do, their insecurities and lack of trust may interfere in ways they cannot even imagine. This type needs to work around supportive people who can give them the attention and affection they need to accomplish all they desire. If they feel comfortable with people, they give great energy to help them. Once they notice any imbalance of give and take in a situation, they may lose interest completely.

JULIA CHILD—August 15, 1912
GENE KELLY—August 23, 1912
ALEX HALEY—August 11, 1921
SEAN CONNERY—August 25, 1930
MITZI GAYNOR—September 4, 1930
WILLIAM FRIEDKIN—August 29, 1939
ELIZABETH ASHLEY—August 30, 1939
LILY TOMLIN—September 1, 1939
ROBERT PLANT—August 20, 1948

SEPTEMBER **7**-1-2

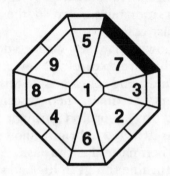

DATES THE MONTHS CHANGE

SEPTEMBER 8–OCTOBER 7, 1894	SEPTEMBER 8–OCTOBER 7, 1948
SEPTEMBER 9–OCTOBER 8, 1903	SEPTEMBER 8–OCTOBER 8, 1957
SEPTEMBER 8–OCTOBER 8, 1912	SEPTEMBER 8–OCTOBER 8, 1966
SEPTEMBER 8–OCTOBER 8, 1921	SEPTEMBER 8–OCTOBER 8, 1975
SEPTEMBER 8–OCTOBER 8, 1930	SEPTEMBER 7–OCTOBER 7, 1984
SEPTEMBER 8–OCTOBER 8, 1939	SEPTEMBER 8–OCTOBER 7, 1993

INTUITIVE
STEADY
EASYGOING
SOCIAL

OBSTINATE
CONSERVATIVE
PASSIONATE
HYPERSENSITIVE

These people tend to be intuitive. Once they get strong feelings, they follow them very independently. They seem to be lucky in making decisions regarding these situations.

They are usually good socially. Whether this type is talkative or not depends largely upon whether or not they are interested in the subject at hand. Their easygoing nature helps them to know many kinds of people, yet they do not really open up easily to people until they know them well. Their sensitivity makes them shy, and often it is difficult for them to express their affections until something important comes up. Once they must face serious emotions, however, they jump right in and become very passionate (especially the women). It may take them some time to be frank about their passion, as they are quite conservative.

They are hypersensitive and obstinate, but because of their easygoing, independent movement, people are not always aware of this.

Women of this type have definite ideas about what their "ideal" relationship is and tend to choose lovers of a particular type, often a very personal taste. This can lead to difficulty. The women must constantly be aware of the conflict between their independent mind and basically dependent nature and must strive to keep a healthy balance between the two. The men are more conservative than the women about developing their lives. Often they do not express themselves strongly enough because they are extremely self-protective.

Moneywise, this type seems to have good luck indirectly. For example, they may choose a good partner who helps develop their business, or a friend's recommendation may lead them to a good money-making opportunity. They can manage money well, yet are conservative in their investments. The same seems to be true of the decisions they make. Something or someone always appears at just the right moment to help them make the proper choice. Their intuition helps at these times, also.

Most important for this type is to know how to balance their considerable steadiness and sensitivity. When they face difficulty, their independent thinking and natural obstinacy can help them break through and overcome their sensitive natures. They must learn to keep an open mind, especially in dealing with others.

RUTHERFORD B. HAYES—October 4, 1822
D. H. LAWRENCE—September 11, 1885
MICHELANGELO ANTONIONI—September 29, 1912
RAY CHARLES—September 23, 1930
FRANKIE AVALON—September 18, 1939
OLIVIA NEWTON-JOHN—September 26, 1948

OCTOBER 7-9-3

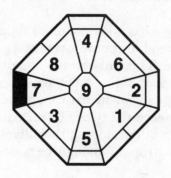

DATES THE MONTHS CHANGE

OCTOBER 8–NOVEMBER 6, 1894	OCTOBER 8–NOVEMBER 6, 1948
OCTOBER 9–NOVEMBER 8, 1903	OCTOBER 9–NOVEMBER 7, 1957
OCTOBER 9–NOVEMBER 7, 1912	OCTOBER 9–NOVEMBER 7, 1966
OCTOBER 9–NOVEMBER 7, 1921	OCTOBER 9–NOVEMBER 7, 1975
OCTOBER 9–NOVEMBER 7, 1930	OCTOBER 8–NOVEMBER 6, 1984
OCTOBER 9–NOVEMBER 7, 1939	OCTOBER 8–NOVEMBER 6, 1993

ENTERTAINING   *SELF-CONSCIOUS*
PROUD   *RASH*
PASSIONATE   *HASTY*
HYPERSENSITIVE   *TALKATIVE*

These people tend to have a two-sided character. Outwardly they are quite polished; they are active, reliable, and strong. However, on the inside, they are passive, sensitive, and often afraid of being alone. They are indeed "two-headed" to those who know them well. They are often persuasive speakers.

These people are outgoing and cheerful and are natural entertainers. They love to be the center of attention. Often easily likable and very talkative, they usually stand out in a crowd and are good in social situations. Their great personal charm and apparent self-confidence make other people assume them to be extremely reliable upon first meeting them. However, once people become better acquainted, they may find this type's inner feelings to be different from the ones they originally presented.

This type gives tremendous energy to their personal expression and their appearance in public. Inside they are self-conscious about their appearance and hypersensitive to criticism; this, combined with their pride, makes them easy prey to flattery.

They also tend to be moody and may move suddenly or aggressively if they face an important change or public challenge. When their mood is calm, their natural foresight, sense of pride, and flexibility combine to allow them to think quite logically, even in times of grave difficulty. However, this type does not always accept another's opinion easily, often trying to push their own ideas through, sometimes to the detriment of others concerned. At this point, they may find fault with others as a means of protecting their own interests. This aspect of their nature is usually not accompanied by the patience necessary to see things through, often resulting in the failure of a project.

Women of this type give much attention to their appearance and are often stunning. They need more attention than people think, because they tend to appear stronger than they really are. The men have a tendency to appear very reliable to people on first contact, but they are often more frivolous than expected. Because of this, they may have difficulty holding on to a lover, despite their charm.

In money matters, this type is quick to take advantage of profitable situations. In long-range planning, however, they may let rashness or impatience intrude and sometimes lose good opportunities. It is hard for them to control money over the long run. To ensure solvency they must follow a plan of conservative saving.

This type can be very passionate and expend great energy on things they really want. Success for them depends upon controlling their hypersensitivity, self-consciousness, and rashness. They must learn to sustain their energies over a longer period of time, always keeping their goals in sight.

JAMES K. POLK—November 2, 1795
THEODORE ROOSEVELT—October 27, 1858
POPE PAUL I—October 17, 1912
YVES MONTAND—October 13, 1921
HAROLD PINTER—October 10, 1930
RALPH LAUREN—October 14, 1939

NOVEMBER 7-8-4

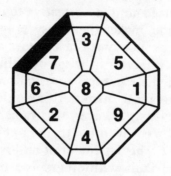

DATES THE MONTHS CHANGE

NOVEMBER 7–DECEMBER 6, 1894	NOVEMBER 7–DECEMBER 6, 1948
NOVEMBER 9–DECEMBER 7, 1903	NOVEMBER 8–DECEMBER 6, 1957
NOVEMBER 8–DECEMBER 6, 1912	NOVEMBER 8–DECEMBER 6, 1966
NOVEMBER 8–DECEMBER 7, 1921	NOVEMBER 8–DECEMBER 7, 1975
NOVEMBER 8–DECEMBER 7, 1930	NOVEMBER 7–DECEMBER 6, 1984
NOVEMBER 8–DECEMBER 7, 1939	NOVEMBER 7–DECEMBER 6, 1993

SMOOTH-MANNERED	*HYPERSENSITIVE*
BRIGHT	*SELF-CENTERED*
SOCIABLE	*NERVOUS*
AMBITIOUS	*OBSTINATE*

This type of Number 7 has many similarities with the February Number 7; however, they are less flexible. They have limited ability to control their hypersensitivity. They are not always able to move step by step. They want what they want, right away!

They are sociable and have a more polished approach than the February Number 7. This makes them appear reliable and helps them to attract other people.

They are loyal to their own feelings and ideas; although they may appear easygoing, their actions are more often self-centered. Their sensitivity makes them easily influenced by the opinions of others and by outside circumstance. This can make them lose their consistency.

Most are bright and ambitious and show a dauntless, smooth manner that helps them get along well socially.

The women of this type tend to have a more independent attitude than the men, and they have a greater ability to control others when calm. Men of this type appear more tender than the women and are attracted to strong women.

Moneywise, this type seems to have good luck in attracting it, but can't seem to hold onto it. They tend to squander cash in an attempt to buy a good reputation, even though they strongly desire to put it away for themselves.

When it comes to making decisions, this type finds it difficult to balance their desires and ambitions against what they are actually capable of, as they are often hurt by their hypersensitivity in the business arena.

They have a keen sense of art and have the potential to achieve recognition in artistic fields if they are patient and willing to build their reputation step by step.

FRANKLIN PIERCE—November 23, 1804
JAMES A. GARFIELD—November 19, 1831
CLAUDE MONET—November 14, 1840
MARIE CURIE—November 7, 1867
DAVID MERRICK—November 27, 1912
JOHN V. LINDSAY—November 24, 1921
PRINCE CHARLES—November 14, 1948
CAROLINE KENNEDY—November 27, 1957

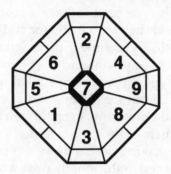

DATES THE MONTHS CHANGE

DEC. 7, 1894–JANUARY 4, 1895	DEC. 7, 1948–JANUARY 5, 1949
DEC. 8, 1903–JANUARY 6, 1904	DEC. 7, 1957–JANUARY 5, 1958
DEC. 7, 1912–JANUARY 5, 1913	DEC. 7, 1966–JANUARY 5, 1967
DEC. 8, 1921–JANUARY 5, 1922	DEC. 8, 1975–JANUARY 5, 1976
DEC. 8, 1930–JANUARY 5, 1931	DEC. 7, 1984–JANUARY 4, 1985
DEC. 8, 1939–JANUARY 5, 1940	DEC. 7, 1993–JANUARY 4, 1994

ORGANIZED　　　　　　　*SELF-CONSCIOUS*
HARDWORKING　　　　　*HYPERSENSITIVE*
CALM　　　　　　　　　*STUBBORN*
ACTIVE LEADERS　　　　*SELF-PROTECTIVE*

These people have naturally detail-oriented minds. Their organizational abilities are very strong, and yet once they focus on a project, they expend so much energy in its organization that their attention to detail and overall structure may be lost completely.

Strongly self-assertive, they build up their lives by combining hypersensitivity and a certain stubbornness. Hypersensitivity can make them agitated by circumstance or by the opinions of others. It also contributes to their frequently changing their minds and growing tired of things easily. They are very self-protective, and although their actions or attitudes may appear confident and firm much of the time, they may feel afraid or weak. When they are calm and reserved on the outside, they may in fact be suspicious inside, and stubborn as well. However, once they decide about something or someone, their expression is very straightforward.

This type tends to consider matters cautiously and tries to take a rational, thorough approach whenever possible. They have a strong desire to control, and they hate "halfway" measures. Although they have a certain natural leadership ability, it is difficult for them to temper their views, so people may consider them stubborn or inflexible. They do not like to be stuck in a situation where someone else is in complete control.

They are hardworking and fairly lucky about money. They love to spend, especially on their favorite social passions. In business, they have a good eye for focusing calmly and using wise judgment when necessary. They prefer high-class kinds of operations.

The men of this type have great energy to give to their job or business and are not naturally domestic people. The women have good luck in their work situations and in finding a relationship but may find marriage difficult at times.

This type has much in common with the March-born type of Number 7. This type, less able to use their detail-minded natures than the March Seven, tends to push outward into a social setting by using self-consciousness in a very straightforward way. Because of this, people think them very strong. They must always be on guard against their hypersensitivity, which makes them lose control if it becomes unbalanced.

ISAAC NEWTON—December 25, 1642
ARTHUR FIEDLER—December 17, 1894
STEVE ALLEN—December 26, 1921
ALVIN AILEY—January 5, 1931
PHIL SPECTOR—December 26, 1939
JACK NICKLAUS—January 2, 1940

JANUARY **7**-6-6

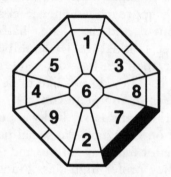

DATES THE MONTHS CHANGE

JANUARY 5–FEBRUARY 3, 1895	JANUARY 6–FEBRUARY 3, 1949
JANUARY 7–FEBRUARY 4, 1904	JANUARY 6–FEBRUARY 3, 1958
JANUARY 6–FEBRUARY 3, 1913	JANUARY 6–FEBRUARY 3, 1967
JANUARY 6–FEBRUARY 4, 1922	JANUARY 6–FEBRUARY 4, 1976
JANUARY 6–FEBRUARY 4, 1931	JANUARY 5–FEBRUARY 3, 1985
JANUARY 6–FEBRUARY 4, 1940	JANUARY 5–FEBRUARY 3, 1994

SOFTHEARTED *HYPERSENSITIVE*
CHARISMATIC *INFLEXIBLE*
INTUITIVE *STUBBORN*
JUDICIOUS *PROUD*

This type of person has natural leadership qualities that are readily apparent. They set their own pace and have their own singular philosophy. Yet they are softhearted and sensitive, attracting others who regard them as leaders.

Many of these people are very proud of these qualities and tend to feel superior. Even though they are sensitive and responsible in taking care of others, their pride and lack of adaptability interfere if they are not careful. They can become too focused on "their way." However, this lack of adaptability can be a good thing. Coupled with their stubbornness, it helps them carry things through according to their preferences. Usually, other people's opinions or ways fail to satisfy them.

They have strong intuition and the willpower to direct their own destiny, which makes it easy for them to move according to their feelings. When they face something serious, they often become very emotional and impulsive. Sometimes, if their hypersensitivity gets out of balance, they may lose their ability to objectively judge a situation. Life can be a series of extreme highs and lows. Usually, however, this type has the faith and stubbornness necessary to ride out the bad times.

In love, they are positive, active, and persistent. They may move more egoistically than they realize, once their feelings are involved. The women are self-reliant and do not expect to depend on someone else. They naturally seek out responsibility at work and at home. The men, also very self-reliant, are less adaptable than the women. Adjustments in domestic situations may be hard for them, and learning to balance home and business may prove to be tricky.

Their hypersensitivity and stubbornness, coupled with an intuitive mind, make them enthusiastic about focusing deeply on one interest. This may make for great success or difficulty, depending upon whether or not they can maintain calm judgment and continue to tap into their strong intuition.

They seem to have luck in money matters but move by feeling here also. The result is that they may have difficulty sustaining a stable financial condition over a long period of time.

Although there are many similarities between this type and the April Number Seven, April is more likely to move by feeling and, as such, is less flexible than this January type. January has more luck with money, devoting more attention to financial matters. This helps them control their emotions more successfully and be more flexible than the April type.

EDOUARD MANET—January 23, 1832
JOHN FORD—February 1, 1895
CARY GRANT—January 18, 1904
GEORGE BALANCHINE—January 22, 1904
RICHARD M. NIXON—January 9, 1913
JAMES EARL JONES—January 17, 1913
DANNY KAYE—January 18, 1913
CAROL CHANNING—January 30, 1922
SAM COOKE—January 22, 1931
GENE HACKMAN—January 30, 1931
❧ *JOHN BELUSHI*—January 24, 1949

FEBRUARY 8-2-2

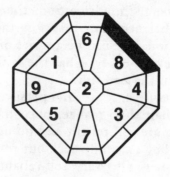

DATES THE MONTHS CHANGE

FEBRUARY 3—MARCH 4, 1893	FEBRUARY 5—MARCH 5, 1947
FEBRUARY 5—MARCH 5, 1902	FEBRUARY 5—MARCH 4, 1956
FEBRUARY 5—MARCH 6, 1911	FEBRUARY 4—MARCH 5, 1965
FEBRUARY 5—MARCH 5, 1920	FEBRUARY 4—MARCH 5, 1974
FEBRUARY 4—MARCH 5, 1929	FEBRUARY 4—MARCH 5, 1983
FEBRUARY 4—MARCH 5, 1938	FEBRUARY 4—MARCH 4, 1992

AMBITIOUS   *DEPENDENT*
STEADY   *WILLFUL*
CURIOUS   *OBSTINATE*
CONSERVATIVE   *PERSISTENT*

These people are bright and ambitious. They appear to be weak and vulnerable but are actually quite willful. They develop their lives by following their own strongly self-motivated minds in a conservative, steady manner.

Their ambitions keep their mind active, seeking out new experiences. They have powerful memories, and their delicate sensitivity is often accompanied by a fine artistic sense. Although they may tend to change focus easily or often, once they really want something, they make a commitment to its attainment and never give up until they succeed.

It is intrinsic to their basic nature to be self-motivated and persistent, but also dependent. As a result it is very important for this type to have attention from others as they work toward their goals.

If they can consider others' views in decision making and achieve a position of stability, their natural steadiness and powers of organization can take over and guide them along.

They may, however, take some time to arrive at this point in their lives. This type needs to experience a great variety of situations in order to build up confidence. Although they are always seeking independence, they cannot do so rapidly. Because they are really dependent, they may be easily swayed by those around them. They always consider their status and may at times take matters too seriously or be overly concerned with appearances. Once they get angry, they hold stubbornly to their own opinions, but if a stronger, more powerful person tries to hold or control them, they cannot always stand firm and may give in easily. For these reasons, they must develop slowly and steadily, being sure to learn how to avoid making any rash or ill-advised decisions, so that they may maintain control.

Once they attain this stability of self, their focus on life can change, especially if they are surrounded by friends or trustworthy coworkers. If comfortable, they can relax and allow their steady, curious minds and dedication to give others free rein. In this way, a person who is introverted, withdrawn, suspicious, and unable to express himself clearly can become openminded, trusting, and able to relate to others. This type must be careful, though, not to go overboard in trying to control events.

Women of this type are strongly self-motivated but are still dependent. Often spoiled when young, they find it easier to succeed later in life. They make excellent assistants or wives and mothers. Men of this type need time to stabilize and must expect a great amount of experience in life. Once they level off, they can use their ambitious spirit and steadiness well.

Many of these people have difficulty in first marriages or in young love because of their self-motivated, dependent natures, which give them high ideals and great expectations.

CHARLES DICKENS—February 7, 1812
JOHN STEINBECK—February 27, 1902
RONALD REAGAN—February 6, 1911
AN WANG—February 7, 1920
OLIVER REED—February 13, 1938

MARCH **8**-1-3

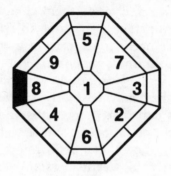

DATES THE MONTHS CHANGE

MARCH 5–APRIL 3, 1893	MARCH 6–APRIL 4, 1947
MARCH 6–APRIL 5, 1902	MARCH 5–APRIL 4, 1956
MARCH 7–APRIL 5, 1911	MARCH 6–APRIL 4, 1965
MARCH 6–APRIL 4, 1920	MARCH 6–APRIL 4, 1974
MARCH 6–APRIL 4, 1929	MARCH 6–APRIL 4, 1983
MARCH 6–APRIL 4, 1938	MARCH 5–APRIL 3, 1992

SELF-MOTIVATED	*IMPATIENT*
INDEPENDENT	*AMBITIOUS*
HONEST	*SENSITIVE*
STRAIGHTFORWARD	*NARROW-MINDED*

These people are self-motivated and express themselves in an honest, straightforward manner. They move ambitiously toward their goals. If allowed to do this, they will be very optimistic, not looking back or worrying.

If this type is restrained or expected to hold their strong desires back, they become very frustrated. Their nature is such that their wants must be expressed outwardly. It is difficult for them to keep their feelings inside or dormant. They want movement.

These people, especially the women, can be very talkative and open socially. They express themselves very clearly. They are capable of "stinging with words" and although they are bright, the surety of their self-motivation can sometimes make their actions appear childish and lead to disagreements. However, they do have good judgment and know how to use it. They can look at people and read them fairly well.

Because they are sensitive and honest, they may be cautious about becoming involved. Once they start working on a project, however, they give great energy to carrying it through. When moving forward on a project, they need to be careful of emotional problems caused by not considering others. Such situations may result in a loss of objectivity of their judgment.

This type gives great energy in caring for blood relations. Although usually social, they sometimes find difficulty in expressing themselves when faced with a serious situation such as love.

This type is usually indirectly lucky about money and knows how to control it once they have it.

These people must learn to control their impatience. They must guard against placing too much emphasis on themselves, their ambitions, and their desires. Otherwise they will tend to rush on to new subjects before they have settled the old.

ANDREW JACKSON—March 15, 1767
L. RON HUBBARD—March 13, 1911
TENNESSEE WILLIAMS—March 26, 1911
TOSHIRO MIFUNE—April 1, 1920
IRENE PAPPAS—March 9, 1929
JAMES COCO—March 21, 1929
RUDOLF NUREYEV—March 17, 1938
ELTON JOHN—March 25, 1947
EMMYLOU HARRIS—April 2, 1947

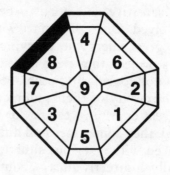

DATES THE MONTHS CHANGE

APRIL 4–MAY 4, 1893	APRIL 5–MAY 5, 1947
APRIL 6–MAY 5, 1902	APRIL 5–MAY 4, 1956
APRIL 6–MAY 6, 1911	APRIL 5–MAY 5, 1965
APRIL 5–MAY 5, 1920	APRIL 5–MAY 5, 1974
APRIL 5–MAY 5, 1929	APRIL 5–MAY 5, 1983
APRIL 5–MAY 5, 1938	APRIL 4–MAY 4, 1992

CREATIVE	*MOODY*
AMBITIOUS	*WILLFUL*
PROUD	*CHANGEABLE*
SELF-MOTIVATED	*EMOTIONAL*

These people are often talented in their work or business. They tend to be gifted with special abilities or skills that enable them to attain a reasonable degree of success. They are always actively in pursuit of money and successful careers. They are often persuasive speakers.

The fact that they are not only creative but proud, moody, and changeable gives their lives an erratic emotional quality. When it comes to unimportant (to them) details in life, they must often depend on others for help.

They frequently appear to be completely in charge of a situation. They are entertaining, confident, and often charming. Inside, however, they can be quite self-conscious about their behavior.

Their decisions usually depend on their mood. When their mood is positive, they are eager and ready to act upon whatever comes their way. When they are dissatisfied, their frustration makes them lose control easily.

Most women of this type are bright and proud, and have greater self-reliance than the men. In fact, they rarely allow themselves to be dependent upon a man. Men of this type like reliable women. Still, they usually like to have things their way and freedom is important. They do well in flexible occupations that give them room for change and development.

It is most important for this type to reconcile their talent and their everchanging minds. They need to focus on fewer activities and avoid emotional ups and downs. They should concentrate more on moving ahead slowly, completing tasks, and keeping their willful ambitions under control.

JAMES MONROE—April 28, 1758
JOAN MIRO—April 20, 1893
HUNTINGTON HARTFORD—April 18, 1911
JACQUES BREL—April 8, 1929
AUDREY HEPBURN—May 4, 1929
CLAUDIA CARDINALE—April 15, 1938
DOUG HENNING—May 3, 1947
KAREEM ABDUL-JABBAR—April 16, 1947

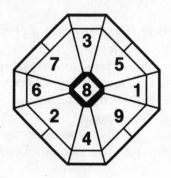

DATES THE MONTHS CHANGE

MAY 5–JUNE 4, 1893	MAY 6–JUNE 6, 1947
MAY 6–JUNE 6, 1902	MAY 5–JUNE 5, 1956
MAY 7–JUNE 6, 1911	MAY 6–JUNE 5, 1965
MAY 6–JUNE 5, 1920	MAY 6–JUNE 5, 1974
MAY 6–JUNE 5, 1929	MAY 6–JUNE 5, 1983
MAY 6–JUNE 6, 1938	MAY 5–JUNE 4, 1992

SELF-MOTIVATED	*WILLFUL*
AMBITIOUS	*STUBBORN*
ENERGETIC	*CHILDISH*
PERSUASIVE	*OPINIONATED*

This type of person usually has unusually powerful drive, ambition, and great energy for pursuing their goals. They possess a sharp wit and a mind that is always active, seeking out new experiences. They have a sense of adventure. This makes them difficult to satisfy; at any time, they may be looking ahead in search of something better.

This constant seeking for new opportunities may prevent them from sticking with one project or person for very long. Their enthusiasm may run hot and cold as they continually change their focus. This can give their lives an up-and-down quality and also affect their finances. Although they are lucky with money, it may be hard for them to maintain stability over a long period of time.

These people appear proud and reliable, and they are often active and ambitious. They catch people's attention easily and have the ability to speak persuasively. Others find them charming, and their observations satisfying.

This type may spread out their energies over many different interests and be unable to focus on one thing. They may get too busy, shifting their focus back and forth among several ideas or projects, and appear either competent or incompetent as a result, depending on the situation. Despite their ambitious spirit, the fact that they are opinionated and changeable often causes this type to take much time before making important decisions.

Men of this type have great goals in life, but sometimes overemphasis on money interferes with their personal pride. Women of this type are more willful and expect more freedom than the men. Many of them seem to have bad luck in their first marriage.

These people have tremendous self-confidence, and at times they tend to be too opinionated. Their great energy and willful behavior can appear childish, although in the face of a stronger person or power, they will soften. This type's weak points are their naïvete, great generosity, easy trusting of others, and willingness to open up to situations that appeal to their self-interest. Ambition may blind them to the whole truth, and they may lack judgment, being biased by their desires and narrow focus.

Despite their energy, pride, and stubbornness, they need to find someone who can back them up. They are outgoing, yet easily cheated, and need someone who understands their great pride and ambition to guide and protect them. Often they are not so independent as they like to think, and how their lives turn out may depend on this other person. When they have good backing, they can utilize their self-motivated energies much better.

MARTHA WASHINGTON—June 2, 1731
MARQUIS DE SADE—June 2, 1740
HARRY S. TRUMAN—May 8, 1884
DAVID O. SELZNICK—May 10, 1902
HUBERT H. HUMPHREY—May 27, 1911
ROSALIND RUSSELL—June 4, 1911
POPE JOHN PAUL II—May 18, 1920
PEGGY LEE—May 26, 1920
BURT BACHARACH—May 12, 1929
BEVERLY SILLS—May 25, 1929
RICHARD BENJAMIN—May 22, 1938
SUGAR RAY LEONARD—May 17, 1956
BROOKE SHIELDS—May 31, 1965

JUNE **8**-7-6

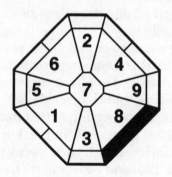

DATES THE MONTHS CHANGE

JUNE 5–JULY 6, 1893	JUNE 7–JULY 7, 1947
JUNE 7–JULY 7, 1902	JUNE 6–JULY 6, 1956
JUNE 7–JULY 7, 1911	JUNE 6–JULY 6, 1965
JUNE 6–JULY 6, 1920	JUNE 6–JULY 6, 1974
JUNE 6–JULY 7, 1929	JUNE 6–JULY 7, 1983
JUNE 7–JULY 7, 1938	JUNE 5–JULY 6, 1992

SELF-MOTIVATED   *OPINIONATED*
ORGANIZED   *HYPERSENSITIVE*
DETERMINED   *STUBBORN*
WILLFUL   *INFLEXIBLE*

Although they can be very self-motivated and opinionated, these people tend to appear retiring or easygoing, which can be misleading. Their determination and organizational ability make them good leaders; however, these traits also tend to make them stubborn and inflexible. When their desires are opposed, they become very frustrated. When there is mutual agreement in a situation, they can use their organized, motivated energy to lead the project to successful completion.

This type can become weak about pursuing goals in which they are not interested, but when interested they can bring their genius into full play.

They tend to be very concerned with details and are often hypersensitive to situations. This can make them self-conscious, and they react by strongly demonstrating what appears as leadership ability to others. However, their self-assertiveness is often too much for others to handle. This type needs to broaden their focus and learn to consider alternate viewpoints.

Women of this type possess the energy necessary to pursue goals and can be very proud, and therefore often independent. The men tend to appear quite retiring, though they are really determined to have their way.

Most of this type are hard workers. Once they find a satisfactory career or business, they give great energy to make it a success.

They become quite involved in their social life. They find it easy to attract people, but if they do not control their tendency to be frank and opinionated, they may have difficulties in sustaining relationships.

The expectations these people have for themselves are often great, and they must be careful not to bite off more than they can chew.

In general this type usually has good luck in developing a successful and productive life if they are careful to choose projects they can stay with.

BJORN BORG—June 6, 1956
THOMAS MANN—June 6, 1875
GUY LOMBARDO—June 19, 1902
RICHARD ROGERS—June 28, 1902
WILLIAM WYLER—July 1, 1902
VITTORIO DE SICA—July 7, 1902
PRINCE ALY KHAN—June 13, 1911
MITCH MILLER—July 4, 1911
JUNE CARTER CASH—June 23, 1929

JULY **8**–6–7

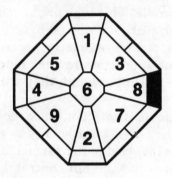

DATES THE MONTHS CHANGE

JULY 7–AUGUST 6, 1893	JULY 8–AUGUST 7, 1947
JULY 8–AUGUST 7, 1902	JULY 7–AUGUST 6, 1956
JULY 8–AUGUST 8, 1911	JULY 7–AUGUST 7, 1965
JULY 7–AUGUST 7, 1920	JULY 7–AUGUST 7, 1974
JULY 8–AUGUST 7, 1929	JULY 8–AUGUST 7, 1983
JULY 8–AUGUST 7, 1938	JULY 7–AUGUST 6, 1992

INTUITIVE   *SELF-MOTIVATED*
STYLISH   *WILLFUL*
IDEALISTIC   *HYPERSENSITIVE*
PASSIONATE   *INFLEXIBLE*

Many of these people appear easygoing, yet they have a strong will. Once they have a goal in mind, they must take immediate practical steps to attain it. They will give tremendous energy and enthusiasm to focusing on interesting activities until they gain satisfaction. Their enthusiasm often helps them build great success.

Their hypersensitivity, however, makes them easily influenced by circumstances, so they may worry at times. Usually, their self-motivation and easygoing nature keep them from worrying for long.

They are moved by their intuitive feelings, which are often correct, yet they may lose adaptability in certain situations as a result, because they tend to go their own way. They need to explain themselves, as others may not be able to understand them

270

readily. Also, they may be opinionated and unlikely to change for others, especially when they face something interesting or important to them. They are strongly self-assertive and try to break through opposition.

Their attitude is tender and stylish, attracting people, yet their discrimination is clearly based on their feelings about others. So, persons of this type may have very different reputations. Their ambitious, adventurous spirit, always seeking new experiences, drives them forward. At times people misjudge them, because Number 8's jump into projects quickly, often without concern for others. Once Number 8's establish a good relationship, however, their concern and consideration for others increases greatly.

These people work very hard and need to play hard as well. In order to enjoy themselves, their feelings must follow, so they are often limited. They are good socially when their self-confidence is with them, or when they are in a position of leadership. Their actions are clear and simple, their minds insightful and original.

Most of the women are proud and ambitious, often seeming to look down on others. Although they may appear hard to get close to, they have their own sense of love and are actually very passionate once they open up to someone. The men have great expectations and lofty ideals about love and affection. They can be quite playful, but once they get serious, they are afraid to be hurt. Both the men and the women may expect to get more in love than they give, because of this fear.

This type has great personal style and needs to attain a certain status. They may suffer silently if this doesn't occur, but if they succeed, they are able to express themselves better.

JOHN QUINCY ADAMS—July 11, 1767
AMEDEO MODIGLIANI—July 12, 1884
GINGER ROGERS—July 16, 1911
MARSHALL MCLUHAN—July 21, 1911
ROBERT TAYLOR—August 5, 1911
LUCILLE BALL—August 6, 1911
YUL BRYNNER—July 11, 1920
BELLA ABZUG—July 24, 1920
JACQUELINE KENNEDY ONASSIS—July 28, 1929
NATALIE WOOD—July 20, 1938
O. J. SIMPSON—July 9, 1947
ARLO GUTHRIE—July 10, 1947
DOROTHY HAMILL—July 26, 1956

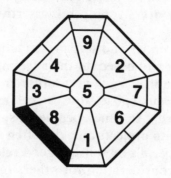

DATES THE MONTHS CHANGE

AUGUST 7–SEPTEMBER 6, 1893	AUGUST 8–SEPTEMBER 6, 1947
AUGUST 8–SEPTEMBER 8, 1902	AUGUST 7–SEPTEMBER 7, 1956
AUGUST 9–SEPTEMBER 8, 1911	AUGUST 8–SEPTEMBER 7, 1965
AUGUST 8–SEPTEMBER 7, 1920	AUGUST 8–SEPTEMBER 7, 1974
AUGUST 8–SEPTEMBER 7, 1929	AUGUST 8–SEPTEMBER 7, 1983
AUGUST 8–SEPTEMBER 7, 1938	AUGUST 7–SEPTEMBER 6, 1992

ENTHUSIASTIC　　　　　*OVERAMBITIOUS*
TALENTED　　　　　　　*OVERPERSISTENT*
LIKABLE　　　　　　　　*CHANGEABLE*
SELF-MOTIVATED　　　　*STUBBORN*

People usually find this type charming and likable. They project a down-to-earth quality that is attractive. They tend to have somewhat unbalanced traits. They can be generous yet self-motivated, ambitious yet hesitant, energetic yet frustrated. They are forceful, but their attitude changes easily. Nevertheless, they give full energy and enthusiasm to whatever they focus on at a particular moment.

Their enthusiasm combined with their talent and ambition helps them carry through their projects. Once they want something, they can be quite stubborn, even losing good judgment. If they persistently pursue numerous goals without steady focus or sufficient energy, undertakings can start well but stall in midstream.

Often their self-motivated behavior becomes childish in a likable way. Since they are somewhat adventurous and are not followers, these people tend to do well on their own. They work well in a free-lance capacity or in situations where they can move around freely and do what they want.

Their connections with their families are usually good, and they are often lucky about money.

Both the men and the women are driven forward by self-motivated ambitions. The women tend to be more uninhibited than the men.

In human relationships they tend to have strong sexual and emotional desires and become extremely serious, causing problems. They may even try to possess another person exclusively, whether the other person is committed to someone else or not.

These people do not usually like to stay long in one place. They are always seeking something new. If they keep their ambitions realistic and manageable, they will be able to direct their energies and talents toward successful goals.

JOHANN WOLFGANG VON GOETHE—August 28, 1749
DARRYL F. ZANUCK—September 5, 1902
CHARLIE PARKER—August 29, 1920
CRAIG CLAIBORNE—September 4, 1920
KENNY ROGERS—August 21, 1938
ELLIOTT GOULD—August 29, 1938

SEPTEMBER 8-4-9

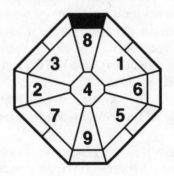

DATES THE MONTHS CHANGE

SEPTEMBER 7–OCTOBER 7, 1893	SEPTEMBER 7–OCTOBER 8, 1947
SEPTEMBER 9–OCTOBER 8, 1902	SEPTEMBER 8–OCTOBER 7, 1956
SEPTEMBER 9–OCTOBER 8, 1911	SEPTEMBER 8–OCTOBER 7, 1965
SEPTEMBER 8–OCTOBER 8, 1920	SEPTEMBER 8–OCTOBER 8, 1974
SEPTEMBER 8–OCTOBER 8, 1929	SEPTEMBER 8–OCTOBER 8, 1983
SEPTEMBER 8–OCTOBER 8, 1938	SEPTEMBER 7–OCTOBER 7, 1992

PROUD
SELF-MOTIVATED
CURIOUS
FORESIGHTFUL

EMOTIONAL
STATUS-CONSCIOUS
EVASIVE
CHANGEABLE

Great curiosity and ambition lead these people into many adventures, as they give great energy to building their lives. Once they get interested in something, they make elaborate plans as to how best to approach the situation. They are very bright, capable of great foresight. Yet at the same time, they try to settle everything on a moment-to-moment basis that makes stability difficult.

Most of these people are proud, bright, and self-motivated. Although they may seem calm and steady, they often vacillate because they are highly influenced by their feelings. Emotional and outwardly evasive, they can be difficult for others to understand. They are very loyal to their own opinions, finding compromising with others difficult. This, along with their pride, may give them an air of arrogant superiority, and their concern about attaining special status can isolate them from other people.

Decisions are made quickly but are always adjustable, depending on the emotional reactions that follow. If they are not satisfied with the immediate results, they change and change again until they are. Their standards are high, and so it may be hard for them to achieve complete satisfaction. Their jobs and residences are also subject to frequent change.

Most of them have been influenced or received great affection from their parent of the opposite sex. This governs their expectations for love and social attention in adult life.

The women of this type like powerful men but do not like to be controlled by them. They cannot compromise easily. The men prefer calm, independent women but need to continue moving their own way.

Once people come into their social circle, they like to take care of them. They are kind to others, yet usually dislike having to deal with complicated situations, often preferring not to get involved. However, they cannot always maintain this detached status.

Although they are hardworking and have a natural leadership potential, other people cannot always follow the movement of their foresighted but changeable minds. They need to explain themselves to others, to avoid appearing arrogant or evasive. Despite their foresight and enthusiasm, these people need to keep their focus and not change too much. If they use their energy in a concentrated effort, they are able to help many people and bring success to themselves at the same time.

CHESTER A. ARTHUR—October 5, 1830
WILLIAM HOWARD TAFT—September 15, 1857
H. G. WELLS—September 21, 1866
J. C. PENNEY—September 16, 1875
ALEXANDER KORDA—September 16, 1893
RAYMOND A. KROC—October 5, 1902
MICKEY ROONEY—September 23, 1920
ARNOLD PALMER—September 10, 1929
STEPHEN KING—September 21, 1947

OCTOBER 8-3-1

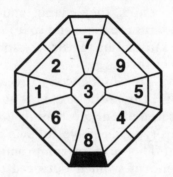

DATES THE MONTHS CHANGE

OCTOBER 8–NOVEMBER 6, 1893	OCTOBER 9–NOVEMBER 7, 1947
OCTOBER 9–NOVEMBER 7, 1902	OCTOBER 8–NOVEMBER 6, 1956
OCTOBER 9–NOVEMBER 7, 1911	OCTOBER 8–NOVEMBER 7, 1965
OCTOBER 9–NOVEMBER 7, 1920	OCTOBER 9–NOVEMBER 7, 1974
OCTOBER 9–NOVEMBER 7, 1929	OCTOBER 9–NOVEMBER 7, 1983
OCTOBER 9–NOVEMBER 7, 1938	OCTOBER 8–NOVEMBER 6, 1993

AMBITIOUS	*SENSITIVE*
PATIENT	*INSECURE*
SELF-ASSERTIVE	*CAUTIOUS*
COMPETITIVE	*SELF-PROTECTIVE*

These people have great ambition combined with patience. They give great energy to developing their life and often overcome difficult circumstances. Most seem to be active and open-hearted, but inside, insecurity can cause them problems. Their sensitivity combined with insecurity can interfere with their natural self-assertion. On the other hand, their insecurity combined with patience can give them the energy and desire to overcome almost anything.

This type is often influenced by a strong mother, who sometimes overprotected them. This can affect their relationships with other people by making them more dependent.

Ambition creates a strong drive toward fame or recognition in these people. Such energy helps them develop possibilities for future success. Because of their curiosity, adventurous spirit, and love of competition, they may appear to be self-confident "big talkers." In fact, their insecurities may cause them inner doubt or worry, and they need a certain amount of attention and admiration from others. They are sensitive and self-protective as well, and if someone takes sides against them, their reaction can be defensively forceful.

Cautious about decision-making, they have great patience. They give full energy to carry through their ambitions once they make a choice. If they cannot decide something, they experience great frustration and loss of self-confidence, which increases their insecurity. The same frustration comes if they are "stuck" in a stable condition; this type needs new activity constantly.

They can judge situations calmly if they are not personally involved. If they are, they tend to protect themselves. Once they like or trust other people, however, they can give much attention. Still, they keep a certain distance much of the time.

Women of this type have more energy to control their desires than the men, especially in family situations. They are patient and can take responsibility for problems that may arise. After they overcome certain difficulties, the strong ambition and active nature of the men combine for great independence. By controlling their energies properly, they can have more peaceful lives.

When they reach a certain degree of success, their energies may spread out or escalate so that they can barely control them. If they try to hold back their explosive feelings or lack the stamina to keep up with the constant push of their ambitions, frustration and worry can take over, causing great physical and emotional stress. They must always be aware of the conflict between their basic ambitious, energetic nature and their insecurity and worry. To balance these two is an ongoing challenge. These people must try to stay strong and physically healthy, if they are to withstand the thrust of their own great drive.

ELEANOR ROOSEVELT—October 11, 1884
ELSA LANCHESTER—October 28, 1902
LARAINE DAY—October 13, 1920
MONTGOMERY CLIFT—October 17, 1920
TIMOTHY LEARY—October 22, 1920
EVEL KNIEVEL—October 17, 1938
RICHARD DREYFUSS—October 29, 1947
CARRIE FISHER—October 28, 1956

NOVEMBER **8**-2-2

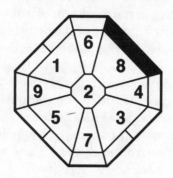

SELF-MOTIVATED	*SENSITIVE*
ACTIVE SOCIALLY	*DEPENDENT*
AMBITIOUS	*OBSTINATE*
CONSERVATIVE	*PROUD*

These people are self-motivated and proud. They have a quiet power that appears tender, making it easy for them to attract and charm other people. Although their expression is usually calm and conservative, they are also willful and ambitious. In a critical moment, they may lose their thoughtful expression, rushing ahead forcefully after something or someone. Once they find something they really want, they never give up until they attain it.

Although they dream of independence and seek high status in life, their dependent, sensitive nature often keeps them from reaching these goals on their own. Their energy is such that they are much better suited to establishing themselves in a secondary position, with a stronger, more powerful ally who can lead the way toward mutually beneficial ends. This arrangement may be hard for them to accept, because their pride and self-motivated nature always push them to try to lead or control people or circumstances. However, if they can establish a stable secondary position, in time they can build a good reputation and gain much valued experience.

Gentle yet hardworking, these people enjoy activity and have an adventurous spirit. Despite their strong self-motivation, bright minds, and calm judgment, they are easily influenced by outside circumstances. Their dependence and sensitivity demand a certain amount of attention and admiration from others. They consider others in their own way, often in a detail-conscious manner that people cannot accept. This type may be misjudged as being inconsiderate or ignoring others' feelings, although this is not the case.

Socially, they are charming and attractive, always drawing others to them. Although they are somewhat cautious and do not open their minds easily, they can become overconfident and alienate people if their pride gets out of hand. They must also guard against obstinacy and not allow their expression to become too forceful with someone who has different opinions. It is always hard for them to admit being at fault.

Women of this type always expect independence and are always trying to move in their own way. They choose to express their adventurous spirit in a very active manner. They may be spoiled when young; still, others find their self-motivation charming. The men express themselves more conservatively than the women, appearing more tender. They can contain their active minds more successfully and are happy staying within their own small circle. Both the men and the women may find it difficult to stay in a first marriage.

This November type has a strong determination to develop matters according to their own ideas, so it is not easy for them to find a supportive staff. Although attention is important to them, their need for it is less intense than that of the February type, who try to surround themselves with like-minded people. The November type is driven by self-motivated energies toward desired status. Often it is through their social life, where their brightness appears so charming, that their best opportunities come.

FYODOR DOSTOEVSKY—November 11, 1821
HARPO MARX—November 21, 1893
RICARDO MONTALBAN—November 25, 1920
VIRGINIA MAYO—November 30, 1920

DICK CLARK—November 30, 1929
GRACE KELLY—November 12, 1929
EDWARD ASNER—November 15, 1929
JEAN SEBERG—November 13, 1938
RICH LITTLE—November 26, 1938
TINA TURNER—November 26, 1938
BO DEREK—November 20, 1956

DECEMBER **8**-1-3

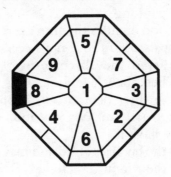

DATES THE MONTHS CHANGE

DEC. 7, 1893–JANUARY 4, 1894	DEC. 8, 1947–JANUARY 5, 1948
DEC. 8, 1902–JANUARY 5, 1903	DEC. 7, 1956–JANUARY 4, 1957
DEC. 8, 1911–JANUARY 6, 1912	DEC. 7, 1965–JANUARY 5, 1966
DEC. 7, 1920–JANUARY 5, 1921	DEC. 7, 1974–JANUARY 5, 1975
DEC. 7, 1929–JANUARY 5, 1930	DEC. 7, 1983–JANUARY 5, 1984
DEC. 8, 1938–JANUARY 5, 1939	DEC. 7, 1992–JANUARY 4, 1993

SELF-MOTIVATED　　　*OPINIONATED*
PROGRESSIVE　　　　 *CAUTIOUS*
INDEPENDENT　　　　 *ANXIOUS*
QUICK-WITTED　　　　*RASH*

These people are endowed with a progressive spirit and are usually candid, expressing themselves freely. They can be quite sensitive to high quality in life and in art. They are, however, rash and this, combined with a self-motivated mind, can make them lose flexibility.

They are quick-witted, hardworking, and rather serious-minded. Despite a usually positive outlook, they tend to worry and become anxious if things do not go the way they want. Once they are frustrated, they find it difficult to be patient, and they may rush forward in search of a quick result.

Socially they clearly like or dislike people, discriminating according to their own views. Their lack of patience and constant movement often make relationships uneven. In their haste, they may not consider others as much as they should. Although they may hold a grudge or become jealous at times, they rarely keep these feelings for very long.

Their self-motivation enables them to exert great energy in one direction, becoming successful but not necessarily popular! They tend to lose flexibility if they become overly preoccupied with their own ideas. When they face difficulties, often a friend will help or something to their benefit will happen at just the right time. They are also usually lucky about money and know how to control it once they have it.

Often this type is the favorite child and may receive much favorable attention from their families. However, they do not like their parents or siblings to control or restrict their activities. They prefer to exert their independence.

Women of this type are often very talkative, and their forceful expression can sometimes cause problems. The men, however, have a quieter expression, and they tend to hold more inside. If they like someone or something, they too become talkative and more forceful.

In general, these people need to be aware of their tendency to be self-assertive and opinionated. Then they can open their minds, learn to keep their relationships smooth, and overcome their impatience.

ANNA PAVLOVA—January 3, 1885
MAO TSE-TUNG—December 26, 1893
RALPH RICHARDSON—December 19, 1902
JULES DASSIN—December 8, 1911
LEE J. COBB—December 9, 1911
DAVID SUSSKIND—December 19, 1920
LIV ULLMAN—December 16, 1938
JON VOIGHT—December 29, 1938
STEVEN SPIELBERG—December 18, 1947

JANUARY **8**-9-4

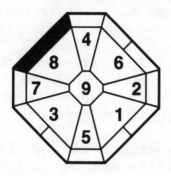

DATES THE MONTHS CHANGE

JANUARY 5–FEBRUARY 3, 1894	JANUARY 6–FEBRUARY 4, 1948
JANUARY 6–FEBRUARY 4, 1903	JANUARY 5–FEBRUARY 3, 1957
JANUARY 7–FEBRUARY 4, 1912	JANUARY 6–FEBRUARY 3, 1966
JANUARY 6–FEBRUARY 3, 1921	JANUARY 6–FEBRUARY 3, 1975
JANUARY 6–FEBRUARY 3, 1930	JANUARY 6–FEBRUARY 3, 1984
JANUARY 6–FEBRUARY 4, 1939	JANUARY 5–FEBRUARY 3, 1993

PROUD	*EMOTIONAL*
AFFECTIONATE	*SHOWY*
TALENTED	*PRETENTIOUS*
SELF-MOTIVATED	*MOODY*

These people have outgoing personalities; they are bright, open-hearted, and proud. Their pride and high ideals make them appear dynamic and "in charge," and they express themselves well in social situations. They have an adventurous spirit and always strive to meet and fulfill great challenges. Indeed, they willingly expend much energy pursuing their own high ideals, especially if success or achievement is within reach. Once they are interested in something, they become very enthusiastic, although they may change their focus quickly.

Most of these people are quite serious and self-confident. They love to gamble, often taking risks without a second thought. Their self-motivation and talent make them want to accomplish much; they are always drawn to new interests. If they face a situation in which they must hold back their desires, they become very frustrated and may lose control. This type is usually cautious about where and when they reveal their frustration, as a public scene could damage their reputation and their chances for future success.

They are moody, and this trait can affect their decision making. If they make hasty decisions, they can lose or disrupt good opportunities and be forced to begin again. This may cause wide fluctuations in their lives, producing frequent ups and downs until middle age.

This type can be very emotional, even stormy, yet quite affectionate. When they feel something, their expression may be very direct, yet childlike at the same time. Most people find them charming, intelligent, and easygoing, all of which adds to their reputation. However, they often make pretentious displays for appearance's sake only and may waste valuable energy that could be put to better use.

In marriage they have high ideals, often seeking perfection. Expecting to find satisfaction quickly, they may overemphasize appearance and so misjudge people again and again. They tend to see events (and people) according to their own particular persuasion. Yet to others, they may appear as a playboy/playgirl type, because they can move so quickly from one love to the next.

Most of the men are proud and give great consideration to their appearance. They need much attention. Women are ambitious and outgoing, yet they cannot be completely independent.

This type moves strongly in their own way, giving great energy to whatever task they choose to pursue. They are considerate of others and expect the same in return. If anyone tries to control them, they become very distressed and disoriented. Despite their strong self-motivation and pride, this type needs a good manager —someone who can handle the seemingly unimportant details for them and keep these people on an even keel. They must always be aware of their emotional nature and the way it affects their ambition and talent. If they can look at themselves calmly and control their moodiness, they can develop their lives more smoothly and fully.

JEROME KERN—January 27, 1885
NORMAN ROCKWELL—February 3, 1894

ERICH LEINSDORF—February 4, 1912
MARIO LANZA—January 31, 1921
SAL MINEO—January 10, 1939
GERMAINE GREER—January 29, 1939
MIKHAIL BARYSHNIKOV—January 28, 1948

FEBRUARY 9-5-9

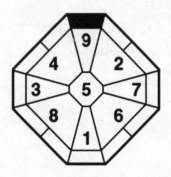

DATES THE MONTHS CHANGE

FEBRUARY 4–MARCH 4, 1892	FEBRUARY 4–MARCH 5, 1946
FEBRUARY 4–MARCH 5, 1901	FEBRUARY 5–MARCH 5, 1955
FEBRUARY 5–MARCH 5, 1910	FEBRUARY 5–MARCH 4, 1964
FEBRUARY 5–MARCH 6, 1919	FEBRUARY 4–MARCH 5, 1973
FEBRUARY 5–MARCH 5, 1928	FEBRUARY 4–MARCH 5, 1982
FEBRUARY 4–MARCH 5, 1937	FEBRUARY 4–MARCH 5, 1991

PROUD	*IMPATIENT*
FORESIGHTFUL	*OVER-CONFIDENT*
ASSERTIVE	*STUBBORN*
BRIGHT	*VAIN*

These people are foresightful, proud, and often talented. They usually make decisions quickly. These qualities make them good leaders, especially in artistic or academic fields. Unfortunately they are impatient when it comes to the study of basic things and since one cannot become a leader in a short time, they may have difficulty reaching goals.

Their proud, assertive manner can come across too strongly, so that they appear haughty, sometimes provoking resentment in others.

They have a great desire to control circumstances and have difficulty restraining their egos. This limitation can interfere with their leadership ability.

They have a stormy nature and like to carry things through

quickly. Since they anger easily and are likely to change their minds, a long-running career is difficult for them to attain unless they can hold their ego in check and consider the feelings and ideas of others.

They sometimes give great attention to appearances to the point of being vain. They can be overly self-confident at times. This can make them less able to see talent and strength in others, thereby missing out on needed help or support.

Women of this type are usually bright and proud, often achieving positions of leadership. Marriage for them can be difficult since they have high ideals about how a marriage should work. Men of this type tend to be more stubborn than the women and somewhat more self-conscious about what others think. They are usually quite concerned about their appearance.

If this type can be patient and consider other people, they can slowly mature into excellent leaders. If not, their bright minds might make them cunning, crafty, and egoistic.

In general, they have close knit relationships with their family. They give attention to money, often using it as a means for maintaining their pride, which is extremely important to them.

VICTOR HUGO—February 26, 1802
THOMAS EDISON—February 11, 1847
JENNIFER JONES—March 2, 1919
ANDREW MORAN GREELEY—February 5, 1928
FATS DOMINO—February 26, 1928
KAREN SILKWOOD—February 19, 1946
SANDY DUNCAN—February 20, 1946

MARCH 9-4-1

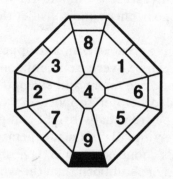

DATES THE MONTHS CHANGE

MARCH 5–APRIL 3, 1892	MARCH 6–APRIL 4, 1946
MARCH 6–APRIL 4, 1901	MARCH 6–APRIL 5, 1955
MARCH 6–APRIL 5, 1910	MARCH 5–APRIL 4, 1964
MARCH 7–APRIL 5, 1919	MARCH 6–APRIL 4, 1973
MARCH 6–APRIL 4, 1928	MARCH 6–APRIL 4, 1982
MARCH 6–APRIL 4, 1937	MARCH 6–APRIL 4, 1991

PROUD　　　　　　　*STUBBORN*
CREATIVE　　　　　　*OPINIONATED*
PATIENT　　　　　　　*INSECURE*
EMOTIONAL　　　　　*CHANGEABLE*

These people are bright, proud, and creative but must always do battle with their insecurity, which has a profound effect on their lives. Their appearance is one of vulnerability, usually being quiet and shy, and may hide the fact that their inner nature is stubborn and stormy. Since they expect perfection, they often need time to reach satisfaction. Fortunately, they have a cautious approach to life, and their patience serves them well.

This type is emotional, but they cannot openly express their feelings. They tend to hold much inside, creating frustration, because their pride and insecurity are entwined. Before they express themselves directly, they want to be sure they are not making a mistake. They try at times to appear stronger than they really are.

In the same way, if someone else hurts their pride, they retaliate unexpectedly, despite their usual calm demeanor.

They can be evasive and changeable, often wavering in their decisions, making it difficult for others to understand them. If they are too introverted emotionally and do not keep an open mind, they can isolate themselves from others. They work hard, because they need to prove that what they are doing is right, and to gain the admiration of other people. This reduces their insecurity and enables them to carry on.

These people devote themselves to accumulating knowledge. They pay attention to details. These qualities give them a certain leadership ability that enhances their reputation. They also are careful about money and make an effort to save it.

They live cautiously and yet need constant activity. Their insecurity increases when things get slow and they may become frustrated. Because of this, they need a good support system—friends or coworkers who will surround them—so they can feel protected enough to fight off problems they may face.

This type may be prejudiced in their relationships, unable to trust others easily. Many were strongly influenced as children by a complicated family situation or received great attention from their parent of the opposite sex. These early impressions tend to color their future views considerably.

Women of this type expect a certain amount of attention at all times and are, to some degree, emotionally dependent. But basically they are more independent than the men. The men are always seeking their own brand of perfection. Natural feminists, they are usually kind and considerate to women and able to keep a certain objectivity once physically involved with someone.

Individuality is important to these people. They choose their own social circle and stubbornly refuse to associate with people they don't like. They are bright and opinionated, yet need time and reassurance if they are to express themselves well. Despite their stubborn streak, they like to analyze and try to be logical. This capacity gives them time and helps them make thoughtful decisions. Their pride and patience enable them to bring even large-scale dreams to completion.

HARRY HOUDINI—March 24, 1874
LON CHANEY—April 1, 1883

AKIRA KUROSAWA—March 23, 1910
EDWARD ALBEE—March 12, 1928
JOSEPH CARDINAL BERNARDIN—April 2, 1928
WARREN BEATTY—March 30, 1937
LIZA MINNELLI—March 12, 1946
PRINCE EDWARD—March 10, 1964

APRIL **9**-3-2

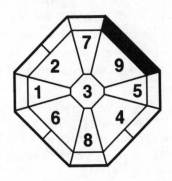

DATES THE MONTHS CHANGE

APRIL 4–MAY 4, 1892	APRIL 5–MAY 5, 1946
APRIL 5–MAY 5, 1901	APRIL 6–MAY 5, 1955
APRIL 6–MAY 5, 1910	APRIL 5–MAY 4, 1964
APRIL 6–MAY 6, 1919	APRIL 5–MAY 5, 1973
APRIL 5–MAY 5, 1928	APRIL 5–MAY 5, 1982
APRIL 5–MAY 5, 1937	APRIL 5–MAY 5, 1991

CONSERVATIVE	*SENSITIVE*
PROUD	*STORMY*
BRIGHT	*PASSIONATE*
FLEXIBLE	*OVERCAUTIOUS*

These people are usually proud and conservative. Although they appear quiet and tender, they are really controlled by high sensitivity and passion. They cannot hold themselves back once their desires are aroused. If they feel or want something strongly, they are compelled toward it with an intensity that often surprises others. It is perfection and complete satisfaction that they seek.

Most have bright, flexible minds, except when pride is involved. They often catch the fresh scent of a new trend before others. Socially their proud, conservative approach may keep them somewhat aloof. It takes time for people to get to know them.

A kind of sensitivity controls their decision making. They may appear indecisive when they are being overcautious. Once they face a serious situation, however, they can become rather stormy inside, expressing their views forcefully. This surprisingly direct expression may interfere with relationships.

Where money is involved, this type has a good sense of balance and flexibility. Their desires are great, and they push to satisfy them. They tend to have high expectations, which can lead to success in their work or disappointment if they fail to live up to them.

Many of this type have strong mothers whose influence deeply affects their lives. Their relationship with their mother has a great bearing on their views of masculinity and femininity later in life. In terms of affection, these people often expect perfect satisfaction, having a difficult love life.

Women of this type may appear more proud and independent than men. They find it hard to handle change themselves, yet they are often attracted to evasive, changeable men. This can be frustrating because they also expect perfection and security. The men often act strong outwardly to cover their sensitivity. Still, inside they are very proud and may find forming harmonious relationships with others difficult.

In general, this type strives for success, fame, or position. They must, however, learn to maintain realistic expectations if they are to develop their lives smoothly. Because they are naturally conservative, they can build a steady, successful life if they are aware of their own stormy nature. Often only a serious situation of some kind propels them into definite action. At those times, they have a better chance of carrying through if they can control their forceful expression, treat their associates with respect, and keep their pride in check.

ROBERT F. WAGNER—April 20, 1910
ANN MILLER—April 12, 1919
CELESTE HOLM—April 29, 1919
BETTY COMDEN—May 3, 1919
SHIRLEY TEMPLE BLACK—April 23, 1928
JAMES BROWN—May 3, 1928
JACK NICHOLSON—April 27, 1937
HAYLEY MILLS—April 16, 1946

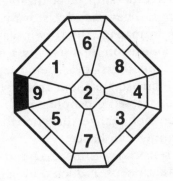

DATES THE MONTHS CHANGE

MAY 5–JUNE 4, 1892	MAY 6–JUNE 5, 1946
MAY 6–JUNE 5, 1901	MAY 6–JUNE 5, 1955
MAY 6–JUNE 6, 1910	MAY 5–JUNE 5, 1964
MAY 7–JUNE 5, 1919	MAY 6–JUNE 5, 1973
MAY 6–JUNE 5, 1928	MAY 6–JUNE 5, 1982
MAY 6–JUNE 5, 1937	MAY 6–JUNE 5, 1991

FORESIGHTFUL *AGGRESSIVE*
PROUD *DEPENDENT*
SOCIAL *PASSIONATE*
ORGANIZED *IMPATIENT*

These people are intelligent, proud, and highly active, with great organizational abilities. Their foresight and progressive approach to life provide them with almost limitless potential. Given their natural talent and capacity for hard work, it is no wonder these people are always giving full energy to the pursuit of success. Yet despite their outward drive, inside they are dependent, and rather delicate emotionally. Easily swayed by their passions, these people desperately need attention and support from others if they are to keep their own balance.

This need for attention makes them give much energy to social life, and indeed it is often there that they can best build their reputation and find the most enticing opportunities. They have good leadership potential, but at times, their conservative inner nature makes *active* leadership difficult for them, despite their independent longings. They may act stormy to gain control of a situation they wish to manage their own way.

Once they make a decision, it is usually a strong one, and they find it difficult to accept others' ideas, being very opinionated. This aggressive attitude can isolate them from others. They become very confused and distressed if people withdraw attention or support. Often they do not realize the alienating effect that their straightforward manner can have.

Their foresight, sensitivity to beauty, and easy sentimentality give them a fine aesthetic sense, which they can use to great benefit in an artistic endeavor. However, they need time and effort to develop and polish themselves if they are to succeed. Though serious and active about their work, they have a conservative side that demands a slow, steady build-up. Life becomes difficult, however, if this steady side tries to hold or control their actions. If their passionate side shines through, it often helps their projects to progress, but they must guard against impatience.

They are sometimes impractical about love, although they give it much energy and interest. They cannot convey their feelings easily; usually their expression is too straightforward or serious. Once in love, they can give great passion to one person. Unfortunately, they usually ignore the other person's wants.

Women are proud and think of themselves as independent. They may, however, be jealous, and need much attention and activity to be happy. Men can give much energy to their social life, yet are more delicate emotionally than the women.

These people are not easily satisfied, as their expectations tend to keep growing. They actively pursue success, but to realize their potential, they must develop their aesthetic sense, become more flexible in communicating with others, and broaden their frame of reference. They require much attention to maintain a good emotional balance. In order to keep the attention they desire, they must learn to consider others more.

DOUGLAS FAIRBANKS, SR. —May 23, 1883
GARY COOPER —May 7, 1901
LAURANCE S. ROCKEFELLER —May 26, 1910
EVA PERON —May 7, 1919

LIBERACE—May 16, 1919
MARGOT FONTEYN—May 18, 1919
GEORGE CARLIN—May 12, 1937
CANDICE BERGEN—May 9, 1946
CHER—May 20, 1946

JUNE **9**-1-4

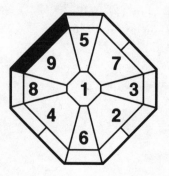

DATES THE MONTHS CHANGE

JUNE 5–JULY 6, 1892	JUNE 6–JULY 7, 1946
JUNE 6–JULY 7, 1901	JUNE 6–JULY 7, 1955
JUNE 7–JULY 7, 1910	JUNE 6–JULY 6, 1964
JUNE 6–JULY 6, 1919	JUNE 6–JULY 6, 1973
JUNE 6–JULY 6, 1928	JUNE 6–JULY 6, 1982
JUNE 6–JULY 7, 1937	JUNE 6–JULY 6, 1991

PROUD *OBSTINATE*
FORESIGHTFUL *SELF-ASSERTIVE*
CONFIDENT *IMPULSIVE*
BRIGHT *TENACIOUS*

These people are usually confident and foresighted, having traits that can help them achieve success. They are often self-assertive and can concentrate tenaciously on a problem to the point of being obstinate. They are usually proud, bright, and independent; these qualities can help them in their work if they are careful not to ignore the feelings and ideas of others. If they allow their impulsive nature to overrule their intelligence, they may have difficulty getting along with people.

A kind of superiority complex can cause them to see only one side of issues. If they realize they have this problem, they can correct it and become good leaders.

They often have close family ties and are protective of outside criticism of the family. Within the family, however, they can be quite critical.

Generally these people are lucky in life. They usually manage to get good positions and make enough money to satisfy their pride.

Their weakness, a tendency to protect themselves too much, can insulate them from the real world.

Sometimes they go to great lengths to retain their superiority in situations, occasionally even using questionable methods to stay on top.

Women of this type are especially proud and self-assertive, but in respect to love or emotion, they tend to become impulsive. This can make it difficult for them to find satisfactory mates. They like tender, conservative men. Men of this type are often especially bright but tend to have trouble attracting mates because of their air of superiority. Both the men and women have leadership potential if they overcome a narrow, self-centered view of life and consider other people and situations fully.

When these people take advantage of foresight and are careful not to let stormy, self-assertive feelings overwhelm others, they can usually become successful and productive.

ACHMED SUKARNO—June 6, 1901
JEANNETTE MACDONALD—June 18, 1901
ROBERT PRESTON—June 8, 1919
E. G. MARSHALL—June 18, 1919
CHE GUEVARA—June 14, 1928
ANNE MURRAY—June 20, 1946
SYLVESTER STALLONE—July 6, 1946

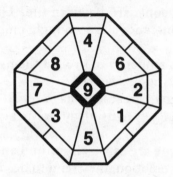

DATES THE MONTHS CHANGE

JULY 7–AUGUST 6, 1892	JULY 8–AUGUST 7, 1946
JULY 8–AUGUST 7, 1901	JULY 8–AUGUST 7, 1955
JULY 8–AUGUST 7, 1910	JULY 7–AUGUST 6, 1964
JULY 7–AUGUST 7, 1919	JULY 7–AUGUST 7, 1973
JULY 7–AUGUST 7, 1928	JULY 7–AUGUST 7, 1982
JULY 8–AUGUST 7, 1937	JULY 7–AUGUST 7, 1991

PROUD	*IMPULSIVE*
FORESIGHTFUL	*MOODY*
GENEROUS	*PRETENTIOUS*
ENTERTAINING	*STUBBORN*

This type is usually proud and foresightful. They like to be the center of attention. Without attention they tend to feel isolated. They appear to be creative in their endeavors but do not always have the organizational ability necessary to carry through.

They can often be entertaining and generous in social situations and are sympathetic to others, attracting people. However, their impulsiveness can make them agreeable one day and disagreeable the next.

This type of person can be very friendly and convincing but may not always provide factual information. They often persuade people to believe they have qualities or knowledge they may not really possess.

Making decisions can be difficult for this type because they are often moody and let their emotions affect their decisions. They sometimes have a tendency to show off or to be pretentious, especially under the influence of a stronger power. Usually, however, they are less confident on their own.

Generally they are not domestic types. They have an outgoing, changeable nature that often leads them to exotic experiences and rich relationships.

Women of this type can be very independent, talkative, and proud, but they need someone to support their ideas and goals if they are to be at their best. The men get along well with women and give the appearance of being very reliable and trustworthy. However, they can be very self-indulgent and stubborn. Both the men and women can be too protective of their pride. Before they have much life experience, they need others' guidance and acceptance. They need reassurance that their ideas and opinions are worthwhile. Choosing the right people, who will support them in sound decision making until they themselves are mature enough to be truly independent, is their key to success.

If these usually generous, entertaining people can control their tendency to be moody and impulsive, they can expect successful lives.

ALEXANDRE DUMAS—July 24, 1802
GEORGE BERNARD SHAW—July 26, 1856
BENITO MUSSOLINI—July 29, 1883
BILL COSBY—July 12, 1937
PETER DUCHIN—July 28, 1937
ALFONSE M. D'AMATO—August 1, 1937
LINDA RONSTADT—July 15, 1946

AUGUST 9-8-6

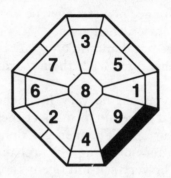

DATES THE MONTHS CHANGE

AUGUST 7–SEPTEMBER 6, 1892	AUGUST 8–SEPTEMBER 7, 1946
AUGUST 8–SEPTEMBER 7, 1901	AUGUST 8–SEPTEMBER 7, 1955
AUGUST 8–SEPTEMBER 7, 1910	AUGUST 7–SEPTEMBER 6, 1964
AUGUST 8–SEPTEMBER 7, 1919	AUGUST 8–SEPTEMBER 7, 1973
AUGUST 8–SEPTEMBER 7, 1928	AUGUST 8–SEPTEMBER 7, 1982
AUGUST 8–SEPTEMBER 7, 1937	AUGUST 8–SEPTEMBER 7, 1991

PROUD　　　　　　*SELF-INDULGENT*
DIGNIFIED　　　　 *VAIN*
AMBITIOUS　　　　*INFLEXIBLE*
INTELLIGENT　　　*OBSTINATE*

Most people of this type tend to be strong on the outside and soft on the inside. They are usually proud and dignified. They also tend to be ambitious and intelligent. Their ambition can be so strong it can at times make them greedy or lead them to lose their ability to be moderate.

Their minds are usually active, and they tend to be quick to sense new trends. Their pride leads them to expect perfection, slowing their ability to make decisions.

Because they tend to be self-indulgent, they search for personal satisfaction and tend to be unsympathetic to the ideas and needs of others.

They often have a dignified appearance and good mind for planning large-scale projects. However, carried too far, this quality can make them vain and obstinate.

Women of this type are usually more proud and ambitious than the men, and they have the ability to shoulder responsibility. However, they must be careful not to become vain or proud, or their self-indulgence will isolate them. They actually are less independent than they want to appear. Men of this type need strong guidance in decision-making. They tend to have a polished or sophisticated way about them that attracts people, but they must not let this quality become overbearing.

Most of this type give great consideration to the accumulation of money or the achievement of fame, and often they are lucky in these areas. If these people are careful to control their pride and vanity and listen to good advice when it is offered, they can usually find success.

HERBERT HOOVER—August 10, 1874
MAE WEST—August 17, 1892
SYLVIA SIDNEY—August 8, 1910
GEORGE WALLACE—August 25, 1919
HENRY FORD II—September 4, 1919
ANN BLYTH—August 16, 1928
DUSTIN HOFFMAN—August 8, 1937
ROBERT REDFORD—August 18, 1937
SUSAN ST. JAMES—August 14, 1946
BARRY GIBB—September 1, 1946

SEPTEMBER 9–7–7

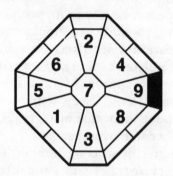

DATES THE MONTHS CHANGE

SEPTEMBER 7–OCTOBER 7, 1892	SEPTEMBER 8–OCTOBER 8, 1946
SEPTEMBER 8–OCTOBER 8, 1901	SEPTEMBER 8–OCTOBER 8, 1955
SEPTEMBER 8–OCTOBER 8, 1910	SEPTEMBER 7–OCTOBER 7, 1964
SEPTEMBER 8–OCTOBER 8, 1919	SEPTEMBER 8–OCTOBER 7, 1973
SEPTEMBER 8–OCTOBER 7, 1928	SEPTEMBER 8–OCTOBER 7, 1982
SEPTEMBER 8–OCTOBER 8, 1937	SEPTEMBER 8–OCTOBER 8, 1991

PROUD　　　　　　　*HYPERSENSITIVE*
ORGANIZED　　　　　*CALCULATING*
EASYGOING　　　　　*PASSIONATE*
GENEROUS　　　　　　*SELF-CONSCIOUS*

These people are usually proud and generous. They can appear easygoing, quiet, and slow-moving, yet beneath the surface often lies a rather passionate, stormy nature. Balancing these opposing qualities can be an ongoing challenge for them.

They usually have a delicate, nervous temperament and, because they can be hypersensitive, they may be touchy, easily influenced by circumstance. Their pride and self-consciousness can make them self-protective, afraid of criticism from others. Although they may not show that they are upset, their sensitivity can seriously affect their physical condition. If they can't balance their stormy natures, their lives can be a series of ups and downs, depending on their emotional reactions.

This type of person often has a naturally calculating mind and an ability to organize most situations very well. They are less successful with their personal affairs, especially if they must face issues they find troublesome, complicated, or unpleasant. They tend to avoid distasteful situations to the point of appearing lax or unable to carry through. They often change directions rather than remain in an unpleasant situation for long. However, once they want something, they usually work very hard for it, expending great energy and giving much attention to detail.

This type can be very generous and will often spend money lavishly on personal pleasure or on friends and lovers. They often have a sense of beauty and good taste but must beware of vanity. Again, caution and balance in these matters are best.

These people are usually looking for someone fun to be with, and in love they are playful but rarely serious. Because of their easygoing approach, they are often misunderstood and may find relationships difficult, despite their passionate search. Their careless expression makes others doubt their sincerity and think them incapable of deep commitment.

Women of this type may be more proud and appear more independent than the men. They usually seek ambitious, self-motivated men. The men may appear unreliable but, in fact, can be very hardworking. They seem to like women who are tender. Both the men and women of this type have the ability to make firm decisions; this gives them excellent opportunities for future growth.

As long as their lives are controlled by pride and hypersensitivity, this type may have a hard time. These people need experience to help them keep their easygoing yet sensitive natures in balance and bring out their self-confidence. They benefit greatly from finding a good assistant, someone who can allow them to be the center of attention, yet who will protect them from negative outside influences that can upset their delicate nerves. Once this type can sustain confidence over a period of time and keep their stormy nature under control, they can give much positive energy to achieving their goals.

WILLIAM PALEY—September 28, 1901
JOSEPH PASTERNAK—September 19, 1901
GEORGE PEPPARD—October 1, 1928
JULIET PROWSE—September 25, 1937

OCTOBER 9-6-8

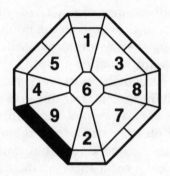

DATES THE MONTHS CHANGE

OCTOBER 8–NOVEMBER 6, 1892	OCTOBER 9–NOVEMBER 7, 1946
OCTOBER 9–NOVEMBER 7, 1901	OCTOBER 9–NOVEMBER 7, 1955
OCTOBER 9–NOVEMBER 7, 1910	OCTOBER 8–NOVEMBER 6, 1964
OCTOBER 9–NOVEMBER 7, 1919	OCTOBER 8–NOVEMBER 6, 1973
OCTOBER 8–NOVEMBER 7, 1928	OCTOBER 8–NOVEMBER 7, 1982
OCTOBER 9–NOVEMBER 7, 1937	OCTOBER 9–NOVEMBER 7, 1991

PROUD	*CAUTIOUS*
INTUITIVE	*SELF-MOTIVATED*
DETAIL-MINDED	*STORMY*
CHARISMATIC	*INFLEXIBLE*

These people are usually bright and intuitive, yet cautious, tending to move according to what they feel will benefit them most at any given time. Although their appearance is usually tender, they are proud and self-motivated. They have a strong desire to control situations and be in positions of leadership. However, their pride and personal ambition can sometimes make them appear self-important. This may isolate them from others, making leadership difficult. They are more successful if they look at facts and circumstances with an open mind and a greater concern for others.

Often they control things by using their keen senses. They usually have naturally intuitive minds and fine powers of concentration and are enthusiastic about applying their energies to one aspect of life. However, their basic nature may also be stormy and changeable, so their focus can shift rather easily. Despite good intentions and persistence, they may have trouble finishing tasks.

These people often inherit money or position or may be taken into an established venture by another person. At times they can be distant from their families, for although they are usually affable in social situations, their domestic or personal relationships may be adversely affected by their sometimes self-important appearance. Their sharp discrimination, coupled with their tendency to give detached criticism, can make others think them heartless or uncaring. If these individuals expect to become good leaders, they must learn to broaden their focus and consider others more, especially when they size up situations and deal with facts.

Once they face opposition, they fight stubbornly to keep control. They are often inflexible. However, because they are not always strong enough to get involved in unpleasant situations, they generally try to avoid them.

Women of this type are intelligent, strong-willed, proud, and often inflexible. Given their strong-willed appearance and high expectations, they may have difficulty finding the right person and being fully satisfied. The men are also proud and strong-willed, driven by a self-motivated ambition that can easily cause them to lose their consideration for others, making leadership problematic. With age they develop a more conservative approach to life.

For these people, intuition and self-motivation are connected. Self-motivation pushes them to hurry ahead, while caution and their intuitive feelings tend to color their decisions and effect how they move, as well. Given their stormy inner nature, this can be changing constantly—up one minute and down the next. If people of this type can keep a focus on one matter over a period of time and learn to consider others more, they are capable of realizing their leadership potential.

MARIE ANTOINETTE—November 2, 1775
RITA HAYWORTH—October 17, 1919
THE SHAH OF IRAN (Muhammad Reza Pahlevi)—October 26, 1919
MARTIN BALSAM—November 4, 1919
BEN VEREEN—October 10, 1946
SUZANNE SOMERS—October 16, 1946
SALLY FIELD—November 6, 1946

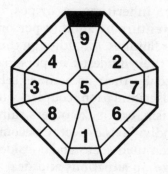

DATES THE MONTHS CHANGE

NOVEMBER 7–DECEMBER 6, 1892	NOVEMBER 8–DECEMBER 7, 1946
NOVEMBER 8–DECEMBER 7, 1901	NOVEMBER 8–DECEMBER 7, 1955
NOVEMBER 8–DECEMBER 7, 1910	NOVEMBER 7–DECEMBER 6, 1964
NOVEMBER 8–DECEMBER 7, 1919	NOVEMBER 7–DECEMBER 6, 1973
NOVEMBER 8–DECEMBER 6, 1928	NOVEMBER 8–DECEMBER 6, 1982
NOVEMBER 8–DECEMBER 6, 1937	NOVEMBER 8–DECEMBER 6, 1991

PROUD　　　　　　　　　*STORMY*
DETERMINED　　　　　　*TENACIOUS*
AGGRESSIVE　　　　　　*PRETENTIOUS*
CANDID　　　　　　　　*HAUGHTY*

These people are often quite proud and aggressive. They can be very determined and hard to satisfy, yet they will make the necessary effort to reach goals.

They are usually candid and their attitude can be overly honest and aggressive, tending to make them appear haughty. Most are willing to accept any challenge and work hard to carry a project through. They are often tenacious and unwilling to give up.

They like to be showy and can be easy prey to people who flatter them. Because they are usually stubborn and stormy, they become impatient easily.

They can often be good leaders but must be aware of their difficulties in creating harmonious relationships with their family or staff. They give much attention to money matters, and their hard work usually helps them earn enough to enjoy life.

Women of this type tend to like stylish, magnanimous men. They may prefer to lead in their relationships. Most of the men become good leaders when they make an effort to create harmony with their associates and to avoid being haughty.

This type, in general, has a strong urge to complete tasks, hating to leave anything unfinished. There is always the possibility for these people to be "heroes." On the other hand, if they fail to make an effort to control their weaknesses—aggressive pride and failure to consider others—they can become completely isolated.

If people of this type try to see the strengths and talents of others, they will be able to better balance their strong nature and become well-adjusted, important members of their group.

ZACHARY TAYLOR—November 24, 1784
WINSTON CHURCHILL—November 30, 1874
SAM SPIEGEL—November 11, 1901
LEE STRASBERG—November 17, 1901
WALT DISNEY—December 5, 1901
MICKEY MOUSE—November 18, 1928
ANDY WILLIAMS—December 3, 1928

DECEMBER 9-4-1

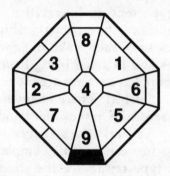

DATES THE MONTHS CHANGE

DEC. 7, 1892–JANUARY 4, 1893	DEC. 8, 1946–JANUARY 5, 1947
DEC. 8, 1901–JANUARY 5, 1902	DEC. 8, 1955–JANUARY 5, 1956
DEC. 8, 1910–JANUARY 5, 1911	DEC. 7, 1964–JANUARY 4, 1965
DEC. 8, 1919–JANUARY 6, 1920	DEC. 7, 1973–JANUARY 5, 1974
DEC. 7, 1928–JANUARY 5, 1929	DEC. 7, 1982–JANUARY 5, 1983
DEC. 7, 1937–JANUARY 5, 1938	DEC. 7, 1991–JANUARY 5, 1992

PROUD　　　　　　*EMOTIONAL*
SERIOUS　　　　　　*INSECURE*
PATIENT　　　　　　*STUBBORN*
ADAPTABLE　　　　　*VAIN*

This type is usually very serious and patient in working toward goals. They are adaptable to new situations but can be stubborn about the importance of details. Generally they do not complain or express their discontent and are therefore easy to get along with.

Usually this type has great pride and tends to be vain. A kind of insecurity leads them to expend great effort to succeed. They often work hard for the applause of others.

Most are serious and have a strong sense of justice and responsibility. If they are pressured unreasonably, they may become unexpectedly stubborn and aggressive, collecting strength from others to fight back.

These people are often bright and quick-witted but slow to make decisions. When they are comfortable, they can be very adaptable. However, if they become insecure and emotional, making decisions becomes even harder for them.

Women of this type tend to be vain. They have strong maternal instincts and may become frustrated if they cannot control those around them. Men of this type are usually very serious about their goals in life. They like quiet, independent women.

In general, many of this type had great influence from their parents when young.

These people give great attention to their finances and tend to spend money to satisfy their vanity as readily as they spend it on their ordinary expenses.

Often they are not easily satisfied in life, tending to strive hard to get ahead. They need to make an effort to focus their minds on what is really important. Then they can expect success.

WOODROW WILSON—December 28, 1856
J. PAUL GETTY—December 15, 1892
SUN MYUNG MOON—January 6, 1920
JACK LORD—December 30, 1928
DYAN CANNON—January 4, 1929
JANE FONDA—December 21, 1937
PATTY DUKE—December 14, 1946

JANUARY **9**-3-2

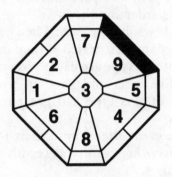

DATES THE MONTHS CHANGE

JANUARY 5–FEBRUARY 2, 1893	JANUARY 6–FEBRUARY 4, 1947
JANUARY 6–FEBRUARY 4, 1902	JANUARY 6–FEBRUARY 4, 1956
JANUARY 6–FEBRUARY 4, 1911	JANUARY 5–FEBRUARY 3, 1965
JANUARY 7–FEBRUARY 4, 1920	JANUARY 6–FEBRUARY 3, 1974
JANUARY 6–FEBRUARY 3, 1929	JANUARY 6–FEBRUARY 3, 1983
JANUARY 6–FEBRUARY 3, 1938	JANUARY 6–FEBRUARY 3, 1992

PROUD　　　　　　　*STRONG DESIRES*
SENSITIVE　　　　　 *PERFECTIONISTS*
STEADY　　　　　　 *SELF-CONSCIOUS*
AGGRESSIVE　　　　 *CAUTIOUS*

Most of these people are proud and sensitive, possessing great physical and spiritual desires. They often consider situations cautiously and, if they remain calm, exercise flexibility of judgment. However, if caution forces them to hold their emotions inside, their sensitive nature may react suddenly and unexpectedly. At times, their feelings explode outward in forceful, direct expression that may be shocking to others. Once their pride is hurt, they may lose their balance completely, becoming surprisingly aggressive, ready to fight to the end.

Despite a rather direct frankness, most have a conservative side. They usually consider others in work or business, making the effort to create good staff relationships. They also generally help their families or blood relations, perhaps assuming additional responsibility in a crisis.

Their great pride may push them to seek perfection in everything they do. They can be fussy over small points. This aspect of their character can make them lose steadiness, and they may hurt themselves by missing opportunities or by pushing past the point of their endurance as they seek their goal. They must be aware of the imbalance between their strong curiosity and their tendency to hold their feelings inside. Indeed, it is difficult for these people to express themselves subtlely. They tend either to hold it all in or release it in a flood. This tendency can affect their reputation.

Many of these people have been strongly influenced by their mothers. The men are a little self-conscious and may strive to appear stronger than they really are. They are proud, expecting perfection in everything. It is often hard for them to express themselves naturally or to find an understanding partner. The women are often proud and sensitive, generally expressing their feelings very directly. Although they are sentimental and tend to seek out love, their desires are strong and not easily satisfied. It is sometimes difficult for them to put themselves in a dependent role. Both the men and the women give great energy to the pursuit of satisfaction, in money matters and in affairs of the heart. They have good business minds, although they may expect perfection in their work.

The main problem for this type is usually the inability to control desires. Their expectation for satisfaction is often so great that they can hardly make use of the natural steadiness that can serve them so well. Before they seek perfection, they need to know how far they can go without hurting themselves. In controlling their desires and developing moderate goals, they can gradually find the means to express their personality and achieve greater success.

D. W. GRIFFITH—January 22, 1875
FEDERICO FELLINI—January 20, 1920
MARTIN LUTHER KING—January 15, 1929
JULES FEIFFER—January 26, 1929
DAVID BOWIE—January 8, 1947

THE BASIS OF THE KI

The modern generation has great mobility and seems to have limitless choices of direction. It is important to think about where you are headed and the consequences of your actions before you move. How are you to know what is right for you when you face an important decision in life?

Individual Ki-energy must work in harmony with the Ki-energy of nature so that life moves along smoothly. Movement that is not in harmony leads to problems.

DIRECTION AND DEGREE

The charts in this study are divided into eight directions. Traditionally, the direction north is located at the bottom segment of the chart. The other directions are read clockwise from there: north —northeast—east—southeast—south—southwest—west—northwest—north.

The four cardinal directions (north, south, east, west) are divided into segments of 30 degrees. The four corner segments (northeast, southeast, southwest, northwest) encompass 60 degree slices.

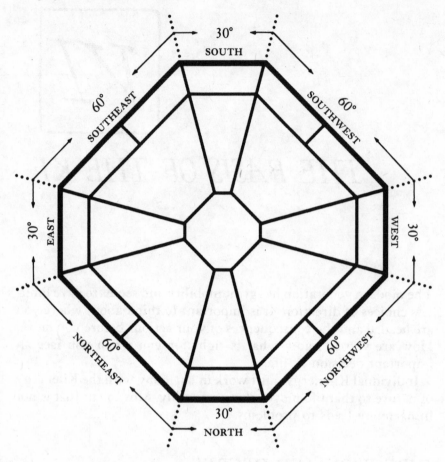

TWELVE ANIMAL ZODIAC SIGNS

In ancient China, farmers heralded the changing seasons observing the growing processes of plants and the activities of animals.

Later, during the Han dynasty (200 B.C.–220 A.D.), the emperor picked twelve familiar animals to represent the zodiac so that farmers who could not read could better adjust to the seasons and the cardinal directions.

In the following charts, the twelve Animal Zodiac Signs and their corresponding months and directions appear in their stationery positions. The Rat (north) represents December; Ox (northeast) represents January; Tiger (east-northeast) represents February; Rabbit (east) represents March; Dragon (east-southeast) represents April; Snake (south-southeast) represents May; Horse (south) represents June; Sheep (south-southwest) represents July; Monkey (west-southwest) represents August; Rooster (west) represents September; Dog (west-northwest) represents October; Boar (north-northwest) represents November.

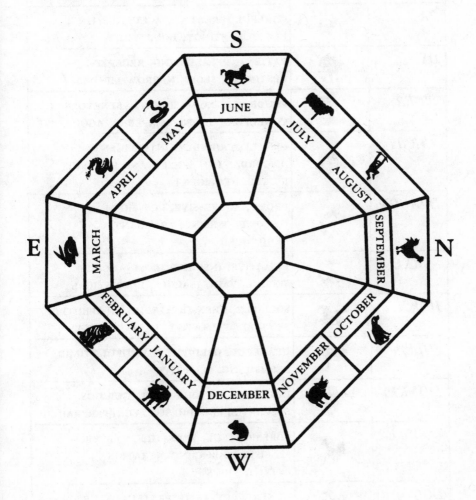

The Animal Zodiac Signs influence the numbers with characteristics as shown on the following chart:

ANIMAL ZODIAC SIGNS

ANIMAL SIGNS		TRAITS
RAT		CAREFUL, CREATIVE, ACCUMULATING, LUSTFUL, STINGY, DOUBTFUL
OX		PATIENT, PERSEVERING, RECEPTIVE, OBSTINATE, SLOW, NARROW-MINDED
TIGER		PRUDENT, COMPASSIONATE, BENEVOLENT, CONCEITED, SHORT-TEMPERED, AGGRESSIVE
RABBIT		GENTLE, FRIENDLY, INTELLIGENT, DISCORDANT IN SPEECH AND BEHAVIOR, FICKLE, NEGLIGENT
DRAGON		PROUD, AGGRESSIVE, POWERFUL, UNCOMPROMISING, ARROGANT, PREJUDICED
SNAKE		INTUITIVE, INSIGHTFUL, FINANCIALLY SECURE, VAIN, JEALOUS, EGOTISTICAL
HORSE		SOCIABLE, KEEN-SIGHTED, HIGH-SPIRITED, SENSUAL, TALKATIVE, EASY TO ANGER
SHEEP		GRACEFUL, OBEDIENT, FAITHFUL, TIMID, PESSIMISTIC, SENSITIVE
MONKEY		INGENIOUS, RESOURCEFUL, CURIOUS, SUSCEPTIBLE, IMPULSIVE, SCATTERBRAINED
ROOSTER		FORESIGHTFUL, VERSATILE, CLEVER, SELFISH, POOR CONCENTRATION, OSTENTATIOUS
DOG		HONEST, LOYAL, RESPECTFUL, STUBBORN, ASSERTIVE, DEMANDING
BOAR		SERIOUS, JUST, GOOD DISPOSITION, RECKLESS, IMPATIENT, INFLEXIBLE

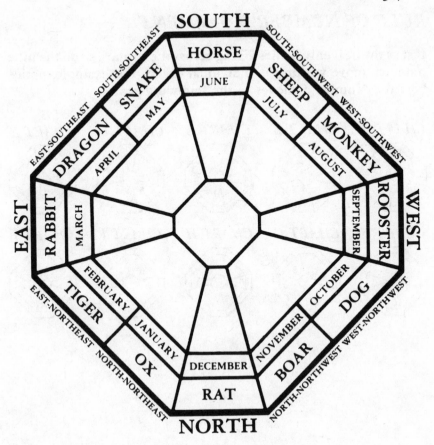

The twelve Zodiac Signs separate into three groups, each of which works with three of the nine numbers:

Rat, Rabbit, Horse, Rooster: 1,4,7

Ox, Dragon, Sheep, Dog: 3,6,9

Tiger, Snake, Monkey, Boar: 2,5,8

For example, the year of the Rat has to fall in a year of 1, 4, or 7. The Rat could not work with 3 or 2.

We use the Animal Zodiac Signs when dealing with direction to help us identify "good" or "bad" movement. Note that although the Monthly Animal Zodiac Chart is fixed, the Yearly Animal Zodiac Sign changes each year for twelve years, then repeats. (see p. 334)

RULE OF NUMBER MOVEMENT

Just as the heavenly bodies zigzag across the cosmos, so do the nine numbers move within the individual charts. For example, notice how the Number 5 moves in the following charts.

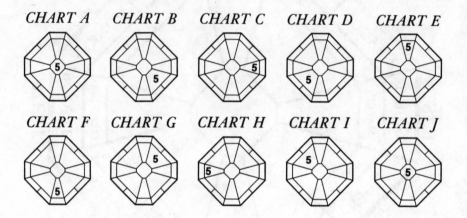

From the starting point in the center of Chart A, Number 5 moves northwest (Chart B) then west (Chart C). Use the following chart to learn how all the numbers move. It will be easier to learn if you follow a number consecutively.

NUMBER	DIRECTION
5	CENTER
6	NORTHWEST
7	WEST
8	NORTHEAST
9	SOUTH
1	NORTH
2	SOUTHWEST
3	EAST
4	SOUTHEAST
5	CENTER

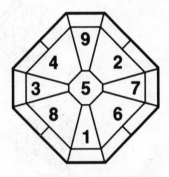

For example, the number in the center always moves northwest, the northwest number always moves west, and so on. (Follow the arrows in the chart.)

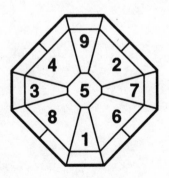

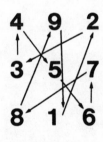

or

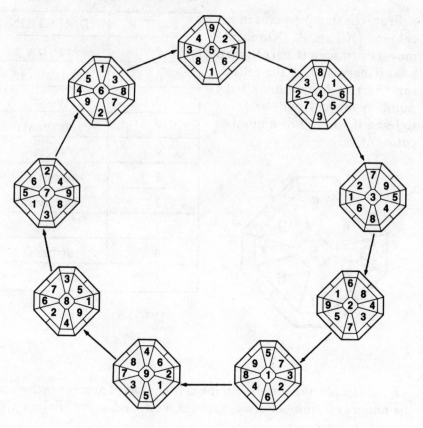

In this manner, the Yearly and Monthly Charts are generated.
This Rule for Number Movement always applies.

DIRECTION OF MOVEMENT

A BRIEF SUMMARY

According to Oriental thought, human beings are a part of nature, and just as Ki-energy fills human life and affects our relationships and communication with others, so it fills nature and the cosmos and affects the direction in which humans and nature move. Ancient Oriental philosophy teaches us to move in directions that are harmonious and to recognize the danger of moving against nature. The nine numbers speak for this fundamental principle as they must move in logical ways that conform to nature.

It is often necessary to think of *movement* literally, using the direction of the chart that follows, to work with the Ki-energy inherent in the patterns evolved by the ancients and incorporated into their charts for Direction of Movement.

By realizing that we are affected by Ki-energy, we establish sensitivity to the energy of natural phenomena and the energy of other human beings. From this opening and understanding, we can derive greater meaning from our daily life.

I would like to tell you about the "movement" of some of my clients as illustration of the importance of Direction of Movement.

Three years after I had advised a very influential lawyer, I was shocked to see the headline in the *New York Post* (dated November 18, 1980) LAWYER INDICTED IN 750G BILK TO PAY FOR HAREM. This was the handsome real estate lawyer who had come to me in 1977. He was a good provider to a wife and five children, and both he and

Designed by Kuni Hashimoto

his father had excellent reputations for their honesty. He had made a potentially destructive move from Brooklyn to mid-Manhattan in 1973. I explained to him that the Ki-energy of the direction in this movement was completely out of harmony and suggested that he leave the new location before he fell into a trap, since he was already beginning to have problems. He agreed, but for some reason never relocated. Eventually he went to jail and the Bar Association took away his license.

Another client, an elderly woman, asked me whether she should live near her son or her daughter after the death of her husband. I checked the time and the direction and suggested her son, but she chose to move near the daughter. A year later her daughter called to tell me that her mother was seriously ill. I told the daughter to find a doctor located in the correct direction from where she lived. She then followed the doctor's advice to have surgery and recovered. I recommended she move in her son's direction, which was again correct for the time. Recently, she called me from there, sounding quite happy. She also told me why she hadn't moved there before: she hadn't wanted to disrupt her son's family life.

As with this elderly woman, wrong *Movement* can be corrected before serious harm occurs, but it calls for patience and a strong will. When faced with an uncomfortable situation, many people simply resign themselves to their fate or assume they're "unlucky." Of course, this is not true, especially if you consider the important role that proper movement plays in your happiness. Let's look at it this way. You do something, and the result turns out poorly for you, but it's a situation you can't avoid. You're then faced with a choice. You can either use a tremendous amount of energy to free yourself from the situation, or you can move to another location to avoid the consequences. Maybe the whole thing never would have happened if you hadn't done what you did in the first place!

But how do you know which way is right for you? Everybody has to make decisions that are hard to live with. If you make a wrong choice, you become disappointed, and if you repeat this process enough, you may begin to doubt your decision-making ability.

To develop self-confidence, you can use the Ki-system to help you make the right decisions. Very often, movement is more important than many people realize. Since this is just an introduction to Direction, I will focus mainly on how the Basic Number works direction-wise in a time chart.

SEVEN KINDS OF DANGEROUS MOVEMENT

The concept of movement is controlled by the nature of the Five Elements. A move toward one will be reciprocated by a result based on the "nature" of the element. For example, Number 5, which is a number of power, will, if opposed, destroy another number. Movement toward this potentially destructive number indicates a dangerous situation.

There are seven kinds of dangerous movement:

1. *Honmei-Satsu*   (Attack of the self)
2. *Honmei-Teki-Satsu*   (Attack of your own mind)
3. *Go-O-Satsu*   (Destruction)
4. *Anken-Satsu*   (Accidental Direction)
5. *Sai-Ha*   (Break-up, lack of energy—yearly)
6. *Getsu-Ha*   (Break-up, lack of energy—monthly)
7. *Joi-Taichu*   (Opposition)

HONMEI-SATSU (Attack of the Self)

When you move on a time chart in the direction of your Basic Number, it is called *Honmei-Satsu*.

CHART OF 1984
(Year of 7)

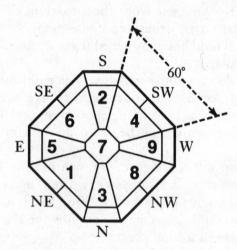

If, in this case, your Basic Number is 4, and you move to the southwest in 1984, this creates the movement of *Honmei-Satsu*. You can cause yourself to have trouble. You attack yourself in a way that can affect your health—possibly developing a serious illness. You may even lose your life.

HONMEI-TEKI-SATSU (Attack of Your Own Mind)

If you move toward the position opposite your Basic Number, it is called *Honmei-Teki-Satsu*. You attack your own mental condition, which leads to disorganization. You can literally lose your mind.

CHART OF 1973
(Year of 9)

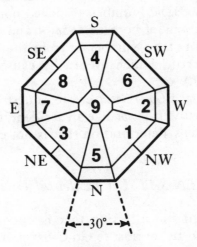

For example, remember the lawyer whose Basic Number was 4. The move from Brooklyn, where his office was, to mid-Manhattan was north, directly opposite his Basic Number 4 during that year, 1973. This movement led to an imbalance in his mental condition —a lack of conscious control over his action. (This represents the rebounding of the substance of his character back against itself.) The movement to mid-Manhattan made his business busier and his social life more active. This was too sudden a change, for he was used to a more conservative, family-oriented situation. As his thinking changed, he became vain, reckless, and thoughtless. He eventually had to face the bitter reality of his actions. Because he had lost his mental balance, he also created *Go-O-Satsu*, which doubled his trouble. (See next example.)

GO-O-SATSU *(Destruction)*

A movement toward Number 5 is called *Go-O-Satsu*. Number 5 has the Ki-energy capability to change and destroy all creatures. A move toward the Number 5 direction can lead you into serious situations: to a serious illness or to being the victim of a crime; to the failure of a business venture, job, or investment; or to some other personal calamity. If you have Number 5 as your Basic

Number, you must be especially careful not to cause *Honmei-Satsu* and *Go-O-Satsu*, which makes for double difficulty. For example, when the lawyer (Basic Number 4) moved north in 1973, it was toward the directions of both *Go-O-Satsu* and *Honmei-Teki-Satsu*. When he moved north (Number 5) from south (Number 4), he made a double error, which eventually caused the ruin of his career. (See chart.)

Movement toward *Go-O-Satsu* creates a destructive effect in us that works gradually. It is *not* like an accident; rather it automatically initiates a slow deterioration that is not easily reversed.

ANKEN-SATSU (Accidental Direction)

Movement toward the direction that is opposite Number 5 is called *Anken-Satsu.* In contrast to Go-O-Satsu, it is movement that affects us suddenly and over which we have no control. It is very difficult to defend ourselves from this kind of accidental trouble. We cannot always avoid traffic accidents, injuries, or troubles that someone else causes, such as fraud or robbery.

CHART OF 1979
(Year of 3)

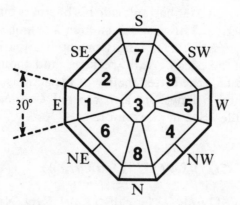

For example, a painter friend of mine moved from California to New York in 1979. A little while later, he was attacked in the elevator of his apartment building and had to be hospitalized. Shortly after his release, unbelievably, he was attacked again. At that point, he was ready to give up. I advised him to move in a direction that would correct this Anken-Satsu movement and prevent further mishaps.

When the reader uses the chart shown here, they show *Anken-Satsu* by making a triangle at the appropriate direction point on the charts using the *ANKEN-SATSU* chart.

This chart shows the direction and the number of *Anken-Satsu* in each year. The first column is a list of the center numbers of the individual charts, Yearly and Monthly.

ANKEN-SATSU

NUMBER OF YEAR AND MONTH	NUMBER OF DIRECTION
1	NORTH 6
2	SOUTHWEST 8
3	EAST 1
4	SOUTHEAST 3
5	
6	NORTHWEST 7
7	WEST 9
8	NORTHEAST 2
9	SOUTH 4

SAI-HA (Yearly: Break-up; Lack of Energy)

Each year, the direction that is opposite the Yearly Animal Zodiac Sign is called *Sai-Ha* on the Yearly Chart. This chart shows the direction of *Sai-Ha* in each Yearly and Monthly Animal position by showing its opposing position. Anyone who takes the direction that is *Sai-Ha* cannot possibly accomplish his purpose. Movement in this direction can cause you to be involved in break-ups, separations, contract failures, and other worrisome problems.

GUIDE FOR SAI-HA AND GETSU-HA
(BREAK-UP, LACK OF ENERGY)

WHEN ZODIAC SIGN	DIRECTION	SAI-H AND GETSU-HA ARE	ZODIAC SIGN	DIRECTION
RAT	N	⟶	*HORSE*	S
OX	NNE	⟶	*SHEEP*	SSW
TIGER	ENE	⟶	*MONKEY*	WSW
RABBIT	E	⟶	*ROOSTER*	W
DRAGON	ESE	⟶	*DOG*	WNW
SNAKE	SSE	⟶	*BOAR*	NNW
HORSE	S	⟶	*RAT*	N
SHEEP	SSW	⟶	*OX*	NNE
MONKEY	WSW	⟶	*TIGER*	ENE
ROOSTER	W	⟶	*RABBIT*	E
DOG	WNW	⟶	*DRAGON*	ESE
BOAR	NNW	⟶	*SNAKE*	SSE

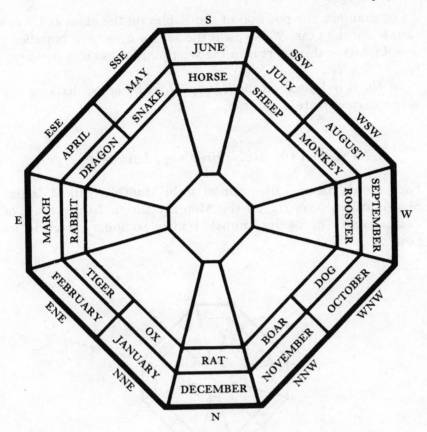

The Yearly Animal Zodiac Sign for 1987 is the Rabbit.

CHART OF 1987
(Year of the Rabbit)

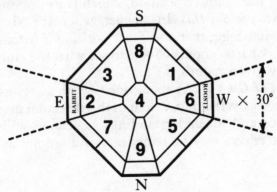

For example, the position of the Rabbit on the chart is always east, so for the year 1987, west is the *Sai-Ha* direction. Number 6 (the Rabbit) in this chart is in the west position, so it is the direction of *Sai-Ha*.

Sai-Ha is indicated on the Yearly Chart by an × marking the appropriate direction point.

GETSU-HA (Monthly: Break-up, Lack of Energy)

Each month, the opposite position of the Monthly Animal Zodiac Sign is called *Getsu-Ha* on the Monthly Chart. In the chart of Zodiac signs, the twelve animals remain stationary, each in its position.

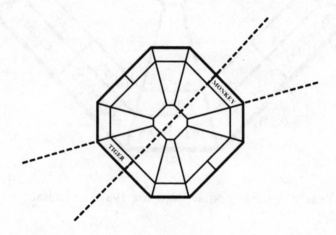

For example, every February, when the Tiger is the Monthly Zodiac Sign, the Monkey position, which is its opposite, is *Getsu-Ha* (see chart for *Sai-Ha*). In August, when the Monkey is the Monthly Zodiac Sign, then the Tiger position is *Getsu-Ha*. (Check the Monthly Charts on pp. 400–408 to see what the Animal Zodiac Sign for any given month is.)

The effect of *Getsu-Ha* is about one-twelfth as severe as that of *Sai-Ha*. This means that movement in this direction may still cause the break-ups and misunderstandings associated with this position, but the effects may be temporary and are not as intense.

JŌI-TAICHU (Opposition)

Of the seven dangerous directions, this is a special case.

Every year, one of the nine numbers appears on the Yearly Chart in a position opposite its position on the Universal Chart, except for the year that Number 5 controls. For example, in 1987, if we compare the Yearly and Universal Charts, we find that Number 9 will be opposite itself (See following charts). This position is known as *Jōi-Taichu*, or Opposition, and for the year 1987, it appears in the north. If you will move toward this direction in 1987, you will not find matters as you expected them; rather, you will meet with opposition. Number 9 will not work like Number 9. Very often it causes little troubles to repeat and pile up until small difficulties (such as family disagreements) became big problems.

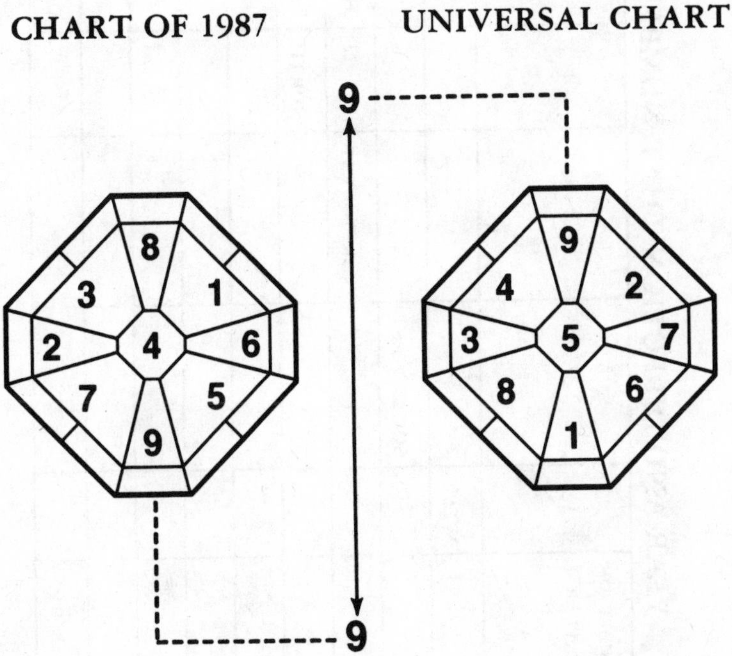

CHART OF 1987   UNIVERSAL CHART

The following chart shows which year numbers are *Jōi-Taichu*, and at which direction points. (Note: *Jōi-Taichu* does not occur during the year of Number 5, when all numbers are in their basic positions for a one-year period.)

Jōi-Taichu also appears in a different position each month (see

YEAR AND DIRECTION THAT NUMBERS ARE JŌI-TAICHU

JŌI-TAICHU NUMBER	NUMBER OF THE YEAR								
	1	2	3	4	5	6	7	8	9
3	WEST								
8		SOUTHWEST							
4			NORTHWEST						
9				NORTH					
5									
1						SOUTH			
6							SOUTHEAST		
2								NORTHEAST	
7									EAST

charts) on the Monthly Charts, and its effects are similar, although for a much shorter period of time. (Note: *Jōi-Taichu* does not occur during a month of Number 5, when all the numbers are in their basic position for a one-month period.) July of 1987 puts Number 4 as the Jōi-Taichu direction for the month, in the position of Northwest.

MONTH OF JULY, 1987   **UNIVERSAL CHART**

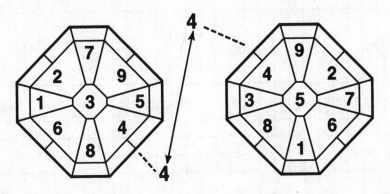

During the times of these seven dangerous directions, you should not consider permanent residence changes, business relocations, or extended trips that would force you to move toward one or more of them. However, if you must take a business trip or want to vacation during these times, select a good month to travel and don't stay for a long period of time. In this way, you can avoid at least some of the negative effects. But you must be careful!

HOW TO USE THE YEARLY CHART SYSTEMS FOR PROPER MOVEMENT

How do you find the correct yearly movement for any Basic Number? With the Yearly Chart Systems given here, it is possible to see which directions are good or bad for any Basic Number in any given year.

Let's suppose your Basic Number is 6. It's 1987 and you're contemplating a move west, to California from New York. How can you tell whether it's a good year to make that move?

THE RELATION OF THE NINE NUMBERS TO THE YEAR AND TWELVE ANIMAL ZODIAC SIGNS

No.	Year	Sign	No.	Year	Sign	No.	Year	Sign	No.	Year	Sign
2	1890	TIGER	8	1893	SNAKE	5	1896	MONKEY	2	1899	BOAR
8	1902	"	5	1905	"	2	1908	"	8	1911	"
5	1914	"	2	1917	"	8	1920	"	5	1923	"
2	1926	"	8	1929	"	5	1932	"	2	1935	"
8	1938	"	5	1941	"	2	1944	"	8	1947	"
5	1950	"	2	1953	"	8	1956	"	5	1959	"
2	1962	"	8	1965	"	5	1968	"	2	1971	"
8	1974	"	5	1977	"	2	1980	"	8	1983	"
5	1986	"	2	1989	"	8	1992	"	5	1995	"

No.	Year	Sign	No.	Year	Sign	No.	Year	Sign	No.	Year	Sign
3	1889	OX	9	1892	DRAGON	6	1895	SHEEP	3	1898	DOG
9	1901	"	6	1904	"	3	1907	"	9	1910	"
6	1913	"	3	1916	"	9	1919	"	6	1922	"
3	1925	"	9	1928	"	6	1931	"	3	1934	"
9	1937	"	6	1940	"	3	1943	"	9	1946	"
6	1949	"	3	1952	"	9	1955	"	6	1958	"
3	1961	"	9	1964	"	6	1967	"	3	1970	"
9	1973	"	6	1976	"	3	1979	"	9	1982	"
6	1985	"	3	1988	"	9	1991	"	6	1994	"

No.	Year	Sign	No.	Year	Sign	No.	Year	Sign	No.	Year	Sign
4	1888	RAT	1	1891	RABBIT	7	1894	HORSE	4	1897	ROOSTER
1	1900	"	7	1903	"	4	1906	"	1	1909	"
7	1912	"	4	1915	"	1	1918	"	7	1921	"
4	1924	"	1	1927	"	7	1930	"	4	1933	"
1	1936	"	7	1939	"	4	1942	"	1	1945	"
7	1948	"	4	1951	"	1	1954	"	7	1957	"
4	1960	"	1	1963	"	7	1966	"	4	1969	"
1	1972	"	7	1975	"	4	1978	"	1	1981	"
7	1984	"	4	1987	"	1	1990	"	7	1993	"
4	1996	"	1	1999	"	7	2002	"	4	2005	"

1. First look through the Yearly Chart Systems and find which one corresponds to Basic Number 6. (Number in the upper left-hand corner of the page.) The nine charts on that page determine proper movement for all people with Basic Number 6. Other Basic Numbers should find their charts accordingly.

2. Since 1987 is the year in question, look at the chart that shows the nine numbers in relation to the years and the Twelve Animal Zodiac signs. Find 1987 and note down the "number of the year" to the left, which is 4, and the Animal Zodiac Sign, which is the Rabbit.

3. Look again at the Yearly Chart Systems for Basic Number 6. The number in the center of each chart represents the year. Locate the chart with 4 in the center. Notice the unshaded, or open, directions. These are the correct directions for a Basic Number 6 to move in 1987.

Note: You must still check for possible *Sai-Ha*, using the chart on page 328. For example, 1987 is the year of the Rabbit (east), so the Rooster (west) is in the position of *Sai-Ha* for the year. And also, west is the position of Number 6 in 1987, which is Honmei-Satsu for Number 6 (see page 323).

Taking all this into account, a person with a Basic Number 6 should not move west (shaded) in 1987. Nor should anyone move west, which is the *Sai-Ha* position. The favorable directions are south, southwest and northeast.

PRACTICE CHART (DIRECTION)

DIRECTION CHART

Name:_____

Date of Birth:_____

Basic Number:_____

When:_____

Zodiac Sign:

DIRECTION CHART

Name:_____

Date of Birth:_____

Basic Number:_____

When:_____

Zodiac Sign:

DIRECTION CHART

Name:_____

Date of Birth:_____

Basic Number:_____

When:_____

Zodiac Sign:

DIRECTION CHART

Name:_____

Date of Birth:_____

Basic Number:_____

When:_____

Zodiac Sign:

YEARLY CHART SYSTEMS

1

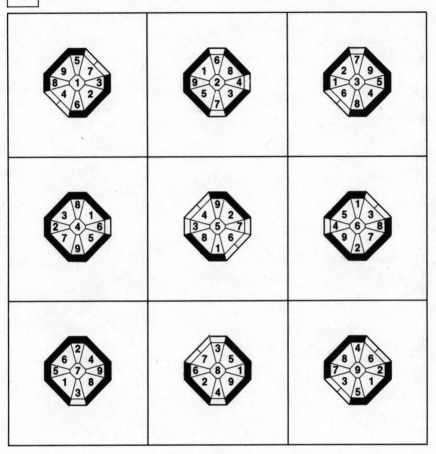

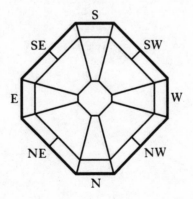

YEARLY CHART SYSTEMS

2

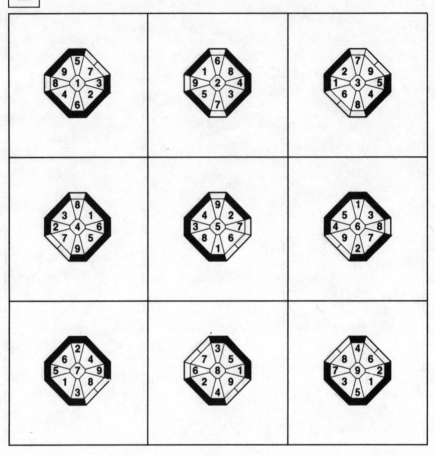

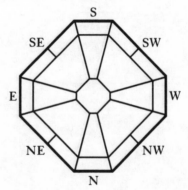

YEARLY CHART SYSTEMS

3

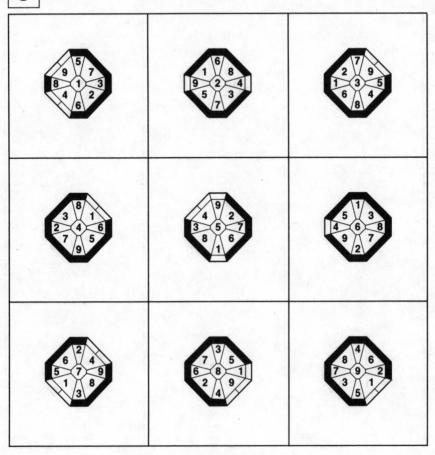

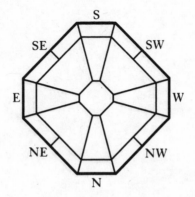

YEARLY CHART SYSTEMS

4

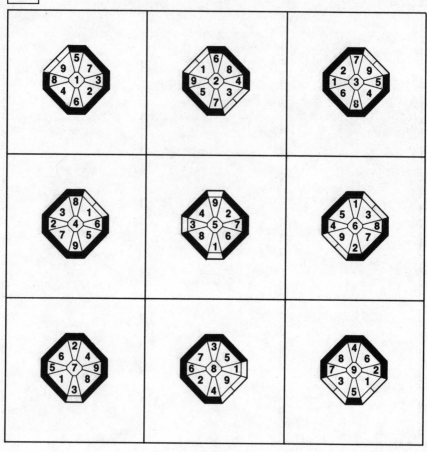

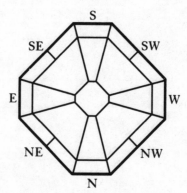

YEARLY CHART SYSTEMS

5

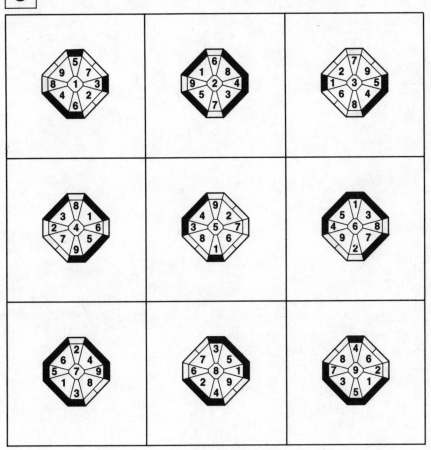

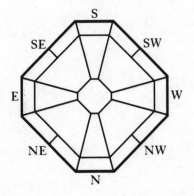

YEARLY CHART SYSTEMS

6

5 7 9 8 1 3 4 2 6	6 1 8 9 2 4 5 3 7	7 2 9 1 3 5 6 4 8
8 3 1 2 4 6 7 5 9	9 4 2 3 5 7 8 6 1	1 3 5 6 8 4 9 7 2
2 6 4 5 7 9 1 8 3	3 7 5 6 8 1 2 9 4	4 8 6 7 9 2 3 1 5

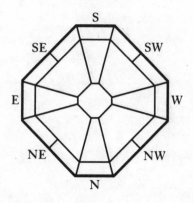

YEARLY CHART SYSTEMS

7

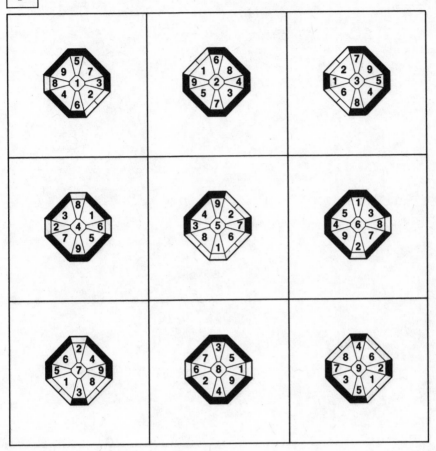

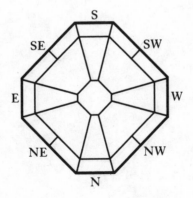

YEARLY CHART SYSTEMS

8

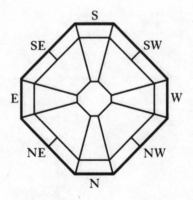

YEARLY CHART SYSTEMS

9

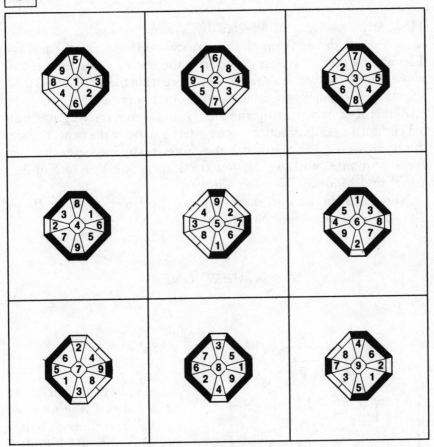

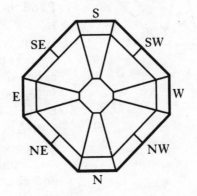

EFFECTS OF DIRECTION ON THE NINE NUMBERS

How, exactly, are you affected by a move toward a particular direction? It depends on the reciprocal relationship of the Five Elements. Clearly, Ki-energy controls the results. This section will show each number in the various directions, and the possible effects of movement in each case on other numbers.

Remember, when using the charts, that your starting position when figuring out direction is considered to be at the center of the chart. However, the number in the center really indicates the time (year or month) with which you are dealing (see Yearly Number Chart and Monthly Number Chart).

Note: You should note on each chart the direction of *Sai-Ha* or *Getsu-Ha* (see Guide for *Sai-Ha* and *Getsu-Ha*).

NUMBER ONE

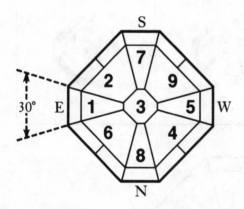

EAST

As shown on this chart of Number 3 (the number in the center), east (Number 1) is opposite Number 5 and therefore is the direction of *Anken-Satsu*, which is not good for anybody.

1. Your crimes may be exposed.

2. You could be stabbed because of sexual violence.

3. You could sustain a great loss because of a business connection that may go bankrupt.

4. You may be deceived by your friends and your employees.

5. You may have surgery.

6. You may become involved in other people's troubles.

SOUTHEAST

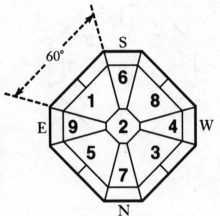

This direction is good for Numbers 4, 6, and, 7. A move to the southeast by Numbers 4, 6, and 7 only will result in the following effects:

1. There is the possibility for improved reputation or a good marriage.

2. You have a chance to meet the right person for your life.

3. You have a chance to meet a good friend from far away who will bring you good luck.

4. There is the possibility for new contracts.

If Numbers 1, 2, 3, 5, 8, or 9 take this direction, its effects are as follows:

1. Problems that cause you to lose your reputation may arise.

2. You encounter trouble from people far away.

3. You may catch a cold or develop an illness.

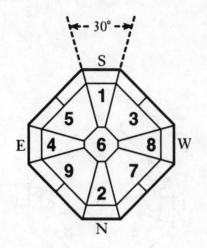

SOUTH

This direction is bad for everybody, because it is the direction of *Joi-Taichu*.

1. This causes divorce problems.

2. You may separate from someone close.

3. You may lose your reputation.

4. You may suffer from eye troubles.

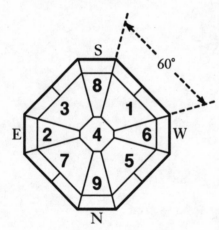

SOUTHWEST

This direction is good for Numbers 3, 4, and 6.

1. You may have a good chance for success.

2. Someone may appear who will help you physically or mentally.

3. Your stomach condition will improve and bring you better health.

This direction is bad for Numbers 1, 2, 5, 7, 8, and 9.

1. You could lose your home.

2. You could lose your job or suffer from dire poverty.

3. You could develop stomach troubles.

WEST

This direction is good for those after middle age because it leads to a kind of settled condition. (It is not a direction to give much energy toward developing life.) This position is good for Numbers 3, 4, and 7.

1. Finances will be better, and financial situations easier.

2. Income will increase gradually.

3. You may expect joy from romance.

This direction is bad for Numbers 1, 2, 5, 6, 8, and 9.

1. You may develop an excessive sexual appetite or a drinking problem.

2. You may develop an illness that will take a long time to recover from, such as lung or kidney problems.

NORTHWEST

This direction is good for Numbers 3, 4, 6, and 7.

1. You have the chance to meet a patron (backer) from whom you will receive financial aid.

2. As a result of a superior's assistance, you may establish a new business.

3. You may have a

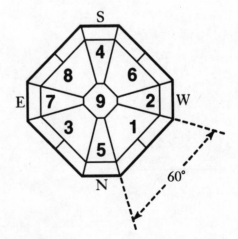

chance to become acquainted with people of high status.

This direction is bad for Numbers 1, 2, 5, 8, and 9.

1. You may lose your home or savings, because of a new venture or investment.

2. You may get a position of leadership, but it could cause you problems.

3. You could have a disagreement with your boss.

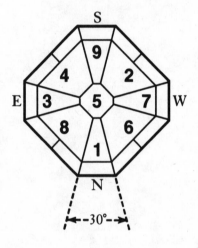

NORTH

This direction is good for Numbers 3, 4, 6, and 7, but good or bad, it is not the direction for a permanent residence, because you cannot expect positive development.

1. Good for retirement, hiding, planning secretly, and quiet living.

2. A chance to get honor from your social conditions.

This direction is bad for Numbers 1, 2, 5, 8, and 9.

1. You may fall into dangerous intrigue or get a sexually transmitted disease.

2. You may develop health problems.

3. You may have sexual problems.

NORTHEAST

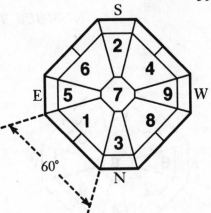

This direction is good for Numbers 3, 6, and 7.

1. You may receive cordial treatment from your relatives and acquaintances.

2. You may expect improvement in your life situation and a turn of events for the better.

3. You may adjust your family situation by adopting an heir.

It is better to use this direction as an emergency aid to pull you out of the fire. If you are in a satisfactory situation now, it is not for you. If you move to the northeast (1) it is better to move there within four years, even if there may be some other, better development, because if you stay there too long, you may lose energy, which can have a bad effect.

This direction is bad for Numbers 1, 2, 4, 5, 8, and 9.

1. You may have many problems caused by your relatives or acquaintances.

2. You may become greedy, leading to failure.

3. You may get lower back pain or aching joints.

NUMBER TWO

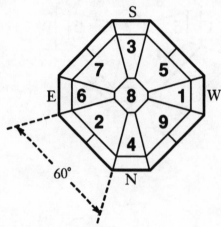

NORTHEAST

This direction is *Anken-Satsu* and also *Joi-Taichu* (see charts on page 327 and page 332) and, as such, is bad for everyone.

1. You may be robbed.

2. You may have constant troubles with your relatives.

3. You may have a recurrence of an old illness or need an operation.

4. You may have a very difficult time in your business or job.

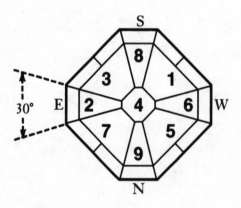

EAST

This direction is good for Numbers 5, 7, 8, and 9.

1. Things may begin to develop the way you want.

2. You may have good health, which will help you accomplish hard work.

3. You may gain efficiency in your work or an outside activity (having the help of strong young labor in business, for example).

This direction is bad for Numbers 1, 2, 3, 4, and 6.

1. Loss of funds may jeopardize your business or job.

2. You may lose your job.

3. You may face the recurrence of an old scandal.

4. A secret fortune you are hiding may be found by someone. You may lose face when it is discovered.

5. Your efforts may be immobilized.

SOUTHEAST

This direction is good for Numbers 5, 6, 7, 8, and 9.

1. You may get a job you have been looking for.

2. You may get profitable advice about real estate.

3. You may find a good person to marry.

This direction is bad for Numbers 1, 2, 3, and 4.

1. You may delay your marriage or break your engagement.

2. A business that has been moving smoothly may become troubled, and you may lose the possibility for new development.

3. You may lose an inheritance.

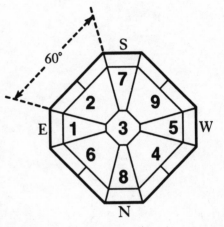

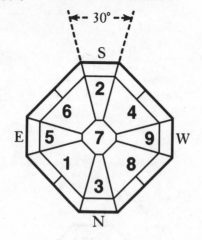

SOUTH

This direction is good for Numbers 5, 6, 7, 8, and 9, but you may face a separation or divorce if you are married. A married person has to be careful about moving in this direction.

1. You may get a creative idea or learn a trick that will help you in your career.

2. You may receive a profit from an investment in real estate.

3. You may improve your business.

This direction is bad for Numbers 1, 2, 3, and 4.

1. You may exercise bad judgment. You may make some costly mistakes.

2. You may become involved in troubles from a trifling matter that, to your discredit, may become public knowledge.

3. You may lose property.

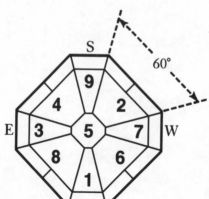

SOUTHWEST

This direction is good for Numbers 5, 6, 7, and 9.

1. You may expect appointment to a sound position in your business, because of your hard work, diligence, and steadiness.

2. You may develop a peaceful life with your family.

This direction is bad for Numbers 1, 2, 3, 4, and 8.

1. This direction may cause you to become lazy and lose your zeal, causing you to lose your reputation.

2. You may develop stomach troubles.

WEST

This direction is good for Numbers 5, 6, 8, and 9. Young people may develop the habit of taking the easy way by depending on someone else.

1. You may expect good profit from buying or selling property.

2. You may receive good income from hard work.

3. You can expect a good chance to marry because of your sex appeal and diligence.

This direction is bad for Numbers 1, 2, 3, 4, and 7.

1. You may develop stomach troubles as a result of irregular eating habits. This may become chronic.

2. You may become emotionally overburdened as a result of losing your job, or a business slowdown.

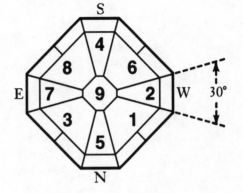

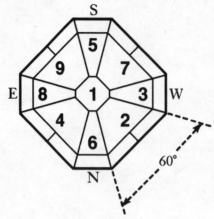

NORTHWEST

This direction is good for Numbers 5, 6, 7, and 8.

1. You may gradually gain a good social reputation after a charitable contribution.

2. Your serious efforts may lead you to gain credit and a chance to succeed in high circles.

This direction is bad for Numbers 1, 2, 3, 4, 5, and 9.

1. You may lose your reputation through bad harmony with the boss.

2. You may face difficulty in your business because of a shortage of capital.

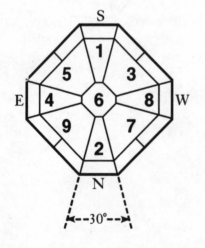

NORTH

This direction is good for Numbers 5, 6, 7, 8, and 9, but married people may face the possibility of a new love affair.

1. You may expect good and hardworking help in your business or job.

2. You may find a happy new relationship.

3. You may receive an increase in income through a second job.

This direction is bad for Numbers 1, 2, 3, and 4.

1. You may face diffi-

culty related to money, health, or robbery. These difficulties may occur again in the future.

NUMBER THREE

SOUTHEAST

This direction is *Anken-Satsu,* and is bad for everyone (see p. 327).

1. You may lose your property in a fire.

2. You may lose prestige because employees run away with your valuables.

3. You may talk carelessly and cause yourself trouble.

4. You may have trouble with your liver or your vocal cords.

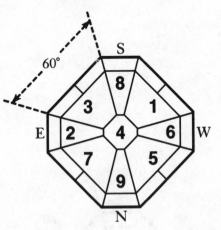

SOUTH

This direction is good for Numbers 1 and 9, but no matter what your number, you may face a divorce or separation if you are married. A married person has to be careful about moving in this direction.

1. You may gain honor for an invention or discovery.

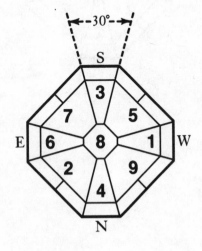

2. You may receive public recognition for your talent or eloquence.

3. You may earn public esteem for a new plan or workshop.

This direction is bad for Numbers 2, 3, 4, 5, 6, 7, and 8.

1. You may unintentionally expose a past misdeed and lose your reputation.

2. You may have a fire.

3. You may suffer problems because of a letter or important papers you may receive.

SOUTHWEST

This direction is good for Numbers 1 and 4.

1. You may develop your business or your job smoothly and steadily as a result of good advice.

2. You may improve your reputation by giving a lecture or teaching a course.

3. You may receive public recognition for previous scholarship.

This direction is bad for Numbers 2, 3, 5, 6, 7, 8, and 9.

1. You may make many mistakes in your new job or business.

2. You may lose your

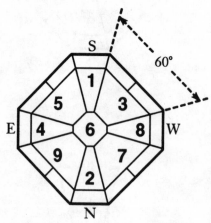

reputation by your false-
hoods and fabrications.

3. You may develop lazy
habits or be dissipated by
pleasure.

WEST

This direction is *Joi-Tai-
chu*, and consequently is
bad for everyone (see p.
332).

1. You may lose your
reputation by a careless expression.

2. You may lose money
by someone's malicious
lies or your own hastiness.

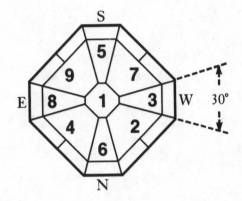

NORTHWEST

This direction is good
for Numbers 4 and 9.

1. Your business or job
may improve and your
reputation increase be-
cause of a new plan.

2. You may have a crea-
tive idea that will develop
into a large-scale project.

3. You may receive capi-
tal or help in a new project.

This direction is bad for
Numbers 1, 2, 3, 5, 6, 7, and
8.

1. You may hope to make
a fortune in a single stroke
and fail.

2. You may waste your

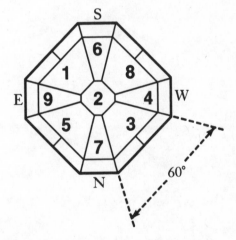

money by expanding your social life.

3. You may earn a bad reputation because of your relatives' possessiveness.

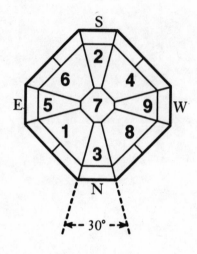

NORTH

This direction is good for Numbers 1, 4, and 9, but married people have to be careful. They may get into trouble because of another love affair.

1. You may succeed because of behind-the-scenes maneuvering.

2. You may develop happiness as a result of a wise decision.

3. You may experience good luck through new social connections.

This direction is bad for Numbers 2, 3, 5, 6, 7, and 8.

1. You may lose your reputation because you are hiding something.

2. You may have trouble with your nervous system.

3. A love affair may lead you to make mistakes.

4. An employee may get you into trouble by lying.

NORTHEAST

This direction is good for Numbers 1, 4, and 9.

1. You may improve your life situation by a decisive action.

2. You may earn a good reputation by helping your relatives.

3. You may hear good news about real estate.

4. This direction is good to use to improve a declining health condition.

However, anyone who takes this direction to establish a residence or business headquarters should move to the next advantageous direction. This direction is bad for Numbers 2, 3, 5, 6, 7, and 8.

1. You may be hurt by the complaining of your relatives or acquaintances.

2. You may cause troubles between your relatives and your friends.

3. You may have troubles in building a home.

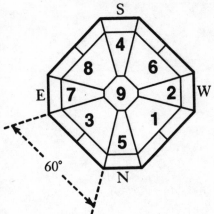

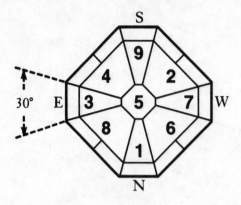

EAST

This direction is good for Numbers 1, 4, and 9.

1. You may get the chance to make a dream an actuality.

2. You may find the energy necessary to develop a new career.

3. You may find you are able to express yourself much better.

4. You may receive recognition for a hitherto unknown talent.

This direction is bad for Numbers 2, 3, 5, 6, 7, and 8.

1. You may lose patience, leading you to failure.

2. Someone else's lie could get you in trouble.

NUMBER FOUR

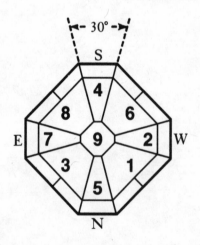

SOUTH

This direction is *Anken-Satsu*, and so is bad for everyone (see p. 327).

1. You may have an argument with your spouse.

2. You may have a separation or break-up as a result of your bad reputation.

3. You may become in-

volved in criminal activity and go to jail.

4. You may have a heart attack or stroke.

SOUTHWEST

This direction is good for Numbers 3 and 9.

1. You may gain a good reputation in the eyes of many people.

2. Someone may help you get a good, steady job.

3. You may earn appreciation from your employer for your ability.

4. You may find good connections that will help expand and improve your business.

This direction is bad for Numbers 1, 2, 4, 5, 6, 7, and 8.

1. You may develop stomach troubles that will take a long time to disappear.

2. You may lose your job.

3. Your business may slow down.

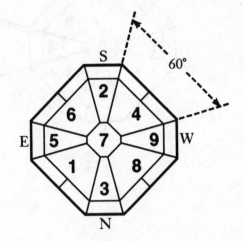

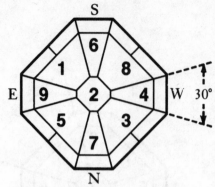

WEST

This direction is good for Numbers 1 and 3.

1. You may have good luck in family or money situations.

2. Single people may expect to find a good person to marry.

This direction is bad for Numbers 2, 4, 5, 6, 7, 8, and 9.

1. You may catch a cold that could lead to pneumonia.

2. You may lend money that becomes irrecoverable.

3. You may cause your family to have trouble.

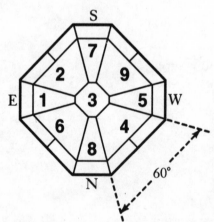

NORTHWEST

This direction is *Joi-Tai-chu,* and so is bad for everyone (see page 332).

1. You may lose your reputation.

2. You may become involved in problems because of participation in a speculative venture.

3. Your new business may fail shortly after it has begun.

NORTH

This direction is good for Numbers 1 and 9, but married persons must be careful about taking this direction. It can lead to finding another lover.

1. You may meet someone from far away and begin a relationship that may lead to marrige.

2. You may receive a big profit from an unknown association or business transaction.

This direction is bad for Numbers 2, 3, 4, 5, 6, 7, and 8.

1. You may lose determination and miss a good opportunity.

2. You may become involved in romantic troubles.

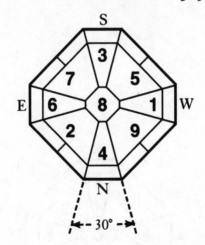

NORTHEAST

This direction is good for Numbers 1, 3, and 9.

1. You may be helped by relatives or friends who are far away.

2. You may change your business or your job, leading to an improvement in your situation.

This direction is bad for Numbers 2, 4, 5, 6, 7, and 8.

1. You may face a sudden

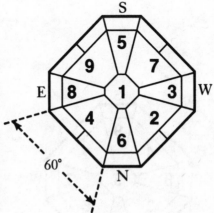

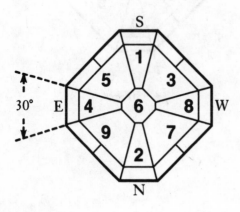

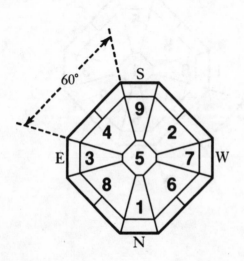

unhappy change in your job or an engagement that has so far proceeded smoothly.

2. Your business may come into difficulty.

EAST

This direction is good for Numbers 1, 3, and 9.

1. You may get a good chance to accomplish your purpose.

2. You may start a new career that will lead to future success.

3. You may discover you have a talent that can bring you success.

This direction is bad for Numbers 2, 4, 5, 6, 7, and 8.

1. You may lose your reputation completely.

2. Your actions cause trouble.

3. You may face difficulty as the result of a failed stratagem or trick.

SOUTHEAST

This direction is good for Numbers 1, 3, and 9.

1. You may become engaged and expect a happy married life.

2. Married persons may expect great developments

in their careers, because of successful planning.

3. You may expect a good contract with a customer from far away.

This direction is bad for Numbers 2, 4, 5, 6, 7, and 8.

1. You may become involved in troubles with someone you helped.

2. You may have troubles with your respiratory system or intestines.

NUMBER FIVE

THIS DIRECTION IS THE DESTRUCTIVE ONE, SO IT IS BAD FOR ABSOLUTELY EVERYONE.

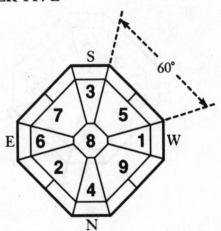

SOUTHWEST

1. You may lose your will to work and you may lose your job or your business will slow down.

2. You may face family disruption.

3. You may become ill.

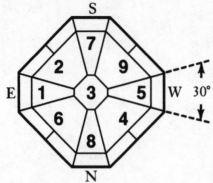

WEST

1. You may have an accident, become wounded, or be injured in an assault or mugging.

2. Your investments may collapse.

3. You may lose your money in pleasure-seeking activities.

4. You may develop a serious illness like tuberculosis or kidney disease.

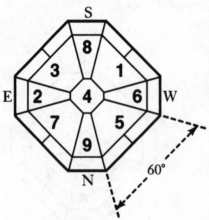

NORTHWEST

1. You may face the death of a father, grandfather, or young child (under four years old).

2. You may cause trouble for your boss and lose your job.

3. You may have to give up your business because of losing a sponsor.

4. You may try to make a fortune in a single stroke (as in investments or speculation) and lose all your money.

5. You may have a traffic accident, heart attack, or stroke or suffer a broken bone.

NORTH

1. You may suffer from fraud or extortion.

2. You may get a serious illness.

3. Your close friends may leave you, and you may become close with bad friends.

4. You may develop venereal disease, a disease of the urinary tract, or hemorrhoids.

5. You may become involved in a sexual scandal.

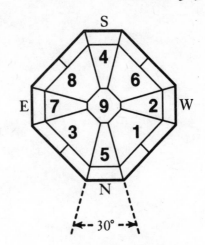

NORTHEAST

1. You may lose your fortune because of cheating by your relatives or friends.

2. You may lose your successor or a close relationship that is very important to your life.

3. You may develop a serious illness relating to the nose, ears, joints, or nerves.

4. You may have troubles with your landlord (or tenant!)

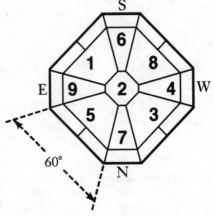

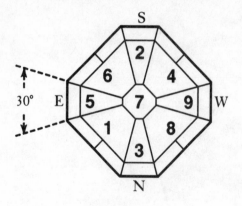

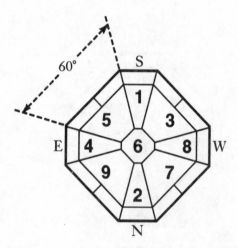

EAST

1. You may be disappointed because of a breakdown in your life's work. You may lose the possibility for future development.

2. You may suffer as a result of your staff or younger people.

3. You may develop a serious illness such as gastric cancer, arteriosclerosis, jaundice, liver problems, nervous prostration, or throat complications.

SOUTHEAST

1. Your engagement may unexpectedly break off.

2. You may lose money or your reputation by falling prey to a malicious trick.

3. You may get a serious illness like a skin disease, respiratory infections, or appendicitis.

SOUTH

1. You may suffer damage because of a legal or criminal case.

2. You may lose money in the stock market.

3. You may lose your reputation by exposure to official corruption.

4. You may develop a serious illness like meningitis, burns, hemorrhage, asthma, eye troubles, or toothaches.

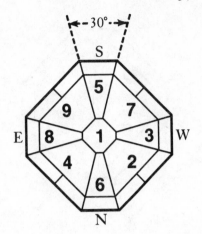

NUMBER SIX

NORTH

This direction is *Anken-Satsu* and consequently bad for everyone.

1. You may lose money in speculation.

2. You may be injured in a traffic accident.

3. You may be driven into a difficult situation by your boss or an older person.

4. You may develop a serious illness like heart disease, high blood pressure, or lung disease.

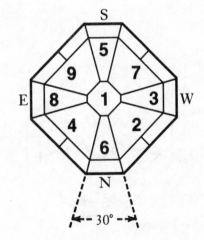

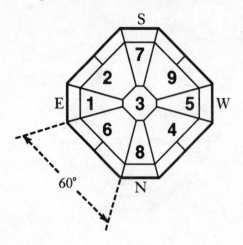

NORTHEAST

This direction is good for Numbers 1, 2, 5, 7, and 8.

1. You may meet a powerful patron who likes your talent.

2. You may get material help from a relative or acquaintance and increase your fortune.

3. You may get a chance to adopt an heir.

This direction is bad for Numbers 3, 4, 6, and 9.

1. You may lose your job unexpectedly.

2. You may quarrel with your relatives or friends.

3. You may get pneumonia.

EAST

This direction is good for Numbers 2, 5, 7, and 8.

1. You may earn a good reputation in your career or position.

2. You may expect good future developments with the help of your boss or an older person.

3. You may receive new support for your new business and have the possibility of future success.

This direction is bad for Numbers 1, 3, 4, 6, and 9.

1. Your overconfidence about a new business or job may bring you troubles.

2. You may become involved in a serious argument with your boss or an older person.

SOUTHEAST

This direction is *Joi-Tai-chu,* and bad for everyone (see p. 332).

1. You may lose money through speculation.

2. You may lose your share of capital.

3. You may catch a bad cold and get pneumonia.

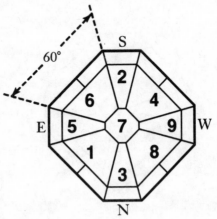

SOUTH

This direction is good for Numbers 1, 2, 5, and 8, but married people may separate.

1. You may come upon a good idea for improving your future planning or present condition.

2. You may receive an honor for an invention or discovery.

3. You may start to work in the political field in order to enhance your future success.

This direction is bad for

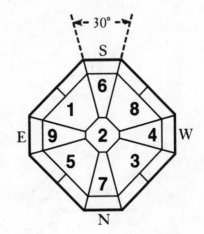

Numbers 3, 4, 6, 7, and 9.

1. Your misjudgment may cause damage to your business or job.

2. You may develop a serious disease of the eyes or of the heart.

SOUTHWEST

This direction is good for Numbers 1, 2, 5, 7, and 8.

1. You may gain a profit from buying real estate.

2. You may get an increase in your income, a promotion by recommendation of your boss or some older person, because of your hard work.

This direction is bad for Numbers 3, 4, 6, and 9.

1. You may lose ambition.

2. You may try to make a quick fortune and fail.

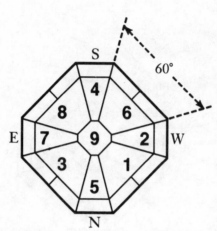

WEST

This direction is good for Numbers 1, 5, 7, and 8.

1. You may expect a superior's help.

2. If you are in business, you may experience an increase in the number of good customers.

3. Your financial condition will improve.

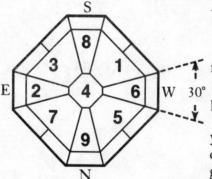

4. You may borrow money necessary for your business.

This direction is bad for Numbers 2, 3, 4, 6, and 9.

1. You may lose your fortune because of personal excess (especially due to sex, but also because of overindulgence in the sensual pleasures—eating, drinking, etc.).

2. A loss of capital may result in business failure.

NORTHWEST

This direction is good for Numbers 1, 2, 5, 7, and 8.

1. You may experience great success through an investment or speculation.

2. You may improve your financial condition because of your hard work.

3. You may be promoted in your position or your reputation.

This direction is bad for Numbers 3, 4, 6, and 9.

1. You may fail in a speculative venture.

2. You may argue with superiors.

3. If you yield to flattery, you can cause troubles.

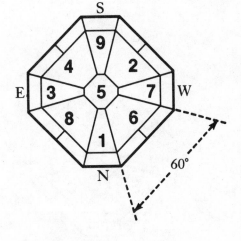

NUMBER SEVEN

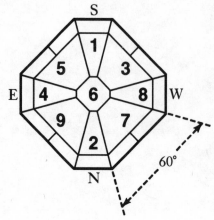

NORTHWEST

This direction is *Anken-Satsu*, and so is bad for everyone (see page 327).

1. You may be wounded.

2. You may have lung or kidney trouble.

3. You may lose your fortune through an affair with the opposite sex.

4. You may lose an inheritance through speculation.

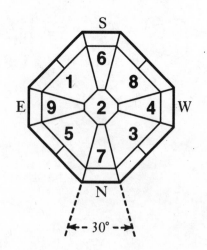

NORTH

This direction is good for Numbers 1, 2, 5, and 8.

1. Your emotional problems may calm down.

2. You may gain extra money from your own excellent idea.

This direction is bad for Numbers 3, 4, 6, 7, and 9.

1. You may give yourself up to sexual situations that lead you to lose your reputation.

2. You may have serious financial difficulties.

NORTHEAST

This direction is good for Numbers 2, 5, 6, and 8.

1. You may get financial help from your relatives or friends.

2. You may expect pleasure from family.

This direction is bad for Numbers 1, 3, 4, 7, and 9.

1. You may overindulge in pleasures, and so lose your steadiness.

2. You may cause an argument with your family.

3. You may get deeper in debt.

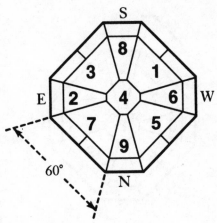

EAST

This direction is *Joi-Tai-chu,* and bad for everyone (see page 332).

1. You may hamper your success by your interference and idle talk.

2. You may be hasty in your plans to achieve success and ruin your career.

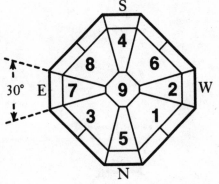

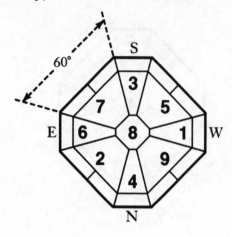

SOUTHEAST

This direction is good for Numbers 1, 2, 5, 6, and 8.

1. Entertaining your clients or people in business may gain you an intimacy that will increase your reputation.

2. Single people may become engaged.

3. If you are looking for a job, someone may help or give advice in getting a good one.

4. You may find yourself in better financial condition.

This direction is bad for Numbers 3, 4, 7, and 9.

1. You may get a cold that develops into a serious respiratory illness.

2. Someone may not pay you; you may incur a bad debt.

SOUTH

This direction is good for Numbers 1, 2, 5, and 6, but married persons have to be careful, as they may face separation problems.

1. Your talent may bring you great success in an artistic field and increase your income.

2. You may gain profit

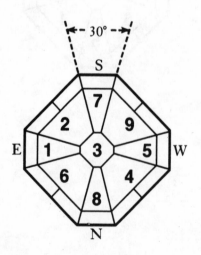

by an investment in stock.

3. You may get a good tip for future investment which will increase your fortune.

This direction is bad for Numbers 3, 4, 7, 8, and 9.

1. You may encounter troubles involving money or sex.

2. Your sharp tongue may cause you to lose your reputation.

SOUTHWEST

This direction is good for Numbers 1, 2, 5, 6, and 8.

1. You may get a steady job or business, connected with money (a restaurant or bar?).

2. You may get the chance to work or have a partnership with a good person.

This direction is bad for Numbers 3, 4, 7, and 9.

1. You may become lazy and slow-witted because of flattery.

2. You may have difficulty as a result of wasting money.

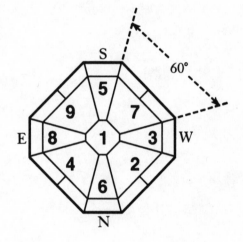

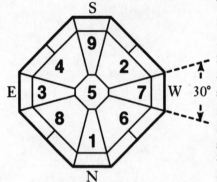

WEST

This direction is good for Numbers 1, 2, 5, 6, and 8. This direction leads to an easy development of life, so young people may lose ambition. They should avoid moving in this direction.

1. You may reach success gradually and expect a comfortable retirement.

2. You may gain enough money to make your life comfortable.

(Conditions 1 and 2 are for people who have made enough of an effort to build a life foundation.)

This direction is bad for Numbers 3, 4, 7, and 9.

1. You may get into the habit of spending money wastefully, and your life may become difficult as a result.

2. You may lose ambition for future planning.

NUMBER EIGHT

SOUTHWEST

This direction is *Anken-Satsu*, and bad for everyone (see page 327).

1. You may face a death in your family.

2. You may lose your savings.

3. You may become involved in your friends' troubles and have difficulties yourself.

4. You may have an operation on your joints, stomach, ears, or nose.

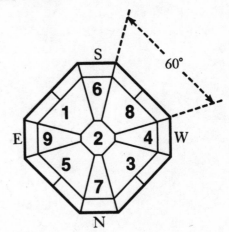

WEST

This direction is good for Numbers 2, 5, 6, 7, and 9.

1. You may receive cooperation and assistance from your relatives or acquaintances, and experience a good career change that will bring you good luck financially.

2. You may expect pleasure at home.

This direction is bad for Numbers 1, 3, 4, and 8.

1. Your relatives or acquaintances may cause financial problems.

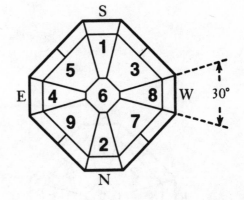

2. Your avarice may cause you irreparable loss.

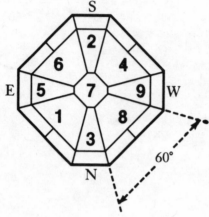

NORTHWEST

This direction is good for Numbers 2, 5, 7, and 9.

1. You may have good luck in finances because a superior becomes your patron.

2. You may improve your finances because of your sincerity and hard work.

This direction is bad for Numbers 1, 3, 4, 6, and 8.

1. You may become involved in troubles with a successor.

2. You may develop a serious illness of the lungs or catch pneumonia, especially if you are the head of your family.

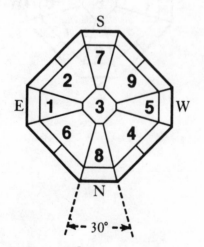

NORTH

This direction is good for Numbers 2, 5, 6, and 9, but married people have to be careful not to become involved sexually with anyone else.

1. You may receive secret assistance from an acquaintance.

2. Your unknown second job may give you extra income.

This direction is bad for Numbers 1, 3, 4, 7, and 8.

1. You may lose your savings by some unexpected misfortune.

2. You may become involved in family problems.

3. You may experience a recurrence of an old illness.

NORTHEAST

This direction is good for Numbers 5, 6, 7, and 9.

1. You may benefit from reorganization and rearrangement.

2. You may increase your real estate by your good judgment.

3. You may become wealthier.

This direction is bad for Numbers 1, 2, 3, 4, and 8.

1. You may have to lend money to your relatives and not be able to get it back.

2. Conditions that have been progressing smoothly may cause you difficulty.

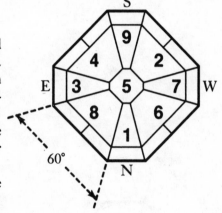

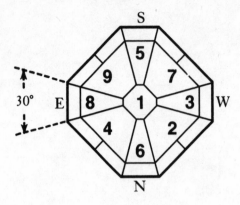

EAST

This direction is good for Numbers 2, 5, 6, 7, and 9.

1. You may reorganize present conditions and gain the possibility of future growth.

2. Your good judgment may bring you better conditions and future success.

This direction is bad for Numbers 1, 3, 4, and 8.

1. You may face a failure in your business or job.

2. Your job or business may be reorganized badly and cause you troubles.

3. You may get neuralgia or hurt your back.

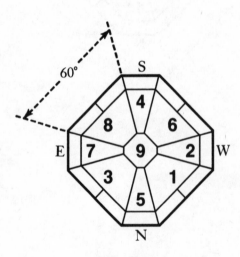

SOUTHEAST

This direction is good for Numbers 2, 5, 6, 7, and 9.

1. Single people may get a chance to marry, because of the help of a relative or acquaintance.

2. You may find a new job through the help of a relative or acquaintance.

3. New development of a social relationship may bring you a positive reorganization of your career or life and promote future success.

This direction is bad for Numbers 1, 3, 4, and 8.

1. Your selfishness and greed may cause you troubles in your married life, and you may be fired from your job.

2. You may become involved in problems with your real estate.

3. Your engagement may break up due to your selfishness, and bring you a bad reputation.

SOUTH

This direction is good for Numbers 2, 5, 6, and 7, but married people must be careful because they may be caused to separate or develop opposing opinions.

1. You may receive great honor for your efforts in an academic or artistic field.

2. You may earn a good reputation from a plan you created.

3. You may get a promotion.

This direction is bad for Numbers 1, 3, 4, 8, and 9.

1. You may have to go to court over inheritance problems.

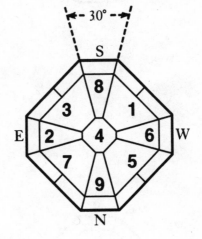

NUMBER NINE

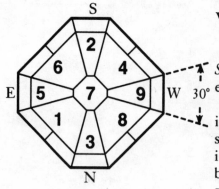

WEST

This direction is *Anken-Satsu*, and so is bad for everyone (see page 327).

1. You may get involved in a lawsuit or experience serious problems pertaining to securities, stocks, bonds, or negotiable instruments.

2. You may become involved in a dispute over a foolish infatuation.

3. You may be hurt by drugs or chemicals.

4. You may have to have an operation of the eyes, face, or brain.

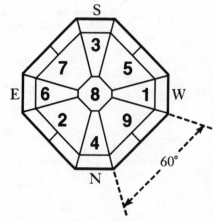

NORTHWEST

This direction is good for Numbers 2, 3, 4, 5, and 8.

1. A person of status or a superior may become your patron because of your talent. You may achieve fame.

2. You may gain a big profit from a sudden rise in stocks.

This direction is bad for Numbers 1, 6, 7, and 9.

1. You may separate

from the head of your family.

2. You may fail in business because of speculation.

3. You may develop a disease of the heart or pneumonia.

NORTH

This direction is *Joi-Tai-chu,* and bad for everyone (see p. 332).

1. Your parents may separate, and you may lead a lonely life.

2. You may have an accident that causes your family and close friends to stay away from you. It may cause you difficulty, both mentally and financially.

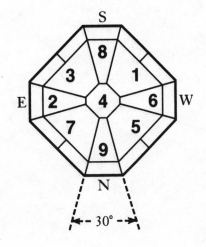

NORTHEAST

This direction is good for Numbers 2, 4, 5, and 8.

1. You may change and reorganize your life, influencing your career favorably.

2. You may remodel or build a new house.

3. You may unexpectedly succeed in real estate ventures.

This direction is bad for Numbers 1, 3, 6, 7, and 9.

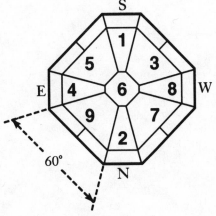

1. You may cause problems with a blood relationship over an inheritance.

2. Your insatiable desires may cause arguments.

Both of these conditions can cause you loss of reputation.

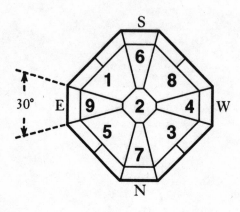

EAST

This direction is good for Numbers 2, 3, 5, and 8.

1. You may receive fame as a result of a successful invention or discovery.

2. You may gain the chance to achieve success because of your talent in an academic or artistic field.

This direction is bad for Numbers 1, 4, 6, 7, and 9.

1. You may be involved in an accident or fire.

2. You may become involved in a scandal, and then have to keep it secret.

3. You may face difficulty because of vanity.

SOUTHEAST

This direction is good for Numbers 3, 4, 5, and 8.

1. You may earn a good reputation on your job through business connected with insurance, shipping or oil.

2. You may expand your business.

3. You may gain a good profit from trade with someone far away.

4. You may expect success through a faraway business.

5. Single people may become engaged.

This direction is bad for Numbers 1, 2, 6, 7, and 9.

1. Your engagement may break up, against your will.

2. You may separate from your wife/husband and family, also against your will.

3. You may have to leave your job.

4. You may make a big mistake in an important document that will cause you troubles.

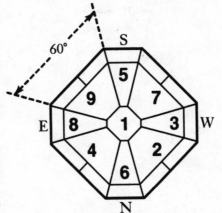

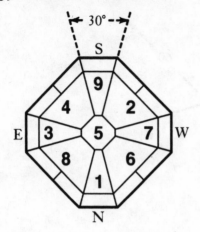

SOUTH

This direction is good for Numbers 2, 3, 4, 5, and 8.

1. You may obtain a promotion and receive honor and status.

2. You may develop a far-seeing intelligence that will bring you future success.

3. You may polish your wisdom and scholarly achievements.

This direction is bad for Numbers 1, 6, 7, and 9.

1. You may lose your reputation by becoming involved in a criminal trial.

2. You may part with a person you relied on.

3. You may become uncomfortable in your own residence.

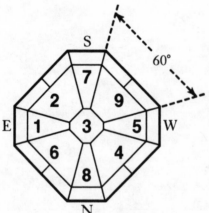

SOUTHWEST

This direction is good for Numbers 2, 3, 4, 5, and 8.

1. You may succeed in business with a partner.

2. You may get a chance to reach future success by your efforts, especially related to the artistic or academic fields.

3. You may get a teaching job in the academic or artistic fields.

This direction is bad for Numbers 1, 6, 7, and 9.

1. You may become involved in a lawsuit and have to dispose of your real estate.

EXAMPLES OF DIRECTION OF MOVEMENT

NAPOLEON BONAPARTE'S DOWNFALL

Birthday: August 15, 1769
Basic Number: 6
Control Number: 8   **6**–8–3
Tendency Number: 3

CHART OF 1812   *NAPOLEON'S CHART*
(**8**)–Number of 1812   **6**–8–3

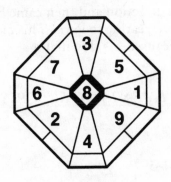

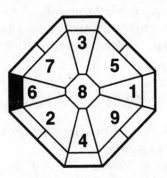

Note that the chart of 1812 is the same as Napoleon's chart! 1812 was a year of Number 8. The directions on this chart show Paris in the southwest and Moscow in the northeast.

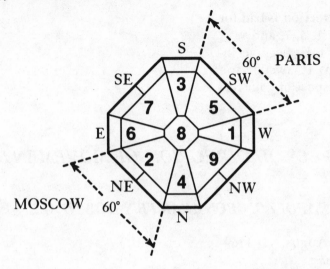

The concept of Direction of Movement is controlled by the nature of the Five Elements. In 1812, the southwest was controlled by Number 5, which we call the *destructive number*. The number opposite Number 5, in this case, Number 2, is in the *Anken-Satsu*, or accidental direction, northeast. So, by moving in 1812 from Paris (southwest) toward Moscow (northeast), Napoleon unwittingly moved toward the accidental direction and then came back toward the destroyer number (5) by retreating to Paris. This movement, *Anken-Satsu* and *Go-O-Satsu*, caused his downfall.

CHARLIE CHAPLIN'S MOVEMENTS TO SUCCESS

Birthday: April 16, 1889
Basic Number: 3
Control Number: 3   **3**–3–5
Tendency Number: 5

CHART OF 1917
(**2**)-Number of 1917

CHARLIE CHAPLIN'S CHART
3–3–5

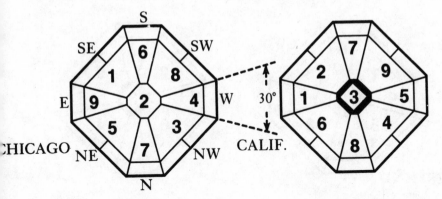

The year 1917 was the year of Number 2. That year, Chaplin moved to California from Chicago, an east-to-west movement. From the Chart of 1917, we can see that Number 4 was in the west position. Since his Basic Number is 3, this move toward Number 4 created a cooperative-relationship response, and the move was not only right for him personally but career-wise.

Also, in 1953, he moved east to Switzerland from the United States. Looking at the Chart for the year 1953, which also was a year of Number 2, we see that again, the west-to-east movement was right for him. Number 9, which was in the east position, created a favorable relationship with his Basic Number, 3. These successive correct movements in his life helped to ensure his success in developing his future.

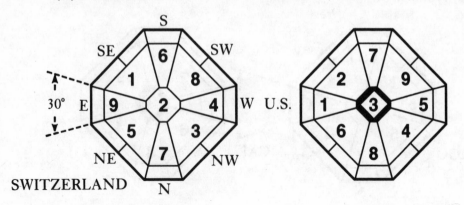

CHART OF 1953
(**2**)-Number of 1953

SWITZERLAND

CHARLIE CHAPLIN'S CHART
3-3–5

U.S.

ROBERT REDFORD

Birthday: **August 18,**
1937
Basic Number: 9
Control Number: 8   **9**–8–6
Tendency Number: 6

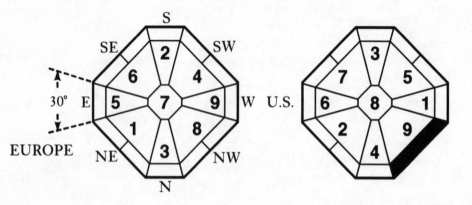

CHART OF 1957
(**7**)-Number of 1957

EUROPE

ROBERT REDFORD'S CHART
9–8–6

U.S.

The year 1957 was the year of Number 7. In 1957, Robert Redford went to Europe to study painting. Europe, which was east in the Chart of 1957, represented movement toward the destructive Number 5 (*Go-O-Satsu*, as pointed out in Napoleon's case). As expected, his life in Europe was miserable.

However, in 1958, the year of Number 6, some of his friends helped him return to the United States during the summertime, a movement from east to west. Looking at the Chart for 1958, we see that Number 8, in the west position, forms an energizing relationship with Redford's Basic Number 9. This corrected direction of movement resulted in a better development of his life.

CHART OF 1958
(**6**)-Number of 1958

ROBERT REDFORD'S CHART
9-8-6

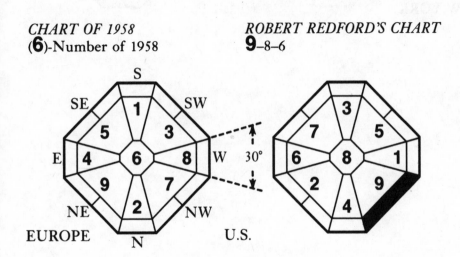

After he made his movie debut (*War-Hunt*, 1962), he returned to Broadway in 1963 and had the chance to play the leading role in *Barefoot in the Park*, which brought him instant recognition and great success. In 1963, Number 8 was in the east position, which corresponds to New York, and so, again, the movement from west to east created a favorable, energizing relationship with Redford's Basic Number 9. Once again, the movement he made was correct for him.

CHART FOR 1963
(**1**)-Number of 1963

ROBERT REDFORD'S CHART
9–8–6

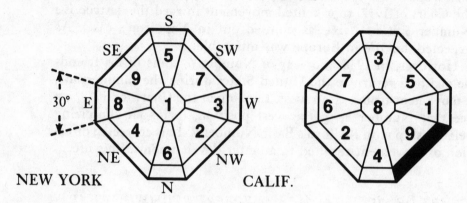

NEW YORK

CALIF.

HOW TO READ THE MONTHLY CHART SYSTEMS

The Monthly Chart Systems give you the proper arrangement of the numbers during any given month. The following example shows the month of February during a year of Number 1, 4, or 7. (The Number of the Year you wish to consult can be found in the graphs at the bottom of the following pages.)

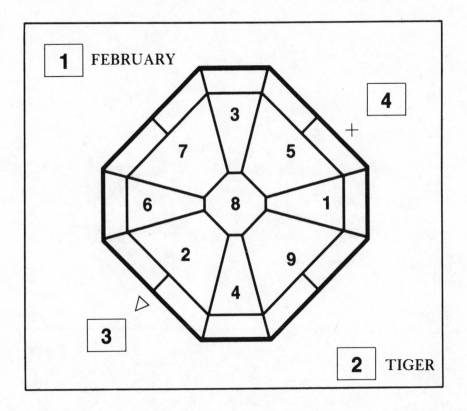

1 FEBRUARY

4

3

7

5

6

8

1

2

9

4

3

2 TIGER

---

1   *Month:* The month in the upper-left hand corner of the chart tells you which month of the year the chart represents. This chart is for February.

2   *Monthly Animal Zodiac Sign:* In the bottom right-hand corner is the Animal Zodiac Sign that corresponds to the month. In February, the Monthly Animal Zodiac Sign is always the Tiger.

| 3 | *Monthly* Anken-Satsu *Direction:* The triangle mark (△) indicates that, for the month of February, Number 2 is in the *Anken-Satsu* position, which is northeast (opposite Number 5). |

| 4 | *Monthly* Getsu-Ha *Position:* The × marking shows that, for the month of February, the direction west-southwest is in the *Getsu-Ha* position (opposite the Zodiac Sign of February). |

The following Monthly Charts appear during the years of 1, 4, and 7. The Yearly Animal Zodiac Signs that combine with those numbers are the Rat, Rabbit, Horse, and Rooster (not to be confused with the Monthly Animal Zodiac Signs listed, which are always the same).

Listed in the table below are Numbers 1, 4, and 7; the years they appear; and the Yearly Animal they combine with. Be sure to check the 108 Personality Types for the dates that the years begin and the months change during each year.

4	1888	RAT	1	1891	RABBIT	7	1894	HORSE	4	1897	ROOSTER
1	1900	"	7	1903	"	4	1906	"	1	1909	"
7	1912	"	4	1915	"	1	1918	"	7	1921	"
4	1924	"	1	1927	"	7	1930	"	4	1933	"
1	1936	"	7	1939	"	4	1942	"	1	1945	"
7	1948	"	4	1951	"	1	1954	"	7	1957	"
4	1960	"	1	1963	"	7	1966	"	4	1969	"
1	1972	"	7	1975	"	4	1978	"	1	1981	"
7	1984	"	4	1987	"	1	1990	"	7	1993	"
4	1996	"	1	1999	"	7	2002	"	4	2005	"

MONTHLY CHART SYSTEMS
(DIRECTION)
Rat—Horse—Rabbit—Rooster

1	4	7

FEBRUARY

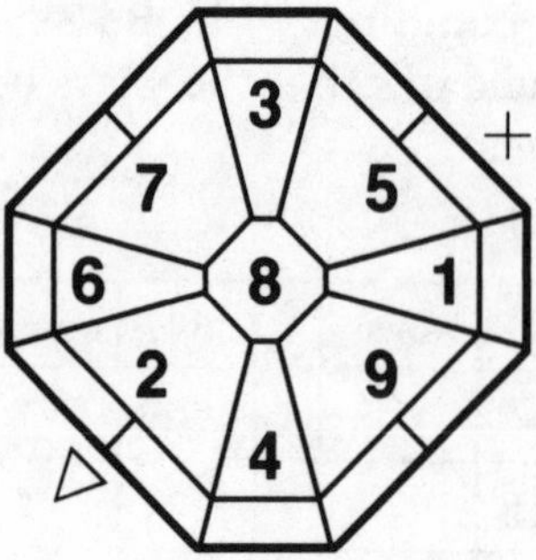

```
    3
  7   5        +
6   8   1
  2   9
    4
```
▷

Tiger

MARCH

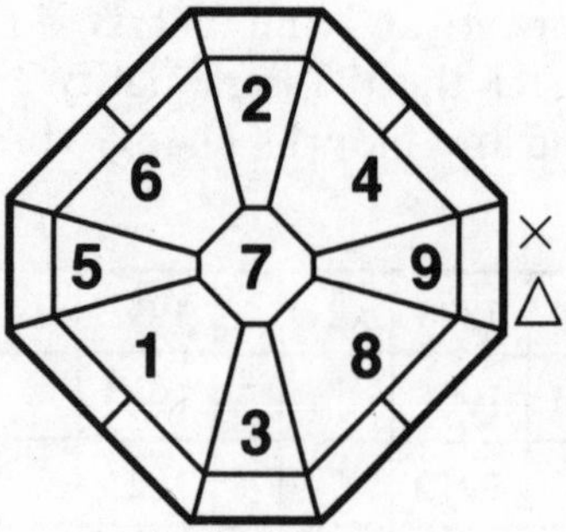

```
    2
  6   4
5   7   9     ×
  1   8       △
    3
```

Rabbit

JUNE

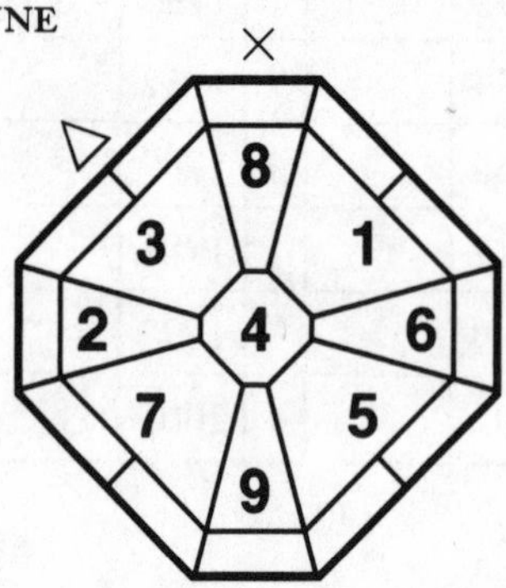

×
▷
```
    8
  3   1
2   4   6
  7   5
    9
```

Horse

JULY

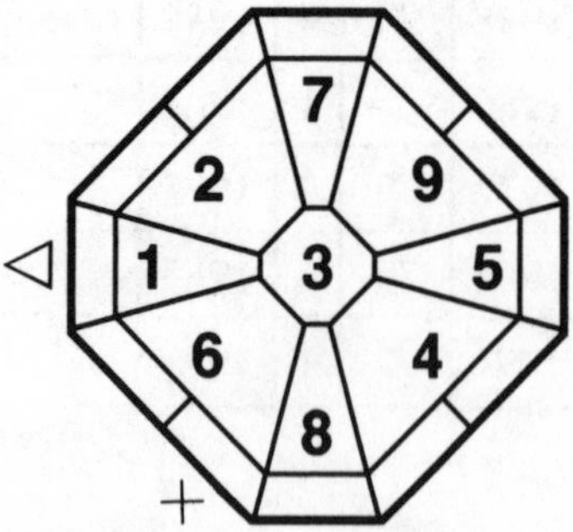

```
    7
  2   9
◁ 1   3   5
  6   4
    8
```
+

Sheep

OCTOBER   △

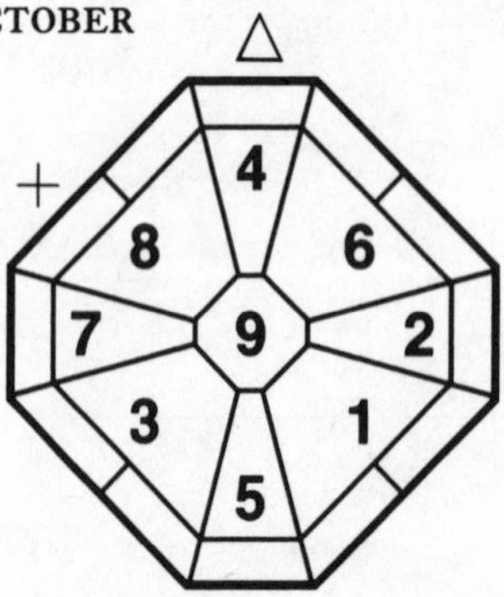

+
```
    4
  8   6
7   9   2
  3   1
    5
```

Dog

NOVEMBER

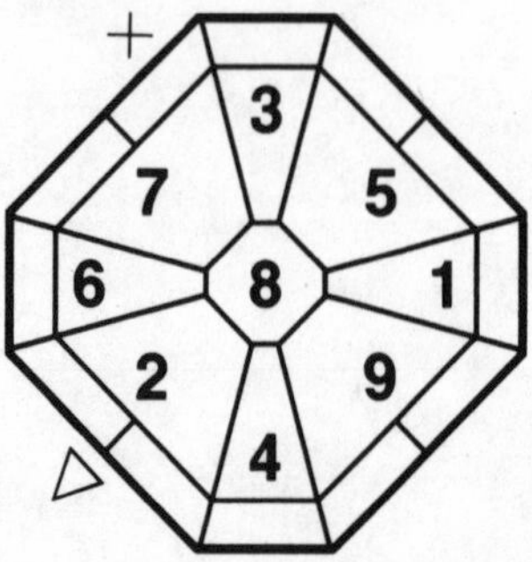

+
```
    3
  7   5
6   8   1
  2   9
    4
```
▷

Boar

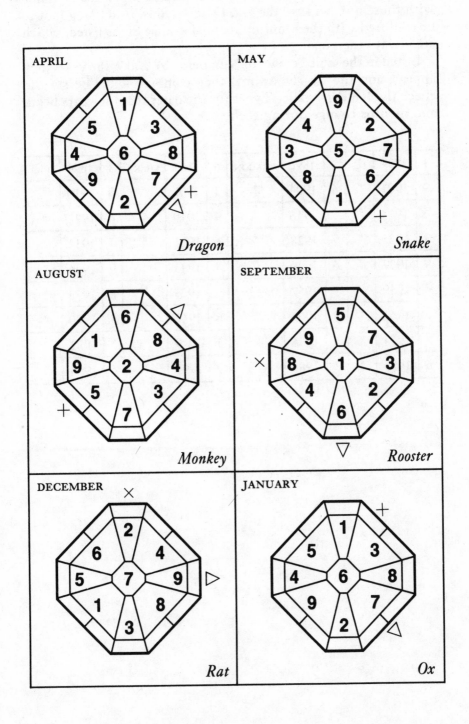

APRIL

Dragon

MAY

Snake

AUGUST

Monkey

SEPTEMBER

Rooster

DECEMBER

Rat

JANUARY

Ox

The following Monthly Charts appear during the years of Numbers 3, 6, and 9. The Yearly Animal Zodiac Signs thatcombine with those numbers are the Ox, Dragon, Sheep, and Dog (not to be confused with the Monthly Animal Zodiac Signs listed, which are always the same).

Listed in the table below are Numbers 3, 6, and 9; the years they appear; and the Yearly Animal they combine with. Be sure to check the 108 Personality Types for the dates that the years begin and months change during each year.

3	1889	OX	9	1892	DRAGON	6	1895	SHEEP	3	1898	DOG
9	1901	"	6	1904	"	3	1907	"	9	1910	"
6	1913	"	3	1916	"	9	1919	"	6	1922	"
3	1925	"	9	1928	"	6	1931	"	3	1934	"
9	1937	"	6	1940	"	3	1943	"	9	1946	"
6	1949	"	3	1952	"	9	1955	"	6	1958	"
3	1961	"	9	1964	"	6	1967	"	3	1970	"
9	1973	"	6	1976	"	3	1979	"	9	1982	"
6	1985	"	3	1988	"	9	1991	"	6	1994	"

MONTHLY CHART SYSTEMS
(DIRECTION)
Dragon—Dog—Ox—Sheep

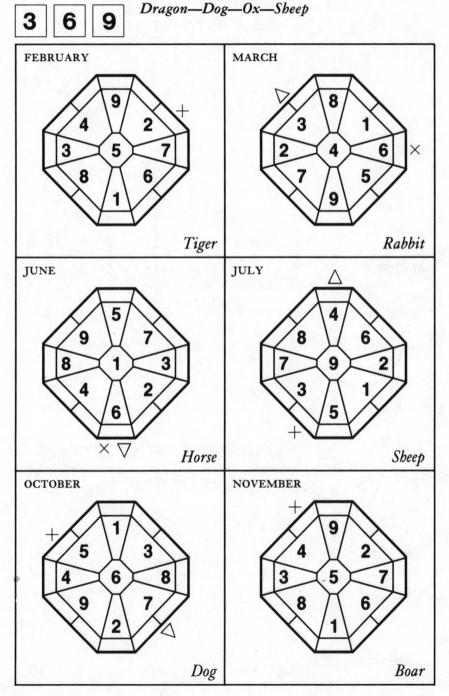

FEBRUARY

9 / 4 / 2 / 3 / 5 / 7 / 8 / 6 / 1 — +

Tiger

MARCH

8 / 3 / 1 / 2 / 4 / 6 / 7 / 5 / 9 — ×

Rabbit

JUNE

5 / 9 / 7 / 8 / 1 / 3 / 4 / 2 / 6 — × ▽

Horse

JULY

4 / 8 / 6 / 7 / 9 / 2 / 3 / 1 / 5 — + △

Sheep

OCTOBER

1 / 5 / 3 / 4 / 6 / 8 / 9 / 7 / 2 — + △

Dog

NOVEMBER

9 / 4 / 2 / 3 / 5 / 7 / 8 / 6 / 1 — +

Boar

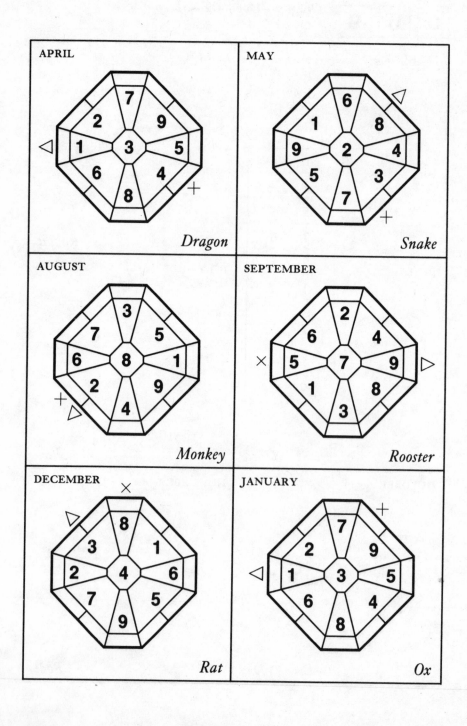

APRIL

Dragon

MAY

Snake

AUGUST

Monkey

SEPTEMBER

Rooster

DECEMBER

Rat

JANUARY

Ox

The following Monthly Charts appear during the years of Number 2, 5, and 8. The Yearly Animal Zodiac Signs that combine with those numbers are the Tiger, Snake, Monkey, and Boar (not to be confused with the Monthly Zodiac Signs listed, which are always the same).

Listed in the table below are Numbers 2, 5, and 8; the years they appear; and the Yearly Animal they combine with. Be sure to check the 108 Personality Types for the dates that the years begin and the months change during each year.

4	1888	RAT	1	1891	RABBIT	7	1894	HORSE	4	1897	ROOSTER
1	1900	"	7	1903	"	4	1906	"	1	1909	"
7	1912	"	4	1915	"	1	1918	"	7	1921	"
4	1924	"	1	1927	"	7	1930	"	4	1933	"
1	1936	"	7	1939	"	4	1942	"	1	1945	"
7	1948	"	4	1951	"	1	1954	"	7	1957	"
4	1960	"	1	1963	"	7	1966	"	4	1969	"
1	1972	"	7	1975	"	4	1978	"	1	1981	"
7	1984	"	4	1987	"	1	1990	"	7	1993	"
4	1996	"	1	1999	"	7	2002	"	4	2005	"

MONTHLY CHART SYSTEMS
(DIRECTION)
Tiger—Monkey—Snake—Boar

| 2 | 5 | 8 |

FEBRUARY

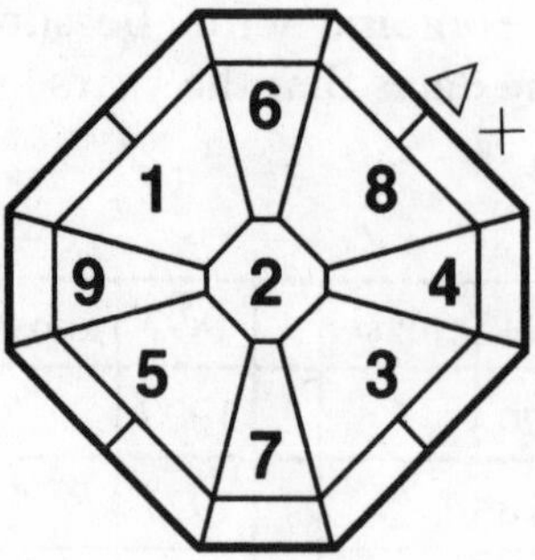

```
    6
 1     8
9   2   4
 5     3
    7
```
△ +

Tiger

MARCH

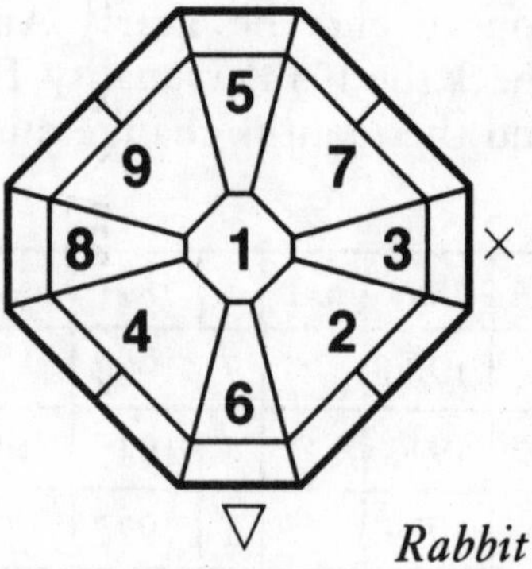

```
    5
 9     7
8   1   3
 4     2
    6
```
× ▽

Rabbit

JUNE

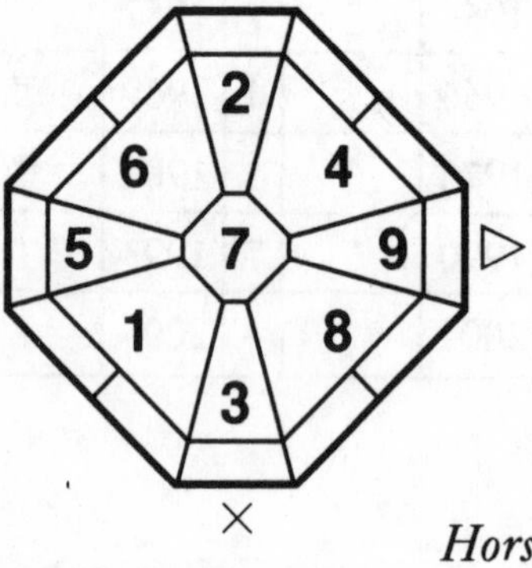

```
    2
 6     4
5   7   9
 1     8
    3
```
▷ ×

Horse

JULY

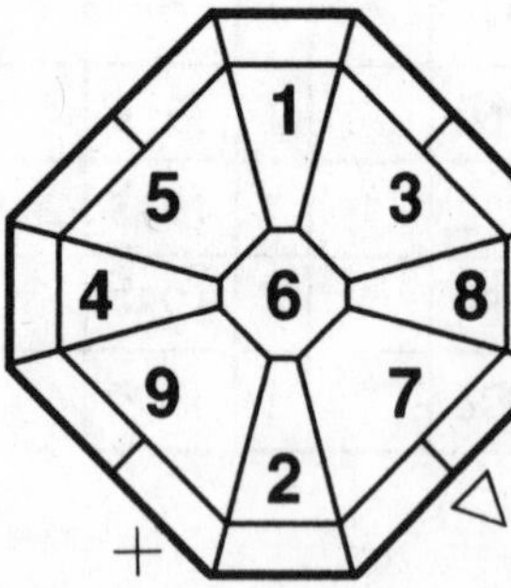

```
    1
 5     3
4   6   8
 9     7
    2
```
△ +

Sheep

OCTOBER

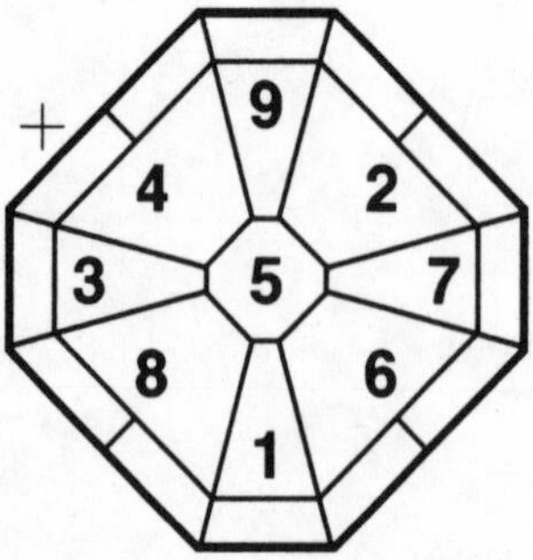

```
    9
 4     2
3   5   7
 8     6
    1
```
+

Dog

NOVEMBER

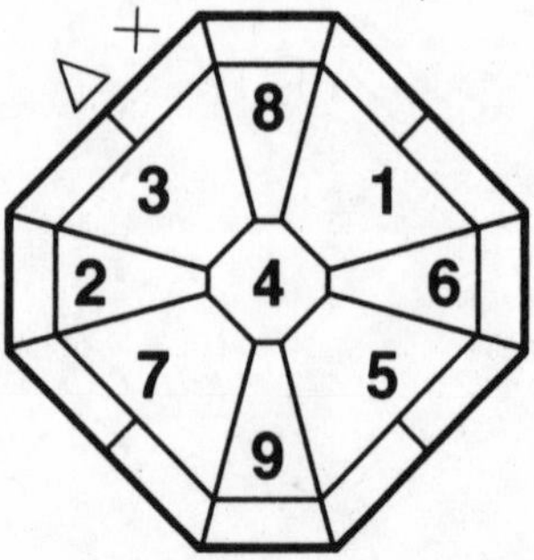

```
    8
 3     1
2   4   6
 7     5
    9
```
△ +

Boar

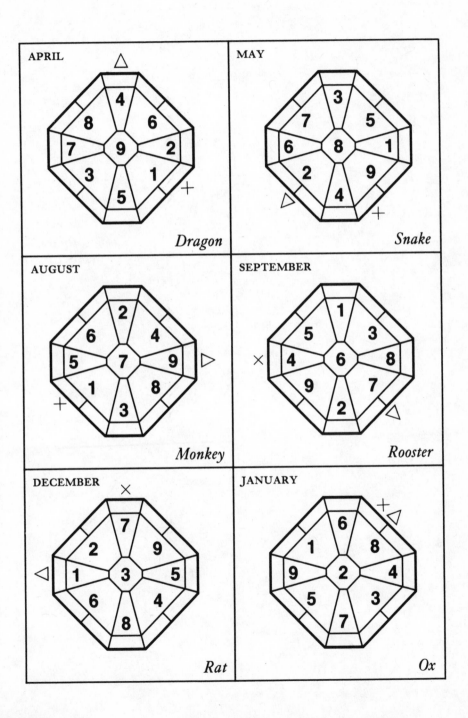

APRIL
Dragon

MAY
Snake

AUGUST
Monkey

SEPTEMBER
Rooster

DECEMBER
Rat

JANUARY
Ox